UTOPIAN AND DYSTOPIAN WRITING FOR CHILDREN AND YOUNG ADULTS

Children's Literature and Culture
Jack Zipes, *Series Editor*

CHILDREN'S LITERATURE COMES OF AGE:
Toward a New Aesthetic
by Maria Nikolajeva

REDISCOVERIES IN CHILDREN'S LITERATURE
by Suzanne Rahn

REGENDERING THE SCHOOL STORY:
Sassy Sissies and Tattling Tomboys
by Beverly Lyon Clark

WHITE SUPREMACY IN CHILDREN'S
LITERATURE:
*Characterizations of African Americans,
1830–1900*
by Donnarae MacCann

RETELLING STORIES, FRAMING CULTURE:
*Traditional Story and Metanarratives in
Children's Literature*
by John Stephens and Robyn McCallum

LITTLE WOMEN AND THE FEMINIST
IMAGINATION:
Criticism, Controversy, Personal Essays
edited by Janice M. Alberghene and
Beverly Lyon Clark

THE CASE OF PETER RABBIT:
*Changing Conditions of Literature for
Children*
by Margaret Mackey

IDEOLOGIES OF IDENTITY IN ADOLESCENT
FICTION
by Robyn McCallum

NARRATING AFRICA:
George Henty and the Fiction of Empire
by Mawuena Kossi Logan

VOICES OF THE OTHER:
*Children's Literature and the Postcolonial
Context*
edited by Roderick McGillis

TRANSLATING FOR CHILDREN
by Riitta Oittinen

CHILDREN'S FILMS:
History, Ideology, Pedagogy, Theory
by Ian Wojcik-Andrews

TRANSCENDING BOUNDARIES:
*Writing for a Dual Audience of Children
and Adults*
edited by Sandra L. Beckett

HOW PICTUREBOOKS WORK
by Maria Nikolajeva and Carole Scott

RUSSELL HOBAN/FORTY YEARS:
Essays on His Writings for Children
by Alida Allison

APARTHEID AND RACISM IN SOUTH AFRICAN
CHILDREN'S LITERATURE 1985–1995
by Donnarae MacCann and Amadu Maddy

EMPIRE'S CHILDREN:
*Empire and Imperialism in Classic British
Children's Books*
by M. Daphne Kutzer

SPARING THE CHILD:
*Grief and the Unspeakable in Youth
Literature about Nazism and the
Holocaust*
by Hamida Bosmajian

INVENTING THE CHILD:
*Culture, Ideology, and the Story of
Childhood*
by Joseph L. Zornado

A NECESSARY FANTASY?
*The Heroic Figure in Children's Popular
Culture*
edited by Dudley Jones and Tony Watkins

WAYS OF BEING MALE:
*Representing Masculinities in Children's
Literature and Film*
by John Stephens

PINOCCHIO GOES POSTMODERN:
Perils of a Puppet in the United States
by Richard Wunderlich and
Thomas J. Morrissey

THE PRESENCE OF THE PAST:
*Memory, Heritage, and Childhood in
Postwar Britain*
by Valerie Krips

THE FEMININE SUBJECT IN CHILDREN'S
LITERATURE
by Christine Wilkie-Stibbs

RECYCLING RED RIDING HOOD
by Sandra Beckett

THE POETICS OF CHILDHOOD
by Roni Natov

REIMAGINING SHAKESPEARE FOR CHILDREN
AND YOUNG ADULTS
edited by Naomi J. Miller

REPRESENTING THE HOLOCAUST IN YOUTH
LITERATURE
by Lydia Kokkola

BEATRIX POTTER:
Writing in Code
by M. Daphne Kutzer

UTOPIAN AND DYSTOPIAN WRITING FOR CHILDREN AND YOUNG ADULTS

EDITED BY
CARRIE HINTZ AND ELAINE OSTRY

Routledge is an imprint of the
Taylor & Francis Group, an informa business

Children's Literature and Culture Vol. 29

Published in 2003 by
Routledge
270 Madison Ave,
New York NY 10016
www.routledge-ny.com

Published in Great Britain by
Routledge
2 Park Square, Milton Park,
Abingdon, Oxon, OX14 4RN
www.routledge.co.uk

Transferred to Digital Printing 2009

Library of Congress Cataloging-in-Publication Data

Utopian and dystopian writing for children and young adults / edited by Carrie Hintz and Elaine Ostry.
    p. cm.—(Children's literature and culture ; 29)
    Includes bibliographical references and index.
    ISBN 0-415-94017-6 (alk. paper)
    1. Children's literature—History and criticism. 2. Young adult literature—History and criticism. 3. Utopias in literature. 4. Dystopias in literature. I. Hintz, Carrie, 1970-. II. Ostry, Elaine, 1967-. III. Series.

PN1009.5.U85U88   2002
809'.93372—dc21   2002011280

ISBN10: 0-415-94017-6 (hbk)
ISBN10: 0-415-80364-0 (pbk)

ISBN13: 978-0-415-94017-7 (hbk)
ISBN13: 978-0-415-80364-9 (pbk)

Contents

v

Acknowledgments

We would like to thank our contributors for two years of creative and intellectual effort. In particular, we would like to thank Kay Sambell and Rebecca Carol Noël Totaro wholeheartedly for their collaboration. Without them, our annotated bibliography would have been much slimmer.

Rebecca has been a tireless adviser on the project, and we thank her for her constant involvement and encouragement.

We thank Lyman Tower Sargent for a list of primary sources that formed a very important part of our investigations, and for his astute reading of our introduction.

We thank Jack Zipes for his help in bringing the project to fruition, and Emily Vail of Routledge.

We thank Tom Morrissey, Daphne Kutzer, and Nicole Pohl for their suggestions on the project and prospectus.

We thank Sarah Winters for being there from the start.

Elaine thanks her family and friends. She thanks her parents, Dan and Adeline Ostry, for their constant and loving moral support. She especially thanks Shawn Murphy for his love, patience, and chowders. She also thanks her colleagues at SUNY-Plattsburgh, especially Tom Morrissey for his expertise in utopia and SF, and her Children's and Young Adult Literature students.

Carrie wishes to thank her parents, Carol and Art Hintz, for their wonderful advice and kindness, Peter Hamilton for peerless conversation, and her colleagues at Queens College/CUNY, especially Nancy Comley, John Weir, Talia Schaffer, Tony O'Brien, Barbara Bowen, Nicole Cooley, Janice Peritz, David Richter, Steve Kruger, and Glenn Burger. Hugh English deserves a special thanks for sharing many utopian schemes. She would also like to thank her Children's Literature students in 2001 and 2002 for their lively engagement with many of the ideas in this book, and Brian Corman for his continued mentorship.

We thank each other for patient and inspired teamwork, and enduring friendship.

Foreword
Utopia, Dystopia, and the Quest for Hope

JACK ZIPES

We are living in very troubled times. More than ever before, we need utopian and dystopian literature. I say utopian *and* dystopian because, despite differences, these kinds of literary works emanate from a critique of "postmodern," advanced technological societies gone awry—and from a strong impulse for social change. As much as we are in need of this literature, especially for young readers, to provide hope for a different and more humane world, we can also use more innovative critical studies such as the present book, *Utopian and Dystopian Writing for Children and Young Adults,* edited with great care and sophistication by Carrie Hintz and Elaine Ostry.

As Hintz and Ostry make clear in their introduction, there was always a utopian element in children's literature from its beginnings in the eighteenth century as it gradually evolved from the oral tradition and became more and more separate from "adult" literary production. It would be misleading to argue that every story written for children is utopian, or to assert that there is an "essential" utopian nature to writing for young people. There is, however, a utopian tendency of telling and writing in general that helps explain why it is we feel so compelled to create and disseminate tales and why we are enthralled by particular stories. The tales, novels, poems, and plays that incorporate this utopian tendency stem from a lack we feel in our lives, a discernible discontentment, and a yearning for a better condition or world. Paradoxically the happiness of the listeners and readers of utopian works depends on the unhappiness of the tellers and writers. Without discontent there is no utopia. Without projections of utopia, our world would be a dismal place, and this is all the more reason why we need utopian and dystopian literature for the young, and not only for the young.

Tomes have been written about utopia, and this is most curious because utopia is allegedly nowhere, a place that has never been seen or experienced. At least this is what Sir Thomas More described in his famous treatise *Utopia,* written first in Latin in 1516 and translated into English in 1551.

Utopia is an imaginary island with a perfect social and political system in which everyone is treated fairly. Yet, since this perfect state of government and existence is imaginary, utopia has also come to mean an impossible idealistic projection. In fact, More's notion of utopia fostered numerous speculative, philosophical and political books from the sixteenth century to the present, and it also promoted all kinds of utopias as well as thousands of stories and novels labeled utopian. But utopia's vague and idealistic premises have led many critics to equate it with idealistic dreaming and unrealistic thinking. To be a utopian is frequently to be somebody out of touch with reality.

Nevertheless, there is a more positive way of looking at utopia that links the conception of utopias to reality and hope, something that the writers in Hintz's and Ostry's collection of essays tend to do with great perspicacity. Although not all of them cite the great German philosopher Ernst Bloch, much of their thinking and views are related to his notion of utopia.

In his monumental three-volume work, *The Principle of Hope,* Bloch proposes that our real life experiences are at the basis of our utopian longings and notions. In our daily lives that are not exactly what we want them to be, we experience glimpses or glimmerings of another world that urge us on and stimulate our creative drives to reach a more ideal state of being. To be more precise, it is our realization of what is missing in our lives that impels us to create works of art that not only reveal insights into our struggles but also that shed light on alternatives and possibilities to restructure our mode of living and social relations. All art, according to Bloch, contains images of hope illuminating ways to create a utopian society. Obviously, not every work that presumes to be art is artful. Nor do all art works necessarily contain a utopian tendency. But inspiring and illuminating images of hope can be detected in low and high art, in a Beethoven symphony or in a rock and roll song, in a grand Shakespeare production or a state fair, or let us say in William Steig's *Shrek,* a picture book for children, and the recent "utopian" film based on it. The utopian tendency of art is what propels us to reshape and reform our personal and social lives. In fact, Bloch points out that there are concrete utopias, short-lived experiments that have given real expression to new social and political relations. These concrete utopias set the building blocks for the future, for once hopes are tested and realized, we cannot betray them for long. We can never fully deny what has been concretized. Among his examples are such major events in the world as the American Revolution of 1776, the French Revolution of 1789, and the Russian Revolution of 1917 as well as the Fourier experiments in France and the Brook Farm "commune" in America, all which have left traces of how we might shape the future. These revolutions and experiments—and there are many more that can be cited—did not entirely succeed because the proper socio-economic conditions to maintain them did not exist. Yet, the very fact that they came into being for a short time reveals a great deal about the validity of our utopian longings that we continue to concretize in different ways.

These longings are recorded in the spoken and written word. These longings are the source of ancient religions and rituals as well as new cults. The belief in a better and just world has always been with us, and this utopian belief assumes a myriad of forms. For instance, the belief in miracles and life after death articulated in religious legends and myths stems from utopian longings. Salvation is predicated on the notion of a just world in which the oppressed will be protected by a powerful divinity. Hundreds of thousands of tales in all religions have been spread with hope that we shall be redeemed after this life. But the more interesting utopian literary works, in my opinion, focus on the present world. The utopian tendency of sacred stories is clear from the beginning. What is not so evident is how our profane and secular stories have a utopian bent to them and are perhaps more appealing and significant because they restore miraculous power to human beings. In other words, they suggest that ordinary people can take power into their own hands and create better worlds for themselves, if they know how to use their gifts.

This is where the dystopian factor plays a role, for the pursuit of perfection, the perfect place and society, can also lead to rigid if not totalitarian societies. Much of what we cite as progress, especially technological progress, has a double edge to it. The cloning of vegetables, animals, and humans that may help overcome hunger and disease may eventually lead to the mechanization of the natural and human world as we know it. The advances in communication may lead to dis-communication and alienation. One could argue that the great drive of human beings to establish fairer, more socialist societies has led to perverted societies, what we might call negative utopias, or what is projected as dystopias in literary works for young and old readers.

As Hintz and Ostry and the authors in their collection demonstrate, there is an intricate link between utopia and dystopia. When asked whether children and young people can handle pure dystopia and what they need to deal with it, Lois Lowry, the author of the provocative novel *The Giver,* responded, "Young people handle dystopia every day: in their lives, their dysfunctional families, their violence-ridden schools. They watch dystopian television and movies about the real world where firearms bring about explosive conclusions to conflict. Yes, I think they need to see some hope for such a world. I can't imagine writing a book that doesn't have a hopeful ending."

Utopian and dystopian literature form a great discourse about hope. The essays in the present volume are part of this discourse, and they make a major contribution toward understanding why such literature has great relevance for young readers. As we all know, there is a real strong "dystopian" tendency in our consumer society to make "better" consumers out of our children. Fortunately, the hope of utopian *and* dystopian literature opposed to this tendency cannot be consumed without deleterious effects—once "struck with hope" for a more humane world, children will want more.

Introduction

CARRIE HINTZ AND ELAINE OSTRY

Neverland, Narnia, Hogwarts, Middle Earth, Oz. Children and young adults imaginatively travel to many fantasy worlds. From Lewis Carroll's nonsensical Wonderland to the contiguous worlds of Philip Pullman's His Dark Materials series, hundreds of children's and young adult books have presented invented "secondary worlds" that go by their own rules and conventions.[1] In many of these alternative worlds, utopian elements abound. Some books present nonexistent societies that, in the utopian and dystopian tradition, are meant to depict environments that are measurably better or worse than the reader's own. With Sarah Fielding's *The Governess or, Little Female Academy* (1749),[2] children's literature begins with a utopian vision of an all-girls' school that teaches ideal social organization. The history of children's and young adult literature is entwined with that of utopian writing from that moment on.

Utopian and dystopian writing for children and young adults has been produced for a variety of reasons, and it has had a range of effects, from play and escape to sustained political reflection. In utopian writing, younger readers must grapple with social organization; these utopian works propose to teach the young reader about governance, the possibility of improving society, the role of the individual and the limits of freedom. Utopian writing for children and young adults examines the roots of social behavior and encourages the child to question his or her own society. It often sets up a confrontation between the child and the adult world. In addition, children and young adults are generally in the center of the action or set of concerns, sometimes even bearing the major responsibility for the formation, survival, or reform of the society.

Some utopian writing for children and young adults offers an idealized, pastoral vision that evokes an Edenic image of the ostensibly unspoiled state of childhood itself. Other texts aimed at a young audience raise questions

1

about political organization and the ideal society, focusing on the built rather than the natural environment.[3] The essays in *Utopian and Dystopian Writing for Children and Young Adults* engage with a variety of texts from the eighteenth century to the present day, encompassing a variety of genres popular in children's and young adult literature: science fiction, fantasy, the school story, and historical fiction. These essays argue for and establish a unique space for children's and young adult utopias and dystopias. They define and explore the category of utopian writing for children, while keeping an eye on the special readership in these books. They link major figures in adult utopian literature to those of children's literature. Ultimately, they provide a context in which we can appreciate the importance of utopia and dystopia in children's and young adult literature, and show how crucial child and adolescent readers are to utopian literature as a whole. In utopian and dystopian writing for children and young adults, the stakes are high: these writings may be a young person's first encounter with texts that systematically explore collective social organization.

We have also included four essays by creative writers who have explored utopia or dystopia in their works. We feel it is important to give voice to creators as well as critics of utopia and dystopia for young readers. James Gurney, Monica Hughes, Alberto Manguel, and Katherine Paterson all add perspectives that complement the essays by academics and enlarge on general themes of utopia. Included as well is an interview with Lois Lowry, whose popular novel *The Giver* (1993)[4] has generated much interest in the field, provoking the kind of troubling, exciting discussion about social organization, individuality, and childhood that this collection seeks to continue.

Utopianism

Utopian writing is a notoriously difficult genre to define. A popular use of the term "utopian" is as a means to dismiss an impractical scheme or vision, but this usage fails to do justice to the seriousness of the body of utopian writing and utopian thought, as well as the variety of purposes for which utopian works are written. Lyman Tower Sargent defines "utopianism," or "social dreaming," as "the dreams and nightmares that concern the ways in which groups of people arrange their lives and which usually envision a radically different society than the one in which the dreamers live" (Sargent, 1994, 3). It often "includes elements of fantasy" (Sargent, 1994, 4). Texts that possess the element of "utopianism" do not necessarily show an elaborated social system, and they may not be radical, but their aspirations toward ideality or amelioration are fundamentally social.

When Thomas More wrote *Utopia* in 1516,[5] he inaugurated a tradition that many writers follow today, but one that has become increasingly complex. Critics differ in their definitions of utopia: Does a text's utopian status

lie within the form of the work, the thematic message of the work, the intention of the author to portray an ideal or nightmarish world, the intentions
and beliefs held by the characters who live in the fictional society, or the
response of the reader? It is impossible to rely on genre, for example, to
establish a text's utopian nature, since the form of utopian works varies.
Furthermore, even a text like *Utopia* is a hodgepodge of elements: travel
narrative, political commentary, theological speculation, and a large portion
of humanist intellectual exercise. Lyman Tower Sargent defines "utopia" as
a "non-existent society described in considerable detail" and reserves
"eutopia" for those societies "that the author intended a contemporaneous
reader to view as considerably better than the society in which that reader
lived," with "dystopia" as considerably worse.[6] Since we are aware of the
difficulty of gauging authorial intention, we add to this definition a consideration of the perception and beliefs of the characters about the ideality of
their society. We use "utopia," a more familiar term for the reader, to signify
a nonexistent society that is posited as significantly better than that of the
reader. It strives toward perfection, has a delineated social system, and is
described in reasonably specific detail. Dystopias are likewise precise
descriptions of societies, ones in which the ideals for improvement have
gone tragically amok.

In this volume, we include the first annotated bibliography of utopian and
dystopian writing for children and young adults. In compiling it, our most difficult task was limiting our definition of utopia. Arguments can be made for
including almost any book for children and young adults, provided that the
definition of utopia is stretched far enough, thus rendering the category less
useful. How does one know a utopian work when one sees it? No one model
captures the range of visions of the ideal society in the Western world. How
does one discern the dystopian as a distinct category from the utopian? As
Sargent notes, "fashions change in utopias; most sixteenth-century eutopias
horrify today's reader even though the authors' intentions are clear. On the
other hand, most twentieth-century eutopias would be considered dystopias
by a sixteenth-century reader and many of them would in all likelihood be
burnt as works of the devil" (Sargent, 1994, 5). To complicate matters further,
several essays in this collection demonstrate how perspectives can change
within a single work, as seemingly ideal societies are exposed as dystopian, or
characters disagree about the ideality of their society.

Are the nonexistent societies of utopian writing even meant to be
attainable? Maureen Moran draws attention to the perennial and productive tension in utopia's oscillation between model and dream: "Some
utopian models offer glimpses of perfection which can never be attained;
possibility 'seems beside the point' for in this modality, fantasy is primarily a compensation for deprivation and an expression of needs which reality can never meet. The very unrealizability of the fantasy draws the reader

reluctantly back to the existing order of things. On the other hand, utopias may be read as agents of change, 'an imperative to drive us onward,' as Karl Mannheim claims."[7] The essays in this collection show both utopian models—models that are sometimes mutually exclusive—as writers show both the unrealizable dream and visions that are meant to lead more directly to social improvement.

Utopia can be more of a space for self-conscious speculation than a model of unrealizable, perfect space or political engagement. As Fredric Jameson argues: "it is less revealing to consider Utopian discourse as a mode of narrative, comparable, say, with novel or epic, than it is to grasp it as an object of meditation, analogous to the riddles or koan of the various mystical traditions, or the aporias of classical philosophy, whose function is to provide a fruitful bewilderment, and to jar the mind into some heightened but unconceptualized consciousness of its own powers, functions, aims and structural limits."[8] The "fruitful bewilderment" of which Jameson speaks might well describe a young person's intellectual process while coping, for example, with the mysteriously colorless world and ambiguous ending of Lowry's *The Giver* (1993). Jameson's remarks solicit political awareness through a renewed consideration of social as well as mental limits and possibilities.

An awareness of social organization, we argue, is necessary for a work to be called utopian; not every text written for young readers that shows a positive environment can be classified as such. As we compiled our bibliography, we saw several texts that portrayed wish fulfillment, where the world, like the Land of Cockaigne, is filled with delights pleasurable to the eye and ear, and even edible.[9] Books that show people immersed in a hedonistic fantasy where they get everything they want are to be distinguished from utopias if the texts do not contain a social dimension for the reader, or offer a system of collective organization. Books about happy families, for instance, are not technically utopias.[10] While Roald Dahl's *Charlie and the Chocolate Factory* (1964)[11] offers a virtual copia of confectionary abundance, it has a claim to the title of "utopia" because of the enclosed nature of its structure (no one is ever seen coming in or out), the strictness of the workers' discipline and an emphasis on beauty in industrial life reminiscent of William Morris. While wish fulfillment and satisfaction of bodily and spiritual cravings undoubtedly form part of a utopia—unfulfilled desire is certainly one catalyst for utopia— the presence of these elements in a work written for children and young adults does not in itself signify a utopia.

Likewise, many books for young readers offer visions of communities that are highly developed technologically or even morally, but which are not necessarily utopian, since they do not represent a significant enough modification of the society to which the reader belongs. Another problematic genre is the Robinsonnade, which portrays solitary civilization or pure adventure devoid of utopian content. Poetry for children often has utopian sentiments, but we have not found any elaborated utopias or dystopias in poetry. In general, picture books are also excluded from our bibliography: we prefer to concentrate on works aimed for a slightly older audience, as picture books rarely develop their social settings. However, we have found some notable exceptions. *Babar the King* by Jean de Brunhoff (1933)[12] presents a fairly comprehensive vision of the ideal city of Celesteville through both text and image. In Celesteville, everyone has a job for which he or she is ideally suited. The city itself is well designed and pleasant: "[t]he Bureau of Industry is next door to the Amusement Hall . . . very practical and convenient" (12–13). When Misfortune threatens to visit Celesteville, it is driven away by "graceful winged elephants who chase Misfortune away from Celesteville and bring back Happiness" (44). Paul Fleischman's *Weslandia* (1999)[13] and James Gurney's *Dinotopia: A World Apart from Time* (1992) and *The World Beneath* (1995) depict whole utopian worlds that describe food, shelter, clothing, recreation, and social relations.[14] An unusual picture book dealing with utopia is *Xanadu: The Imaginary Place* (1999).[15] We do not include it in our bibliography, since it is not fiction, but rather a school project from North Carolina that invited children to express their own utopian hopes. It adds the actual voices of children to the study of utopianism.

What are we to make of the many examples of historical fiction that treat a highly developed social organization? One could easily argue that Holocaust literature is dystopian;[16] we have, however, excluded this genre as simply too broad and deserving of its own study.[17] Historical fiction demands an attention to the complexities of history that detract from the abstract formulation of utopia and dystopia. Likewise, there are a number of fictional texts that dramatize the lives of children in a communal setting such as a Shaker colony.[18] For the most part, we have chosen to exclude these books in favor of a concentration on fantasy texts not rooted in specific historical events. We have chosen texts that focus on the roots, abstract dreams, and plans of utopia and dystopia. Even when one limits the investigation to the fantasy genre, utopian and dystopian writing exhibits a variety of political ideologies, formal techniques, and intended audiences.

The Association of Childhood and Utopia

Children's and young adult utopias are in particular need of sustained study for two reasons. First of all, there is a long tradition of thinking of childhood itself as utopian, a space and time apart from the corruption of everyday adult life.[19] The second reason is the unique function that utopianism and utopian writing plays in children's socialization and education.

Childhood is often viewed as a space sheltered from adult corruption and responsibility. This perspective comes from the Romantic conception of childhood. To the Romantics and their heirs, children were innocent and pure, close to nature and God, possessing greater imaginative powers than adults. They were emblems of hope and the future, capable of converting adults to a better way of life. Usually unconsciously, Romantic children cast a "critical eye" on the adult world of material gain, corruption, and outdated ways of thinking. Childhood was also a time in which individuality could flourish before the conformity of the adult world took hold. The Romantic conception of childhood is one of the most prevalent cultural myths of the Western world. As we teach children's literature, we are astonished at how fervently students cling to the image of the Romantic child. This image is a construction that served the ideological purposes of the Romantics and others since.

In reality, children are more complex and less . . . nice.[20] The Romantic child fits a utopian frame easily, but real children face a variety of social and psychological pressures. No child knows utopia. The Romantic conception of the child empowers the child in one sense and limits him or her in another. The child holds the key to personal and social change, pointing the way to utopia. In Johanna Spyri's *Heidi* (1880),[21] the title character turns the most antisocial and atheistic of Alp-Uncles into a churchgoing pillar of the community. She is the youngest and seemingly most helpless of the characters, but she is the one who makes both Dörfli and Frankfurt better places, drawing people together and giving them mental, emotional, physical, and spiritual health. On the other hand, the image of the perpetually innocent child removes it from the complexities of development and the responsibility to understand the world. Utopias for children reflect this duality.

The Romantic vision of the child influenced educational programs such as that of Friedrich Froebel, inventor of the kindergarten, which considered play and imaginative activity crucial for intellectual and emotional growth. This concept is now universally held in the Western world. Utopian writing intervenes explicitly in children's development. As child or adolescent readers enjoy speculative fiction that treats imaginary worlds significantly different than our own, they develop their imaginative powers. Escapism also plays a role; individuals under pressure form imaginative havens where none exist in real life. Some critics stress the compensatory nature of imaginative literature to those who suffer materially, and the way in which fantasy or folklore directly addresses the specific scarcity experienced by audiences or tellers.[22] As one example, the socialist paradise of L. Frank Baum's *The Emerald City of Oz* (1910) is set against the economic hard times of late nineteenth-century America.[23] Fantasy can also mirror and criticize reality, forcing readers to consider reality, ironically at the same time as they are escaping from it. Fantasy texts, especially those with specifically utopian or dystopian concerns, can be more than escapist: they can offer an improved vision of the future, or address deep and possibly unresolvable fears.

Learning about Society

As we seek to articulate a definition of utopian and dystopian writing for children and young adults, it is important to acknowledge the "dual focus" of this literature. Working with children's literature necessarily commits the scholar to some awareness of reader response, because the literature speaks to young readers in different ways. Children's literature specializes in "cross writing," that is, writing on two levels for two different audiences, adult and child, "a dialogic mix of older and younger voices."[24] Most children's literature, no matter how fanciful, contains lessons to be learned. It is an inherently pedagogical genre, and with cross writing, children learn more as they reread at different times in their lives. Likewise, utopian literature is "generally didactic" (Sargent, 1994, 6). Combined with children's and young adult literature, it can be a powerful teaching tool.

Through utopian and dystopian writing, children learn about social organization. Gurney's *Dinotopia* (1992), for example, is characterized by a remarkable unity between human and animal characters, and a repeated affirmation of the need for cooperation. All of the characters in the series learn that they need to work with others to achieve their individual and collective goals. More specifically, they learn that such cooperation can and must take place across difference—bridging gaps as large as those between human beings and dinosaurs. Similarly, Soinbhe Lally's *A Hive for the Honeybee* (1996)[25] shows both the harmony and tensions of bee life, where the good of the hive ultimately overcomes personal doubts about the society. With drones echoing Marx, it is also a good example of cross writing.

Utopian literature encourages young people to view their society with a critical eye, sensitizing or predisposing them to political action. In the long tradition of utopian literature, an imagined encounter with another culture urges readers to reflect on their home society, a reflection that sometimes takes the form of satire or social criticism. A utopian society likely has solved some of the problems besetting the "real" world, or else its flaws can teach the reader about social improvement. The pedagogical focus of writing for young people invests utopian satire with particular urgency.

The conundrum of many utopian and dystopian books for young readers is as follows: At what point does utopian cooperation become dystopian conformity? At one end of the spectrum, Gurney's *Dinotopia* and its numerous sequels indicate the pleasures and advantages of a strong community, and putting others first. At the other end, however, lies the chilling Camazotz of Madeleine L'Engle's *A Wrinkle in Time* (1962),[26] where all of the children on the street bounce their balls in strictly exact unison. In dystopias for young readers, conformity kills individual creativity, resulting in a dull, oppressive society, as in Louise Lawrence's *Andra* (1971).[27] In Sonia Levitin's *The Cure* (1999),[28] any sign of nonconformity is immediately noted in a citizen's file as a sign of deviance. The hero, Gemm 16884, realizes that he is different, and is singled out for the "cure": he is thrust into the body of a Jewish boy during the Black Death. His experience with discrimination initially leads him to reject difference, but he soon realizes the need to celebrate it in order to foster love. Young readers, faced with the pressure to conform in their own lives, can learn from these texts not to be ashamed of how they may differ from the norm.

Much of children's literature pits the child against the adult world and, in "showing up" the adults, is subversive. Subversion and social criticism are shared by utopian literature; both genres focus on how society might change for the better. The sharp division between the child and the adult world allows for the social criticism that utopias contain. Through the child, the writer casts a "critical eye" on the world. The Romantic association of the child with hope for the future links the child to utopias even further. Utopias for young readers suggest that children can achieve a state of ideality that adults cannot; at times, the impetus for the fictional child to fix society's problems exerts a powerful pressure on the child itself. This can be seen in O. T. Nelson's *The Girl Who Owned a City* (1975),[29] in which everyone over the age of twelve has been killed by a mysterious disease; hence the children cannot rely on adult figures. Violent gangs roam the streets, creating a dystopian, violent society; it is up to the surviving children and the book's protagonist, Lisa, to rebuild from the devastation.

Utopian fiction reveals the social foundations of our own world—and the cracks that form in them. Class systems come under much scrutiny in utopias and dystopias for young readers. Like Ursula K. Le Guin's short story "The Ones Who Walk Away from Omelas" (1975),[30] with its seemingly perfect world, many texts are predicated on the discovery of a society where the sufferings of some allow for the pleasure, comfort, and exaltation of others. We see this pattern, for example, in Zilpha Keatley Snyder's Green-sky Trilogy (1975–1977).[31] In these books, the utopian treetop life of the Kindar is explicitly contrasted to the misery of the bottom-dwelling Erdlings, and, as Carrie Hintz argues in her essay, it is precisely that inequity that the Kindar ultimately must correct. The class system of the real world is exaggerated and criticized in John Christopher's *The Guardians* (1970),[32] H. M. Hoover's *Children of Morrow* (1973),[33] John Tully's *NatFact 7* (1984),[34] Robert Swindells's *Daz 4 Zoe* (1990),[35] among many others. Writers often pull no punches in depicting the brutality of class inequality taken to an extreme. In Tom Browne's *Red Zone* (1980),[36] for instance, twenty-second-century Britain echoes imperial Rome, as the privileged Inner Zone citizens watch the Red Zone denizens fight to the death.

Exposure to these types of texts can lead young readers to see inequality in their own communities and countries, and even lead them into a finer understanding of how the industrialized world exploits developing nations.

Encountering these phenomena in fiction as a young person prepares the reader for a more sustained consideration of the nature of justice and other elements of ideal social life. Indeed, many of the texts we have found openly discuss the nature of democracy, typically in contrast to totalitarianism. The texts mirror political systems that the young readers are just beginning to learn about in school. The fundamentals of democracy are shown in Deborah Moulton's *Children of Time* (1989),[37] in which a postnuclear community, the "Demosee," struggles to make fair, consensual decisions rather than give in to barbaric impulses. G. R. Kestevan's *The Awakening Water* (1977)[38] contains a society guided by the all-powerful Party, and a democratic resistance movement led by youths. Long before child readers encounter *Nineteen Eighty-Four* (1949)[39] and *Brave New World* (1932),[40] they have access to the themes of these classics.

These texts confront the tensions between individual freedom and the needs of society. In many dystopias, totalitarian societies assert the power of determining who lives and who dies. Euthanasia—often called, in Orwellian fashion, "release" or "recycling"—figures prominently in these books. In Lowry's *The Giver* (1993) and *Gathering Blue* (2000),[41] and Nina Bawden's *Off the Road* (1998),[42] the old and sick are put to death as useless members of the community. In Sonia Levitin's *The Cure* (1999), death is the punishment for nonconformity and dissidence. Books like this challenge young readers to consider the value of every individual to the community, as well as the need to keep society from dismantling individual rights.

Learning about the Self through Utopian Writing

How do depictions of utopia and dystopia in young adult literature differ from those in children's literature? For starters, young adult utopias and dystopias tend to be elaborated in greater detail than those directed toward children. The system behind the utopia or dystopia is analyzed for the reader, and its components enumerated. In creating the annotated bibliography, we discovered that utopias predominate in children's literature, whereas dystopias are far more common in young adult literature. This is hardly surprising. It reflects the way in which young children are rarely depicted to themselves as suffering, especially collectively. Furthermore, adolescence frequently entails traumatic social and personal awakening. The adolescent comes to recognize the faults and weaknesses of his or her society, and rebels against it. A common trope in such literature is the emphasis on the lie, the secret and unsavory workings of the society that the teen hero uncovers. Dystopian literature thus mingles well with the coming-of-age novel, which features a loss of innocence.

Indeed, dystopia can act as a powerful metaphor for adolescence. In adolescence, authority appears oppressive, and perhaps no one feels more under surveillance than the average teenager. The teenager is on the brink of adulthood: close enough to see its privileges but unable to enjoy them. The comforts of childhood fail to satisfy. The adolescent craves more power and control, and feels the limits on his or her freedom intensely. Denied legal and social power, teenagers in these books often wield awesome mind control. The adolescents in Stephanie S. Tolan's *Welcome to the Ark* (1996)[43] are trapped in an isolated group home for troubled youth; through mind control, they contact similarly gifted children around the world, and combine forces to conquer violence.

Sometimes the "growing pains" of a society moving toward utopia or away from dystopia are framed as synonymous with adolescent growth itself, and the development of agency. In Monica Hughes's *The Tomorrow City* (1978),[44] adolescents defend free will against an all-controlling computer, invoking the metaphor of a teenager who must learn to make his or her own decisions to mature fully.[45]

During adolescence, one is indeed faced with decisions that mirror those made by society as a whole: What are the proper limits of freedom? To what extent can one rebel? At what point does conformity rob one of his or her identity? The bloom is off the rose, as society views the teenager in far more negative terms than it does the child. In contemporary literature, there is no "Romantic teenager" following the Romantic child. Little wonder that books featuring adolescents who successfully rebel against an oppressive adult society are so common. In the average young adult dystopia, the adolescent knows best.

Utopian and dystopian fiction does give teenagers an important Romantic characteristic, as they often save the world from destruction. This literary pattern reverses the hierarchy in which real children and young adults are at the bottom. The idea of children "saving" adults is a Romantic concept. As we mentioned before, this act is traditionally unconscious; in these books, however, teenagers are fully aware of the role they play. If "[u]topia caters to our ability to dream, to recognize that things are not quite what they should be, and to assert that improvement is possible" (Sargent, 1994, 26), then perhaps young adults possess this ability, this hope, in greater quantities than their jaded elders. Agents of hope, they come to embrace their ability to lead. This leadership may take the form of individual command. Talon in Neal Shusterman's *Downsiders* (1999)[46] leads his underground utopian community in their defense against the Topsiders, and then into their new kingdom of rooftops. He shines as particularly resourceful among the eminently practical Downsiders. In many of these books, children and adolescents form groups that resist the dystopian system under which they suffer. In Garth Nix's *Shade's Children* (1997),[47] a band of young adults (who have managed to escape the state slaughter of all children over fourteen) tries to end the domination of aliens. The young boys in John Christopher's The Tripods

Trilogy (1967)[48] infiltrate the city of the Masters and fight against them. In these books, children and young adults learn about the need for leadership, the stresses of decision making, and the dynamics of group cooperation against a common enemy. They learn how to use limited resources to over-come incredible odds, and become more powerful and capable than they ever could have imagined.

Utopian Writing and Technological Fear

Technology in utopian writing for children and young adults can represent both darkest fears and brightest hopes, as young readers are exposed to anxi-eties about technology while being shown the wonders that it can perform. A large-scale technological intervention in human affairs, such as the construc-tion of an entire domed society, could be seen as a positive response to human needs and an improvement in humanity's lot, or the worst possible step imaginable. In Claire Cooper's *Earthchange* (1985),[49] the only possibil-ity of shucking off dystopia lies in finding and working with scientists who have the proper knowledge to help people advance. Gerry Turner's *Stranger from the Depths* (1967)[50] displays a city replete with technological wonders, including ones that actively combat disease. By contrast, sometimes the vision of technology is anything but sanguine. In Ben Bova's *City of Dark-ness* (1976),[51] a domed New York City of the future is the only place where it is possible to live, but it is marred by violent warfare. Shirley Parenteau's *The Talking Coffins of Cryo-City* (1979)[52] shows a world where a computer pro-grams everything connected to the well-being of a city, including the weather. The city's slogan is "PERFECT WEATHER FOR A PERFECT WORLD" (*Talk-ing*, 13). This is a positive state of affairs until it becomes apparent that any deviant behavior is punished by banishment to cryogenic coffins. You are thawed out later when your major character flaw can be corrected—but long after everyone you know has died.

Above all, portrayals of technology alert young people that no matter what technology is used, and the extent to which it is used, it must be used wisely. Some writers strongly emphasize the need to achieve a balance, espe-cially in such works as *The Secret Under My Skin* by Janet McNaughton (2000),[53] in which the democratic Weavers Guild wants slowly to bring back technology, which has been condemned outright after the environmental dis-aster called the "technocaust." Technology is hastily ushering in a "posthu-man" age: our very bodies are being altered, human cloning looms on the horizon, artificial intelligence is a real possibility.[54] Writers are projecting future scenarios of such developments and mining them for significance; utopian and dystopian literature provides them with an ideal forum for this exploration. Young readers are invited to consider what it means to be human in the twenty-first century.

Children have a great deal to worry about, especially in the wake of the September 11, 2001, terrorist attacks. We remember fearing nuclear war during our 1980s adolescence (a fear fueled not just by the Cold War but by TV movies like *Threads* [1984][55] and *The Day After* [1983][56]) as well as global warming and overpopulation. A startling number of works in the dystopian mode for young adults deal with post-disaster and environmentally challenged scenarios. For example, Robert C. O'Brien's *Z for Zachariah* (1975)[57] is set after a nuclear war, and includes a consideration of what kind of society will be built from the ashes, and Robert Swindells's *Brother in the Land* (1984)[58] explores tensions between people in a postnuclear society. The enormous pressure on our environment is in the forefront of dozens of young adult dystopias from the 1970s to the present day. One of many examples is Adrien Stoutenburg's *Out There* (1971),[59] in which entrepreneurs and developers are eager to exploit even the few pristine parts of the environment. Concern for the environment and the preservation of natural resources in these books are related to class issues because both phenomena relate to the equitable stewardship of what we have on earth. Dystopias function as cautionary tales for a young audience, warning them to take care of the Earth and each other.

When children were asked to express their own utopian dreams in *Xanadu: The Imaginary Place* (1999), many of the entries showed a strong concern for the environment, and a desire for beautiful surroundings. The Land of Cockaigne lived on with children's wishes for such things as "houses made of Hershey Kisses" (*Xanadu*, 8). One child, Synovia Smith, writes, "My favorite thing to do on a Saturday would be to eat a hole in my [candy] house, then fix it" (18). Many children responded with a more social view of utopia that would have cured the problems plaguing their own communities: "My Xanadu has peace in the world. Girls can go outside without getting hurt. And boys can walk down the street without getting shot," writes LaToya Cunningham (21). There would be no prejudice in many of their Xanadus. The teachers involved in this project reported that the exercise of building a fictional utopia made the classroom community stronger and more harmonious (27).

Utopian and dystopian fiction is a productive place to address cultural anxieties and threats as well as to contemplate the ideal; therefore, we expect that this genre will become increasingly popular and provocative. Utopian and dystopian literature talks about the fears, questions, and issues that interest children and young adults. Although these books are written by adults, they allow young readers to take control, if only imaginatively. Jack Zipes argues in *Sticks and Stones: The Troublesome Success of Children's Literature from Slovenly Peter to Harry Potter* (2001)[60] that American children are becoming more controlled, every minute of their time measured out in supervised, organized activity, and increasingly influenced by the market and media. Zipes claims that such control leads to a great need for children and young adults to take charge when they can. As children become progressively more controlled, so will the need for books that address the desire for agency increase. What could give more freedom to children and young adults than to open the vistas of new worlds through speculative fiction, and ultimately inspire them to change the world around them?

From Train Travel to the Postnuclear Age

The essays in our first group, "Planes, Trains, and Automobiles: Utopia in Transit," discuss how trains and planes not only lead children into utopias, but are also utopian spaces in themselves. The next section, "Community and Socialism," examines how utopias in children's literature are created, linking utopia to education and cooperation. Moving from this discussion of the social basis of utopia, the final two sections, "Child Power" and "From the Wreckage: Post–World War II Dystopias and Utopias," focus on the individual child's role in utopias and dystopias. Far from being helpless and passive, children and young adults often wield power against their societies, acts of rebellion born of disillusionment and social criticism. These children and young adults thus come to a greater understanding of whether the society their elders have created for them is utopian or dystopian.

One of the first challenges an author of utopian fiction faces is how to transport characters to utopia. More than just the means of transportation, trains and planes in children's utopias are gateways to perfect worlds, and are even utopias in themselves. Alice Jenkins's "Getting to Utopia: Railways and Heterotopia in Children's Literature" discusses how authors convey characters and readers to a utopia. The steam train in particular has been a common means of solving this problem in fantasy literature for children. The train is more than a mode of transportation; it is a space in which the themes of the works are dramatized. Jenkins suggests that the railway plays an important, even subversive, role in the text, and she uses Foucault's theory of heterotopia to analyze this utopian space.

Just as the railroad captured the imagination of the nineteenth century, the airplane captured that of the twentieth. Fred Erisman's "American Boys' Series Books and the Utopia of the Air" examines thirty series of aviation-related books published for American boys between 1920 and 1945 and comprising more than two hundred titles that offer a striking vision of the utopian society that may be achieved through mastery of the air. The books, from Thomson Burtis's Russ Farrell Series (1924–1929) through Canfield Cook's Lucky Terrell Series (1942–1946), assume the coming of a world in which the airplane is a part of the life and work of every citizen. In this world, the delights and discipline of flying, initially restricted to the aviator, will become a part of democratic life. Every citizen will share in the excitement of flight, and, more to the point, the entire society will share in the exaltation and the intellectual/spiritual cleansing that only flight can offer. The books project a sense of a progressive future, in which the young will become the shapers of a technologically oriented flying society. Led by progressive America, all mankind will thus ascend to a new and higher level of human capacity.

We complete this section with Alberto Manguel's piece, "Travels Through Dystopia: H. G. Wells and *The Island of Dr. Moreau*," on his adolescent reading of H. G. Wells's *The Island of Dr. Moreau* (1895),[61] and how this dystopia influenced him. Manguel is the coeditor, with Gianni Guadalupi, of *The Dictionary of Imaginary Places* (1999),[62] and the editor and writer of numerous anthologies and books.

In the section "Community and Socialism," essays examine the social underpinnings of utopia, emphasizing social criticism and social contracts. They stress that not only is it vital to have an ideology of social cooperation in a utopia, but it must also be passed on to the next generation. Sara Gadeken's "Sarah Fielding's Childhood Utopia" examines the ways in which Fielding's *The Governess, or Little Female Academy* (1749) inculcates the technologies of self necessary for her female utopia, through a system that her narrator calls "a Method of being very happy" (*Governess*, 8). This book was the first English children's novel intended for children to read for themselves; therefore, the genre of children's novels began with utopian thinking. The stories that make up *The Governess* are told in an attempt to restore unity after the schoolgirls have been fighting. Following social models that preceded Locke, the novel expresses the social nature of identity and relationships in a way that conceives of value as rooted in communal practice, and argues that the community should be constructed and guided by values that emphasize communal rather than individual good. The development of the imagination is fundamental to the formation of this utopian community.

Cathrine Frank brings together a major figure in utopian literature, H. G. Wells, and an important writer for children, E. Nesbit; these writers knew each other and shared social agendas. In "Tinklers and Time Machines: Time Travel in the Social Fantasy of E. Nesbit and H. G. Wells," Frank reads two of E. Nesbit's children's novels, *The House of Arden* (1908)[63] and *Harding's Luck* (1909),[64] together with H. G. Wells's *The Time Machine* (1895),[65] and seeks to illuminate the way both authors' involvement in the socialist Fabian Society shaped their sense of the function and style of both adult and children's literatures. These novels pair their real social concerns with fantastic modes of expression that render them innovative in both adult and children's genres. Specifically, both Nesbit's and Wells's narrative use of time travel ironically but firmly situates them between two eras. Their emphasis on the realistic characters' temporal movement out of contemporary England links their dissatisfaction with fictional realism to their participation in the Fabian Society and its political disapproval of real turn-of-the-century social conditions. Their implementation of time travel asks readers to transport themselves out of their everyday dystopias to gain through their imagination a perspective that makes those ills visible.

Holly V. Blackford's "The Writing on the Wall of *Redwall*" shows how Brian Jacques's work presents a utopian community of monk mice to its readers. The mice live in harmony with each other, the land, God, and a traditional way of life. Yet when the rats threaten the abbey, the mice not only engage in, but embrace, war. The peaceful tradition of the monastery is undermined by the legend of Martin the Warrior of Redwall, which inspires their military goals. In fact, the community relies on inequalities of gender, species, class, and church authority for its so-called harmony.

Carrie Hintz's " 'Joy But Not Peace': Zilpha Keatley Snyder's Green-sky Trilogy" describes the way in which the Kindar people, denizens of the idyllic treetop "Green-sky" community, find out that their society is based on the deprivation and imprisonment of the Erdlings, who are held below the root. The article focuses on the Kindar's decision to dismantle the peaceful, happy utopia and allow the Erdlings into their society, disrupting their ideal culture. Children play a large role in that transformation, making it possible for the Kindar to seek justice despite the upheaval involved.

We complete this section with two essays by creative writers. In "Terrible Lizard Dream Kingdom," James Gurney, creator of Dinotopia, discusses how his utopia of dinosaurs and humans living in harmony developed. Katherine Paterson, author of *Bridge to Terabithia* (1977),[66] has written a brief essay for us, "Bridge to Utopia," on utopianism in this book, and how readers have used her utopia to create their own.

In the "Child Power" section, the essays focus on the agency of children and young adults dealing with a faulty society. The child or young adult sees society's flaws for the first time. In real life, children and young adults are the most powerless individuals in a citizenry. In children's literary utopias and dystopias, however, they emerge as powerful, understanding more than their elders, often taking control and doing their best to alter society's course.

In "Suffering in Utopia: Testing the Limits in Young Adult Novels," Rebecca Carol Noël Totaro shows how four contemporary authors of young adult novels take on the challenging task of creating complex utopian and dystopian worlds in which suffering at the most basic level threatens or afflicts their heroes. In Madeleine L'Engle's *A Wrinkle in Time* (1962), Lois Lowry's *The Giver* (1993) and *Gathering Blue* (2001), J. K. Rowling's *Harry Potter and the Philosopher's Stone* (1997),[67] and Sonia Levitin's *The Cure* (1999), the protagonist suffers from an inability to fit in with respect to physical size, level of maturation, the ability to experience the world through the five senses, or some combination of ailments. The heroes then embark on a voyage to another world or dimension of their own. Ultimately, by experiencing the contrast between two different worlds, the heroes come to understand the nature and degree of their suffering as well as the nature of their communities of origin as primarily utopian or dystopian.

Maureen Moran's "Educating Desire: Magic, Power, and Control in Tanith Lee's Unicorn Trilogy" explores the utopian and dystopian alternative worlds represented in Tanith Lee's fantasies for young adolescents: *Black Unicorn* (1991), *Gold Unicorn* (1994), and *Red Unicorn* (1997).[68] It draws theoretically on two contending models of utopia: a construct that serves either as an unrealizable expression of desire, or as an agent of social change, a hopeful "anticipation and catalyst of emergent reality." Using Lee's Trilogy as a case study, the essay examines the applicability of such theorizations of utopia to literature for children with its emphasis on the moral, social, and emotional education of the individual (and, at least in part, the legitimization of certain dominant ideologies). It investigates how the heroine Tanaquil's journeys to utopian and dystopian societies offer opportunities for an evaluation of alternative ways of being and living, emphasizing how magic conveys power and offers a bridge between reality and desire often missing in adult, "theoretical" utopias.

Monica Hughes is the author of *The Keeper of the Isis Light* (1980)[69] and numerous other young adult science fiction books that explore issues of utopia and dystopia. In "The Struggle Between Utopia and Dystopia in Writing for Children and Young Adults," she emphasizes the need to maintain hope for the young reader even in the most horrible of dystopias as she reviews her oeuvre.

The horrors of World War II and the threat of nuclear destruction have inspired dystopias in children's and young adult literature, and have made the theme of hope more difficult to emphasize, yet perhaps all the more crucial. These essays in the section "From the Wreckage: Post–World War II Dystopias and Utopias" focus on science fiction and show the child or young adult in conflict with a world that seems to have dangerously lost control.

Kay Sambell's "Presenting the Case for Social Change: the Creative Dilemma of Dystopian Fiction for Children" explores the formal dilemmas that face authors who seek to adapt the dystopian genre for the young. In the past thirty years, the dystopian novel has become the dominant genre model within futuristic fiction published for young readers. The essay considers the features that set a children's dystopian novel apart from classic "adult" dystopias, and particularly focuses on the ways in which moral meaning is typically carried in these cautionary novels. It suggests that children's writers are prone to compromising the narrative strategies on which the "adult" dystopian novelists rely to highlight their dire warnings. It outlines the ideological and imaginative fractures that result from the tendency of children's authors to supply hope within the text itself, rather than leaving it implicit or barring it, as adult dystopian novelists do.

Karen Sands-O'Connor's "The Quest for the Perfect Planet: The British Secondary World as Utopia and Dystopia, 1945–1999" argues that children's literature has a great effect on national image because it is often a young person's first understanding of a place and its people. This essay examines how national image is portrayed in the secondary world children's novel in Britain after 1945, when Britain was redefining itself. Does British fantastic fiction face the future, or does it return to its paradigms of Empire, and what does the answer to this question mean for child readers and the notion of childhood, both in Britain and throughout the world? These books present an image of a "perfect" England/Britain as almost exclusively male, white, and regressive, which is then contrasted with the imaginary worlds of the authors.

We follow this last section with an interview with Lois Lowry, author of *The Giver* (1993), thus rounding out our collection with the voice of the most well-known (and widely taught) dystopia for young adults.

Children's and young adult utopian literature offers a number of opportunities for future scholarship. The annotated bibliography included at the back of this volume testifies to the scope and variety of utopian and dystopian visions for young readers—from Edenic innocence to the darker dystopias of regimentation, warfare, and conformity. Many of the utopian and dystopian texts we have uncovered are worthy of further scholarly analysis, and inclusion in new literary histories.

Many questions remain in the field. Future studies will no doubt continue to engage with the complexities of the definition of utopia. Historical and biographical works will uncover connections between adult writers in the utopian tradition and writers for a young audience. There is also ample opportunity for research on historical events and time periods as they are reflected in utopian and dystopian writing for children and young adults from the "golden age" of children's literature to the posthuman age. Finally, new utopias and dystopias for children and young adults are being written today, reflecting the uncertainties and possibilities of our time. Utopian and dystopian writing for children and young adults will continue to be central, both for the young readers who are shaped by its questions and challenges, and for those who seek to trace its significance through scholarship.

Notes

1. Lewis Carroll, *Alice's Adventures in Wonderland* and *Through the Looking-Glass and What Alice Found There* (1865, 1871) (New York: Oxford University Press, 1982). Philip Pullman's His Dark Materials Trilogy consists of *The Golden Compass* (New York: Alfred A. Knopf, 1996); *The Subtle Knife* (New York: Alfred A. Knopf, 1997) and *The Amber Spyglass* (New York: Alfred A. Knopf, 2000).

2. Sarah Fielding, *The Governess or, Little Female Academy* (1749) (London: Pandora, 1987); hereafter cited in text as *Governess*.

3. Lyman Tower Sargent makes a distinction between "body utopias or utopias of sensual gratification" and "city utopias or utopias of human contrivance." This is a useful distinction for writing for a young audience, which includes both artificial utopias and pastoral, natural utopias. See "The Three Faces of Utopianism Revisited," *Utopian Studies* 5 (1994): 4; hereafter cited in text.

4. Lois Lowry, *The Giver* (New York: Bantam Doubleday, 1993).

5. Thomas More, *Utopia* (1516), ed. and trans. George M. Logan and Robert M. Adams (Cambridge: Cambridge University Press, 1989).

6. Lyman Tower Sargent, "Introduction," in *British and American Utopian Literature 1516–1985: an annotated, chronological bibliography* (New York and London: Garland Publishing, 1988), xii.

7. Tom Moylan outlines a particular type of "critical utopia" of the 1980s and 1990s. These texts, he claims, "reject utopia as blueprint while preserving it as dream." See *Demand the Impossible: Science Fiction and the Utopian Imagination* (New York: Methuen, 1986), 10.

8. Fredric Jameson, "Of Islands and Trenches: Neutralization and the Production of Utopian Discourse," review of Louis Marin, *Utopiques: Jeux d'Espace*, *Diacritics* 7.2 (Summer 1977): 11.

9. Herman Pleij writes of the Land of Cockaigne, "work was forbidden . . . and food and drink appeared spontaneously . . . one only had to open one's mouth and all that delicious food practically jumped inside." See *In Search of Cockaigne*, trans. Diane Webb (New York: Columbia University Press, 2001), 3.

10. Maria Nikolajeva divides her consideration of utopian children's writing into pastoral, domestic, and social utopias. See *From Mythic to Linear: Time in Children's Literature* (Lanham, Md.: Scarecrow Press, 2000). We tend to focus on the first and last categories, bracketing domestic utopias as an interesting phenomenon, but one that would encompass too many texts for this study.

11. Roald Dahl, *Charlie and the Chocolate Factory* (1964), illus. Joseph Schindelman (New York: Puffin Books, 1988).

12. Jean de Brunhoff, *Babar the King* (1933), trans. Merle S. Haas (New York: Random House, 1935), 12–13; 44–55.

13. Paul Fleischman, *Weslandia*, illus. Kevin Hawkes (New York: Walker Books, 1999).

14. James Gurney (author and illustrator), *Dinotopia: A Land Apart from Time* (Atlanta: Turner Publishing, 1992); *The World Beneath* (Atlanta: Turner Publishing, 1995).

15. Maya Ajmera and Olateju Omolodun, eds., *Xanadu: The Imaginary Place. A Showcase of Artwork and Writings by North Carolina's Children* (Durham: SHAKTI for Children, 1999); hereafter cited in text as *Xanadu*.

16. For more on utopia and totalitarianism, see Frédéric Rouvillois, "Utopian and Totalitarianism," in Roland Schaer, Gregory Claeys, and Lyman Tower Sargent, eds., *Utopia: The Search for the Ideal Society in the Western World*, (New York and Oxford: The New York Public Library/Oxford University Press, 2000), 316–33.

17. See, for example, *Canadian Children's Literature*'s special edition devoted to Holocaust literature: *Children of the Shoah: Holocaust Literature and Education. CCL* no. 95, vol. 25:3 (1999).

18. Examples include Jane Yolen, *The Gift of Sarah Barker: A Novel* (New York: Viking, 1981) and Mary Lyn Ray, *Shaker Boy* (San Diego: Harcourt Brace, 1994).

19. José Lebrero Stals speaks of "the utopic journey into childhood" through certain forms of artistic practice: "the adult recreation of what is proper to childhood: play." See "Childhood, Path of Escape," *Utopias*, special issue *Public 12*, trans. Adriana Benzaquén (Toronto: Public Access, 1995), 74–82.

20. A contrast to the Romantic vision of the child is William Golding's *The Lord of the Flies*, in which British schoolboys left to their own devices regress into savagery (London: Faber and Faber, 1954).

21. Johanna Spyri, *Heidi*, trans. Eileen Hall (New York: Puffin Books, 1994).

22. Robert Darnton explains that wishing in the fairy tales of eighteenth-century France "usually takes the form of food in peasant tales . . . and it is never ridiculous . . . in most of the tales, wish fulfillment turns into a program for survival, not a fantasy of escape." See "Peasants Tell Tales: The Meaning of Mother Goose," in *The Great Cat Massacre and Other Episodes in French Cultural History* (New York: Basic Books, 1984), 33–34.

23. Jack Zipes notes that *The Emerald City of Oz* "lays out the principles of Oz as a type of socialist paradise, an alternative to the United States, which by the end of the book must be made invisible because of encroaching technology and capitalist expansion." See "Introduction," in *The Wonderful World of Oz* (*The Wizard of Oz, The Emerald City of Oz, Glinda of Oz*) (Harmondsworth, England: Penguin Books, 1998), xxv.

24. U. C. Knoepflmacher and Mitzi Myers, "From the Editors: 'Cross-Writing' and the Reconceptualizing of Children's Literary Studies," *Children's Literature* 25 (1997): vii.

25. Soinbhe Lally, *A Hive for the Honeybee* (New York: Scholastic, 1996).

26. Madeleine L'Engle, *A Wrinkle in Time* (New York: Bantam Doubleday Dell, 1976).

27. Louise Lawrence, *Andra* (London: Collins, 1971).

28. Sonia Levitin, *The Cure* (New York: HarperCollins, 1999).

29. O. T. Nelson, *The Girl Who Owned a City* (Minneapolis: Lerner Publications Co., 1975).

30. Le Guin, Ursula K., "The Ones Who Walk Away From Omelas," *Utopian Studies* 2.1–2 (1991): 1–5.

31. Zilpha Keatley Snyder's Green-sky Trilogy consists of *Below the Root*, illus. Alton Raible (New York: Atheneum, 1975); *And All Between*, illus. Alton Raible (New York: Atheneum, 1976); and *Until the Celebration*, illus. Alton Raible (New York: Atheneum, 1977).

32. John Christopher, *The Guardians* (Harmondsworth, England: Puffin Books, 1970).

33. H. M. Hoover, *Children of Morrow* (New York: Four Winds Press, 1973).

34. John Tully, *Natfact 7* (London: Methuen, 1985).

35. Robert Swindells, *Daz 4 Zoe* (London: Hamish Hamilton, 1990).

36. Tom Browne, *Red Zone* (London: Macmillan Topliner Tridents, 1980).

37. Deborah Moulton, *Children of Time* (New York: Dial Books, 1989).

38. G. R. Kestevan, *The Awakening Water* (London: Chatto, 1977).

39. George Orwell, *Nineteen Eighty-Four* (1949) (New York: Oxford University Press, 1984).

40. Aldous Huxley, *Brave New World* (1932) (New York: Harper and Row, 1989).

41. Lois Lowry, *Gathering Blue* (New York: Houghton Mifflin, 2000).

42. Nina Bawden, *Off the Road* (New York: Puffin Books, 1998).

43. Stephanie S. Tolan, *Welcome to the Ark* (New York: HarperCollins, 1996).

44. Monica Hughes, *The Tomorrow City* (Toronto: HarperCollins, 1978).

45. For a consideration of the linkage of the adolescent developmental narrative with utopian literature, see Carrie Hintz, "Monica Hughes, Lois Lowry, and Young Adult Dystopias," *The Lion and the Unicorn* 26.2 (April 2002): 254–264.

46. Neal Shusterman, *Downsiders* (New York: Aladdin, 1999).

47. Garth Nix, *Shade's Children* (New York: Harper Trophy, 1997).

48. John Christopher's The Tripods Trilogy consists of *The White Mountains, The City of Gold and Lead*, and *The Pool of Fire* (Harmondsworth, England: Puffin Books, 1967).

49. Claire Cooper, *Earthchange* (Minneapolis: Lerner Publications Company, 1985).

50. Gerry Turner, *Stranger from the Depths* (New York: Doubleday and Company, 1967).

51. Ben Bova, *City of Darkness* (New York: Scribner, 1976).

52. Shirley Parenteau, *The Talking Coffins of Cryo-City* (New York: Elsevier/Nelson Books, 1979); hereafter cited in text as *Talking*.

53. Janet McNaughton, *The Secret Under My Skin* (Toronto: HarperCollins, 2000).

54. See Francis Fukuyama's *Our Posthuman Future: Consequences of the Biotechnology Revolution* (New York: Farrar, Straus and Giroux, 2002).

55. Mick Jackson, *Threads*, 35 mm, 114 mins. BBC World Enterprises, 1984.

56. Nicholas Meyer, *The Day After*, 35 mm, 126 mins. ABC Pictures, 1983.

57. Robert C. O'Brien, *Z for Zachariah* (London: Victor Gollancz, 1975).

58. Robert Swindells, *Brother in the Land* (Oxford: Oxford University Press, 1984).

59. Adrien Stoutenburg, *Out There* (New York: Viking Press, 1971).

60. Jack Zipes, *Sticks and Stones: The Troublesome Success of Children's Literature from Slovenly Peter to Harry Potter* (New York: Routledge, 2001).

61. H. G. Wells, *The Island of Dr. Moreau* (New York: New American Library, 1987).

62. Alberto Manguel and Gianni Guadalupi, eds., *The Dictionary of Imaginary Places* (Toronto: Alfred A. Knopf, 1999). Expanded from 1980 edition.

63. E. Nesbit, *The House of Arden* (1908) (New York: Dutton, 1967).

64. E. Nesbit, *Harding's Luck* (1909) (London: E. Benn, 1949).

65. H. G. Wells, *The Time Machine* (London: J. M. Dent, 1993).

66. Katherine Paterson, *Bridge to Terabithia* (New York: HarperCollins, 1977).

67. J. K. Rowling, *Harry Potter and the Philosopher's Stone* (London: Bloomsbury, 1997).

68. Tanith Lee's Unicorn Trilogy consists of *Black Unicorn* (London: Orbit Books, 1994), *Gold Unicorn* (London: Orbit Books, 1995), and *Red Unicorn* (New York: Tor/Tom Doherty, 1997).

69. Monica Hughes, *The Keeper of the Isis Light* (1980) (New York: Aladdin, 2000).

PART I

Planes, Trains, and Automobiles: Utopia in Transit

1

Getting to Utopia: Railways and Heterotopia in Children's Literature

ALICE JENKINS

The English narrator of Thomas More's *Utopia* (1516)[1] travels only as far as Antwerp in Belgium. There he meets Raphael Hythlodaeus, a Portuguese sailor who journeyed to the New World with Amerigo Vespucci, remained behind when Vespucci left, and made his way by various unplanned voyages to the island of Utopia; it is Hythlodaeus who describes the way of life of the Utopians. Utopia makes comparatively little play with the experience of physical journeys, but later utopian texts, from *Gulliver's Travels* (1726)[2] on, have not followed its example in this respect. Among the challenges that utopian imagining presents to the writer of fiction is the problem of how to convey characters and readers to the envisioned utopia. This paper considers the tradition that reaches from Lewis Carroll to J. K. Rowling of using the railway train as a means of solving this problem in the context of fantasy literature for children. Train journeys occur at initiatory or climactic moments of large numbers of classic children's utopian fantasies; in these journeys, the railway functions as a protean, paradoxical space, not merely instrumental but instead active. Long after it vanished from the landscapes of the real world as a functional means of transport, the steam train in particular continues to feature in works of fantasy aimed at children, operating by laws often unlike those of the realms through which it passes, and providing a space for the dramatization of spiritual and emotional adventure. This paper attempts an anatomy of these spaces, and argues that railway journeys serve an important role within the metaphorical as well as the narrative economy of utopian texts; this role is sometimes a subversive one, and ultimately calls into question the relationship of reader to text.

Railway trains in utopian fantasy literature operate like alternative worlds, allowing space and time within the narrative for establishment, subversion, and clashing of the logics and values of the other realms of the text. In this way they can be described in terms of Foucault's well-known formulation of "heterotopia": "counter-sites . . . in which the real sites, all the other real sites that can be found within the culture, are simultaneously represented, contested and inverted. Places of this kind are outside of all places, even though it may be possible to indicate their location in reality."[3] Foucault describes ships as "heterotopia par excellence" because as well as being heterotopic in their own spatiopolitical functions, they are a means of transport connecting other heterotopic spaces, including colonies and brothels (Foucault, 27). But similar claims to heterotopic status can be made for railway trains. Cinemas, theaters, and gardens are heterotopia for Foucault because they are "capable of juxtaposing in a single real place several spaces, several sites that are in themselves incompatible" (Foucault, 25). These examples bring different sites together in space, but a train, traveling between points of departure and destinations, brings them together in time. Juxtaposing does not necessarily require instantaneousness; the train achieves it more literally than the cinema, though less immediately. Foucault reminds his reader that carpets "were originally reproductions of gardens," and that "the rug is a sort of garden that can move across space" (Foucault, 26). His reference is to the portability of rugs, but in the context of children's literature there are numerous instances of flying carpets that can literally move across space, juxtaposing different sites while themselves providing a location for action.[4] If a ship or a flying carpet can be a heterotopia, surely we must accept the possibility that a train can also.

Most important for the study of the heterotopic in narrative, Foucault describes heterotopia as functioning "at full capacity when men arrive at a sort of absolute break with their traditional time" (Foucault, 26). He gives the examples of cemeteries, museums, and fairgrounds as spaces that relate the human to a nonhabitual time-scheme, or "heterochrony" (the infinite, the historical, and the ephemeral, respectively) (Foucault, 26). The disruption and remodeling of traditional notions of time that was caused by the advent of the railways in the nineteenth century has been well documented. A national standard of timekeeping became necessary; local time gave way to "railway time" as the demands of time-tabling enforced consistency from one end of the country to the other. As well as this nationalization of the temporal, nineteenth-century writers commented on the way in which the extraordinary speed of railway travel changed their conception of time and its relation to space. The Victorian popularizer of science Mary Somerville was characteristic of her period in seeing the advent of steam-powered travel as carrying humanity toward a utopia in which nationalism, provincialism, and ignorance would be wiped away: "The history of former ages exhibits nothing to be compared with the mental activity of the present. Steam, which annihilates time and space, fills mankind with schemes for advantage or defense; but however mercenary the motives for enterprise may be, it is instrumental in bringing nations together, and uniting them in mutual bonds of friendship. The facility of communication is rapidly assimilating national character.

Society in most of the capitals is formed on the same model; individuality is only met with in the provinces, and every well educated person now speaks more than one of the modern languages."[5] But in later years, when the experience of traveling by train became a common one, open to almost everyone in Britain, this astonished acknowledgement of a decisive alteration in the understanding of time and space gave way to a perception of a kind of heterochrony whereby the train traveler's condition of isolation, removed from familiar surroundings, restricted as to movement in space for potentially long periods of time, engenders a sense of temporal unsettlement. In nonrealist writing, this unsettlement or instability can be put to use in blurring the boundaries between different narrative or historical moments, juxtaposing them (to return to Foucault's term) to allow rapid transitions for readers and characters.

The most recent example of the railway train in children's fantasy, and surely one of the most widely read, comes in the early stages of J. K. Rowling's *Harry Potter and the Philosopher's Stone* (1997).[6] Harry, the persecuted orphan who becomes a wizard-in-training, first encounters the utopian world of Hogwarts Academy of Witchcraft and Wizardry in the form of the Hogwarts Express, an anachronistic steam train operating from the magical platform Nine and Three-Quarters in the very mundane King's Cross Station in London. Hogwarts Academy provides an untypical modern utopia: its strictly defined hierarchies of authority based on seniority, sports teams, and a prefect system combine with its separation of children from domestic and parental influences to create a vision of a controlled, protective environment, which must be rigorously defended against incursions from exterior threats, even when those threats have hidden themselves within the community of the school. Although the connotations of its oligarchical, stratified system may make its utopian imagining a political disappointment to many, it might perhaps be termed a readerly utopia, in that it provides an ideal place for enthusiasts to inhabit in their imaginative life.

The experience of Hogwarts, then, for characters and readers, begins with a railway journey, which Rowling uses in time-honored fashion as a privileged space and time in which many of the main characters of the novel are introduced. Other, less fantastical school fictions have often adopted the same device. In the novels discussed in this essay, however, trains tend to have a peculiarly ambiguous status, negotiating between and blurring the boundaries of the home, "real" world and the utopian, dystopian, or fantasy world. In Alan Garner's *The Weirdstone of Brisingamen* (1960), the two child protagonists Colin and Susan are introduced to the reader on a railway journey, but unlike Rowling, Garner acknowledges and utilizes the uneasy capacity that train travel has for separating travelers from their habitual emotional frame, and so initiating the momentum of fantasy, in which habitual frames of all kinds are disrupted: "Susan began to clear away the debris of the journey—apple cores, orange peel, food wrappings, magazines, while Colin pulled down their luggage from the rack. And within three minutes they were both poised on the edge of their seats, case in hand and mackintosh over one arm, caught, like every traveller before or since, in that limbo of journey's end, when there is nothing to do and no time to relax. These last miles were the longest of all."[7] In this passage from the opening page of the novel, Colin and Susan move from agency to entrapment, from having power over the objects of their life to being objects themselves, "poised" and "caught" in a pattern larger than their own wills. The railway train as a motif engages with the realist and the subversive strands in children's fantasy literature, and provides a sealed space that insulates characters from the landscapes they traverse and which temporarily extracts them from the laws of cause and effect that determine the rest of the fantasy world.

Railway trains may convey characters to a utopia, as in C. S. Lewis's *The Last Battle* (1956),[8] where all the main characters of the Chronicles of Narnia discover they have been killed in a rail crash and are now literally in heaven; or to a dystopia, as in Diana Wynne Jones's *Fire and Hemlock* (1985),[9] in which a train carries the heroine, Polly, and a string quartet of possible superheroes, to a very malign Elfland. The train in Kenneth Grahame's *The Wind in the Willows* (1908)[10] allows the escaping Toad to return to the utopia of Toad Hall, now made dystopian by the invasion of working-class stoats and weasels. In many other instances, though, the destination is not so clearly demarcated as in these novels, and trains take characters to places in which they must prove their worth.

Two contradictory impulses operate in fantastic writing: the impulse toward realism, anchoring the characters and reader in the known world of everyday objects, and that toward imaginative subversion of realism. Tzvetan Todorov's influential study of the genre insists on this doubleness: fantastic texts must make the reader "hesitate between a natural and a supernatural explanation of the events described."[11] He adds: "this hesitation may also be experienced by a character" (Todorov, 33). Utopian fantasy for children, however, generally approaches its subject with less hesitancy than the texts of Todorov's analysis. At the end of *The Last Battle*, the reader discovers that events which have up to now been interpreted literally are in fact to be read allegorically, but this is really self-correction rather than hesitation. The Harry Potter novels, once past the initiatory stages in which Harry does not yet realize he is part of a magical world-within-a-world, provoke and display little of Todorov's hesitancy; each event, spectacle, or sensation is to be understood as real and "natural" within the logic of the books' universe. The characters' and reader's hesitancy is in interpreting the chain of cause and effect as if in a realist detective novel, rather than in determining the ontological status of the underpinning physical laws of the magical world. Even Susan Cooper's fantasy sequence, The Dark Is Rising, which is immensely more subtle and imaginative than Rowling's work, requires the reader to accept the extraordinary experiences narrated as "natural" in Todorov's terms; characters are rarely in doubt as to whether a particular episode really happened, and readers are not asked to doubt the sanity of the characters or the reliability of the narrator through whom these episodes are rendered.

This investment in the reality of the imagined world is a large part of what allows these texts to approach the utopian despite the fact that the worlds themselves are neither perfect nor presented as ideal models. Utopia, as a mode, is very different from Todorov's account of the fantastic: its interest in practical particulars, its historical association with the plain style, and its tendency toward encyclopedism mean that utopian writing, although it may be surrounded by a fantastic frame-narrative and may contain "supernatural" beings or facts, maintains an intimate relationship with realism. Hesitancy in reading utopias is ideological, not narratological. How are readers to be brought to the new kind of reality that utopia offers? In linking the natural and supernatural landscapes of fantasy for children, in drawing together the different planes of reality in which a fantastic narrative operates, railway trains seem to provide a particularly compelling, and certainly recurrent, motif.

Michel Foucault, in his suggestive lecture "Of Other Spaces," notes that "a train is an extraordinary bundle of relations because it is something through which one goes, it is also something by means of which one can go from one point to another, and then it is also something that goes by" (Foucault, 23). The adventures of the child characters in E. Nesbit's *The Railway Children* (1906)[12] take place around, rather than on board, railway trains. The trains deliver the children and other important characters, including a Russian dissident and eventually their unjustly imprisoned father, to the main location of the novel, but throughout the narrative the railway is seen from the point of view of a nontraveling observer, a trainspotter, as it were. The trains are, for the children, "something that goes by," as Foucault puts it (Foucault, 23). But more often, and particularly in utopian or other fantasy fiction, it is the first two elements of Foucault's formulation of the train's "relations" that are put in play.

Unlike a car, in which one is not free to leave one's seat, a train offers the possibility of movement within a space which is itself moving. In this way it enacts contradictory power relations: a passenger in a train is both passive, being carried willy-nilly to the train's destination, and active, capable of travel on foot within the body of the train. Like all enclosed means of transport, a train is a miniature world that is both part of and distinct from the larger world surrounding it; but only ships and, to a lesser extent, airplanes, are analogous to trains in their internal navigability and inhabitability. This capacity for ambiguous power relations allows trains to be used as quasi-magical spaces, moving between two worlds and often creating a third within themselves. In terms of Arnold van Gennep's classic exposition of liminal spaces in *The Rites of Passage* (1913)[13] a train journey is the crossing of a threshold, but a crossing that may have extended temporal duration (in contrast to most pedestrian threshold crossings, which are almost instantaneous), thus cocooning the person making the crossing within a bubble of space and time, in which the established logics of both sides of the threshold may be vulnerable.

Van Gennep regards thresholds as the vestigial remains of much larger "neutral zones" between magically or spiritually determined spaces, and notes that means of transport, as well as geographic areas, can have thresholds and hence demand the performance of threshold rites by the traveler: "the acts of embarking and disembarking, of entering a vehicle or a litter, and of mounting a horse to take a trip are often accompanied by rites of separation at the time of departure and by rites of incorporation upon return" (van Gennep, 23). This observation opens the question of what the traveler's magico-religious status has been while he or she was in the vehicle or on the horse. Has the traveler assumed a new spiritual status with each demarcated area he or she moves into? Or has he or she carried around a single status, conferred by the rites of separation and hence belonging to the home community's belief system even while signaling exile from it, so that changes of place outside the community have not affected the traveler? Trains in utopian and fantasy literature generate the second of these situations: a train may carry the passenger through various "zones," either geographical areas, spiritual states, or different kinds of reality, but by enclosing the traveler in a bubble with its own internal logic and physical or magical laws, it shields the passenger from the logic and laws of the places it passes. This shielding may be protective or entrapping; benign, neutral or dangerous.

In what is probably the initiatory text of this tradition in children's literature, Lewis Carroll's Alice travels by train across the first of the "little brooks" that separate each square of the chessboard landscape of *Through the Looking-Glass* (1871).[14] The passengers in her carriage subject her to contemptuous scrutiny so wildly fantastical that her recognizability as a human being is put into jeopardy. "She'll have to go back from here as luggage!" comments a beetle, and other travelers add: "she must go by post, as she's got a head on her—" (envisaging Alice as a stamped envelope), "[s]he must be sent as a message by the telegraph—" and "[s]he must draw the train herself the rest of the way—" (*Looking-Glass*, 219).

The reader's anxiety about a young female passenger surrounded by threatening male fellow travelers draws on continuing fears about the gendered nature of the space of a train, perhaps related to its rather phallic forcing of a way through surrounding territory, and certainly derived from its being a sealed, enclosed arena. The possibility of entrapment was particularly strong in compartment trains, used in Britain throughout the age of steam, in which small seating areas were located to one side of a corridor running the length of each carriage. Once the doors of the compartment were closed, the space became surprisingly private and hermetic, and hence a place of possible harassment of vulnerable passengers.

As the example from Carroll demonstrates, railway trains cannot be utopian spaces in themselves, because of their ability to shelter and transport the morally repugnant as well as the deserving. The heterotopic space of the train can indeed become dystopian, a space of threat and vulnerability, as is frequently stressed in literature for children. Early in Joan Aiken's historical fantasy *The Wolves of Willoughby Chase* (1962),[15] for instance, the young and ill-nourished Silvia undertakes a long train journey made hazardous by winter weather, circling wolves, and a dubious male stranger who forces himself on her attention. Silvia has been crying with homesickness, and the man, who emerges later in the novel as a callous villain, manifests himself, like the much more benign gnat in *Through the Looking Glass*,[16] as a voice disconcertingly close to her:

> "Here, this won't do," said a voice in her ear suddenly, and she looked up in alarm to see that the man at the other end of the compartment had moved along and was sitting opposite and staring at her. Sylvia gave her eyes a final dab and haughtily concentrated on her reflection in the dark window, but her heart was racing. Should she pull the communication cord? She stole a cautious glance at the man's reflection and saw that he was standing up, apparently extracting something from a large leather portmanteau. Then he turned towards her, holding something out: she looked round enough to see that it was a box of chocolates about a foot square by six inches deep, swathed around with violet ribbons.
>
> "No, thank you," said Sylvia, in as ladylike a tone as she could muster. "I never touch chocolate." . . .
>
> "Now come along—do," said the man coaxingly. "All little girls like sweeties, *I* know."
>
> "Sir," said Sylvia coldly, "if you speak to me again I shall be obliged to pull the communication cord." (*Wolves*, 24)

In this case, the privacy of the compartment imposes a strict set of social conventions on Silvia, involving the reinforcement of class and gender boundaries (icy politeness, physical distancing, denial of appetite) despite an onslaught of sensory temptation. Her unwanted companion, by virtue of his masculinity, his age, and his comparative lack of refinement, is less disempowered by the enclosure of the compartment than Silvia. Male freedom of movement is contrasted with female stasis, and is perceived as threatening.

A similar scene occurs in Diana Wynne Jones's *The Crown of Dalemark* (1993).[17] Maewen, another young girl traveling alone by train, is more assured than Aiken's Silvia but nonetheless vulnerable to violation of her personal space by an intrusive older male. Jones's description of the man's "wriggly grey hair" may be an allusion to the curly beard and horns of the male, besuited goat sitting opposite Alice in John Tenniel's illustration of the railway carriage in *Through the Looking-Glass*, and the man's mild yet faintly menacing manner suggests a sexuality that draws on this hint of goatishness:

> "Are you travelling far, young lady?" asked the passenger opposite, making her jump again. He must have got on the train at Orilsway or somewhere. She looked at him, trying to remember, and decided she must have been asleep when he got on, because she had certainly not noticed him before. He was one of those wide kind of old men who are almost bell-shaped sitting down. He had a sheet of wriggly grey hair on either side of his wide, plump face. Maewen was not sure she liked the way his eyes were half-hooded in fat eyelids—it made him look cunning and rather cruel—but his question had been perfectly polite and she supposed she had better answer. . . .
>
> For one horrid moment Maewen thought he was going to pat her knee. She surged herself right to the back of her seat, but that did not seem nearly far enough away. (*Crown*, 64–65)

Again, the enclosed space and enforced bodily proximity of train travel result in a situation where good manners demand social behavior that the instinct of the female protagonist revolts against. The conditions are ripe for the development of intimacy between the characters—this is why the train is such a useful setting for the opening of school stories, in which relationships need to be established quickly—but because that intimacy is not desired by the girl, the possibility of danger emerges.[18]

The same possibilities for danger apply to travel in (say) a horse-drawn coach, which like a railway compartment organizes strangers into physical nearness, sitting opposite one another; but coaches do not often feature in twentieth-century fantasy except in explicitly "historical" settings such as Aiken's disturbingly dystopian *Midnight Is a Place*.[19] Indeed, they make comparatively few appearances even in Victorian children's fantasy. The profusion of railway journeys in these novels cannot be ascribed simply to the enduring physical reality of trains in the "real" world. This would not explain why steam trains figure in late twentieth-century texts so much more often than the diesel and electric trains of contemporary reality. Neither would it explain why writers tend to imagine trains rather than another familiar means of transport in which one is forced into relationships with strangers: aircraft. There is a particular symbolic resonance in the motif of the steam train that enables it to act potently in the landscapes of fantasy.

In airplanes, as in trains, passengers can move around even as they move through the air. But aircraft do not occupy the same important place in fantasy literature as trains. Their liminality is too visible, too extreme; the linearity of a railway journey, which cannot deviate from predetermined and impersonal tracks, provides the fantastical imagination with a necessary literalness that flight, with its transcendence of borders and determining lines, lacks.

Ships and boats, too, operate without linear determination, but they are limited to one plane, to two dimensions. Ships nonetheless make much more frequent appearances in fantasy novels for children than do aircraft. Vessels often appear in connection with railways, and this is one reason why it is steam rather than diesel or electric trains that dominate in these contexts. Steam trains, as the name reminds us, have a strong connection with water, and it is from the protean qualities of water that they draw part of their strength in symbolic uses. The vapor that steam trains produce quickly condenses in the course of these texts into water that must be crossed. Water moves easily between levels of metaphoricity and so is particularly congenial to a genre where negotiation between different determinations of the real is a necessary part of each text. The children traveling to Hogwarts in the Harry Potter books disembark from their steam train only to board boats that magically steer themselves across the lake to the school. Pidge and Bridget, in Pat O'Shea's *The Hounds of the Mórrígan* (1985),[20] take a wholly anachronistic steam train from contemporary Galway into the realm of Faery, but their journey is not complete until they cross a misty lake in a small boat. The otherworldly steam train at the climax of Susan Cooper's *Silver on the Tree* (1977),[21] itself the climax of The Dark Is Rising series, metamorphoses into a boat (*Silver*, 761). Sometimes after a train journey the trope of water emerges as metaphor rather than location, as in Garner's *The Weirdstone of Brisingamen*. Immediately after the passage quoted at the beginning of this essay about the unsettling liminality of the final stages of train travel, the narration continues: "The platform of Wilmslow station was thick with people, and more spilled off the train, but Colin and Susan had no difficulty in recognising Gowther Mossock among those waiting. As the tide of passengers broke round him and surged through the gates, leaving the children lonely at the far end of the platform, he waved his hand and came striding towards them" (*Weirdstone*, 1). Garner uses a string of metaphors to associate the unpredictable, shifting movements of water with the emotional state of the children, and to use the contrast between the potential danger of the sea and its benign naturalness to establish the contrast between the dangerous multitudes who will attack and harass the children later in the novel, and the heroic individualism and warmth of Gowther, who will protect them. Gowther appears first as a rock that breaks the flow of departing passengers, and then as a metaphorically watery being himself, giving a wave to the children who have been stranded by the spill and surge of the tidelike mass of people. In other instances, train travel and water are linked for structural purposes, as in Jones's *The Crown of Dalemark*, where narratives set in different times but the same fantasy location hinge in the mind of a girl traveling on a train but dreaming about water:

> Maewen came back to the present with a jump. For a moment there, it had seemed as if the noise of the train was not the beat of wheels on tracks, but the sound of water rilling over stones. She had almost seemed to see young leaves rustling overhead, casting a mix of sunspots and shadow on the racing water. . . .
>
> Nonsense, of course. She must have dropped off to sleep while the train was rushing into this deep green cutting—such a deep one that there was no sign of the mountains beyond—and the glint had to be the gold buttons of the guard, just passing on his regular walk down the corridors. (*Crown*, 61)

The events in Maewen's "dream" occurred in the past, but have just been narrated to the reader and will be brought to conclusion later in the novel by Maewen herself during an extended episode of time traveling. In the second paragraph, the train's passage through a railway cutting subtly mimics the passage of a boat through heavy, "deep green" seas, and is likened to the process of losing consciousness. The first paragraph associates Maewen and her railway journey with Norith (Maewen's double in the past) and her crossing of a river in which she finds the golden figure of a god. Jones uses a chain of alliterating gerunds ("rilling," "racing," "rushing") to link together the water and the train in a sonic metaphor that repeats the sensory confusion experienced by Maewen as she tries to make sense of her real but impossible dual vision. So although Maewen does not herself add a boat journey to her train travel, this "dream" adds her double's water-crossing to her own railway experience. Water and trains are thus joined in the spatial and temporal continua of the novel. The mechanics of the steam engine force themselves into the metaphorical dimension of these texts' imaginary landscapes.

Having carried readers and characters to the good place, the next major problem faced by writers in this genre is to keep their utopias from becoming dystopian. It is a commonplace that twentieth-century writers and readers have had greater difficulty than their forebears in making a sustained emotional commitment to the possibility of utopia. I want to conclude this essay with a few observations about Susan Cooper's *Silver on the Tree*, which is the most utopian, and yet the least realistic, novel discussed here. Its utopianism, like that of Philip Pullman's millennarian trilogy, His Dark Materials, is made possible and at the same time made radical by humanism: both sequences reject the possibility of even benign supernatural intervention in humanity's future, insisting instead on the necessity for humans to mature into guardians of their own best interests, to build, as Pullman's characters put it, "the republic of heaven where we are."[22] In Todorov's terms, there is a great deal of "hesitation" involved in reading Cooper's novel: its intense and sometimes bewildering metaphoricity causes the reader to waver between realist and allegorical interpretations. Like Pullman's *The Amber Spyglass*, this concluding novel in a wide-ranging and many-charactered series does not manage to achieve the same clarity of purpose and of imagination as its predecessors; like *The Amber Spyglass*, too, it meditates on the nature of utopia and on its place in a human world.

In *Silver on the Tree*, Cooper uses a mystical steam train for all of the purposes I have outlined in this essay: as a means of transferring readers and characters among locations in time and space; as a means of bringing characters into physical intimacy; and as a space of potential threat, where malignity may cloak itself as familiar and casual. The steam train becomes a symbol, among many others, of the power of the forces of goodness in the sequence's moral universe; but because this novel is hesitant in Todorov's sense, the materiality of the train is eventually dissolved as the forces of goodness dissipate.

In one episode, Barney, Bran, and Will, three boys brought up in the twentieth century, possessing varying levels of supernatural power, have been conveyed to the fourteenth century as part of a quest. Having completed this part of their mission, they experience "a whirling and a turning of the air about them, and a long, strange, husky shrieking in their ears, and when the giddiness went out of their minds they were in a different place and a different time" (*Silver*, 751). The children have been transported to a magical railway station, where they board a train that has also swept up their allies in the quest, who up to this point have been in the world of the twentieth century:

> Simon and Jane had left the dunes and crossed the golf course, coming to the wire fence edging the railway track, when they heard the strange noise. It rang out over their heads on the wind: a clear startling metallic clang, like the single blow of a hammer on an anvil. . . .
>
> And they saw in the distance, against the growing grey clouds, a long plume of white smoke, and heard the rising roar, closer and closer, of a fast-moving train. Then it came into sight, round the distant bend, and grew clearer, rushing at them, and it was like no train they had ever seen before.
>
> Simon gave a great whoop of astonished joy. "Steam!" (*Silver*, 751–52)

In both passages quoted, the train is perceived first as a surprising sound and a disturbance of the air; both phenomena are partly explicable after the reader's realization that it is a steam train, but the impression of uncanniness, or "hesitation," remains. The anachronism of the train contributes to the impression that it is not really of this world. This train is "the great formless vehicle of the Light," a protective heterotopia within which the questers are carried into a mystical landscape where the final battle between Light and Dark is to be fought (*Silver*, 760). But as with the novels discussed earlier, the space of this train contains an element of threat that makes its presence felt first by asking a question about the destination of a young female passenger (*Silver*, 754). The beneficent wizard Merriman Lyon (Merlin) disposes of this threat by banishing it from the privileged space of the train: " 'The Light throws you from this stream of Time,' he said, his voice ringing as the song of the train had rung through the hollow land. 'We drive you before us. Out! Out! And save yourself as best you can, when you fly forth ahead of this great progress, and the terrible force of your Dark falls upon you thinking to ambush the Light' " (*Silver*, 760). In Lyon's phrase, which harks back to the ideological disputes arising from the early days of the railways in Britain, this is not just a train but a "great progress." In a radical rewriting of Lewis's Christian utopia in *The Last Battle*, the progress Cooper's train makes is towards a kind of existentialist state, a recognition of the loneliness and responsibility of human will set free from magical guidance and exploitation. The wizard's valedictory speech in the coda to the novel is curiously untriumphant and muted: "We have delivered you from evil, but the evil that is inside men is at the last a matter for men to control. The responsibility and the hope and the promise are in your hands—your hands and the hands of the children of all men on this earth. The future cannot blame the present, just as the present cannot blame the past. The hope is always therein, always alive, but only your fierce caring can fan it into a fire to warm the world" (*Silver*, 783). Since the reader has, by the time he or she reaches this speech, journeyed through the five novels of Cooper's sequence and become entirely accustomed to its magically determined moral universe, and since, within the logic of the text, the victory and subsequent abdication of the Light ushers in an entirely new era in human history, we might argue that it is this new world, the world of human responsibility rather than the world of magic and mysticism, that represents the heterotopic at this moment in the narrative.

Foucault's most basic distinction between utopia and heterotopia is that the latter is "real" while the former has "no real place." Utopias "are sites that have a general relation of direct or inverted analogy with the real space of Society. They present society itself in a perfected form, or else society turned upside down, but in any case these utopias are fundamentally unreal spaces" (Foucault, 24). Such a distinction must be inadequate in the context of the study of fiction. Not even a place that is well known and easily locatable in the nontextual world can be said to be "real" when it appears in a work of fiction, whether utopian, fantastic, or realist. The difference between the "reality" of King's Cross Station and that of Hogwarts Academy, or of Galway City and Faery, as they feature in Rowling's and O'Shea's texts, can be no more—and no less—than a matter of convention. As the inversion of the real and unreal, or natural and supernatural during the course of Susan Cooper's The Dark Is Rising series indicates, the stability of the valorization and recognizability of utopia and heterotopia is easily disruptable. It is easy to envisage a text in which a "real" place was written about in such a way as to appear more fantastical, more outside the dominant logic of the text's universe, than Faery, Utopia, or Narnia. For an account of the relationship between utopia and heterotopia that is more accommodating to fiction, despite its origin in sociology, we might turn to Kevin Hetherington: "Heterotopia are sites associated with alternate modes of social ordering that are expressions of a utopic spatial play. They are the spaces, defined as Other, relationally, within a spatializating process, which, I believe, have this distinct utopic associated with them. Almost like laboratories, they can be taken as the sites in which new ways of experimenting with ordering society are tried out."[23] Heterotopia, in this model, would allow readers and writers to maintain optimism about the possibility of utopia, since by providing a space of play or experimentation, they permit the construction of possibly utopian configurations but can be quickly excised should the utopian become dystopian.

For Hetherington, heterotopia are "margins in the sense of the unbounded and blurred space-between rather than the easily identified space at the edge" (Hetherington, 27). Adopting this insight, we might argue that literary heterotopia are the spaces that do not fit the prevailing interpretative system; thus in the context of the novels I have been discussing, they belong to neither the realist, the utopian, nor the fantastical modes. The protean, fluid, and ambiguous symbolic qualities of the railway train in imaginative literature mean that as a space of encounter between opposing moral forces and negotiation between intratextual economies, trains do indeed constitute such a "space-between."

Notes

1. Thomas More, *Utopia* (1516), trans. Paul Turner (Harmondsworth, England: Penguin, 1964).
2. Jonathan Swift, *Gulliver's Travels* (1726) (London: Pan Books, 1977).
3. Michel Foucault, "Of Other Spaces," trans. Jay Miskowiec in *Diacritics* 16 (1986): 24; hereafter cited in text.
4. See, for instance, the eponymous carpet in E. Nesbit's *The Phoenix and the Carpet* (1904) (London: Puffin Books, 1994).
5. Mary Somerville, *Physical Geography* (London: John Murray, 1848), 121.
6. J. K. Rowling, *Harry Potter and the Philosopher's Stone* (London: Bloomsbury, 1997).
7. Alan Garner, *The Weirdstone of Brisingamen* (1960) (Glasgow: Collins, 1975), 1; hereafter cited in text as *Weirdstone*.
8. C. S. Lewis, *The Last Battle: A Story for Children* (1956) (Harmondsworth, England: Penguin Books, 1964); hereafter cited in text as *Last*.
9. Diana Wynne Jones, *Fire and Hemlock* (London: Methuen, 1985).

10. Kenneth Grahame, *The Wind in the Willows* (1908) (Oxford: Oxford University Press, 1983).

11. Tzvetan Todorov, *The Fantastic: A Structural Approach to a Literary Genre*, trans. Richard Howard (Ithaca: Cornell University Press, 1975), 33; hereafter cited in text.

12. E. Nesbit, *The Railway Children* (1906) (Oxford: Oxford University Press, 1991).

13. Arnold van Gennep, *The Rites of Passage* (1913), trans. Monika B. Vizedom and Gabrielle L. Caffee (London: Routledge & Kegan Paul, 1960); hereafter cited in text.

14. Lewis Carroll, *Through the Looking-Glass and What Alice Found There* (1871) in *The Annotated Alice* (1965) (Harmondsworth, England: Penguin Books, 1970); hereafter cited in text as *Looking-Glass*.

15. Joan Aiken, *The Wolves of Willoughby Chase* (1962) (London: Red Fox, 1992); hereafter cited in text as *Wolves*.

16. The gnat makes its presence felt by Alice first as "an extremely small voice, close to her ear" (*Looking-Glass*, 219).

17. Diana Wynne Jones, *The Crown of Dalemark* (London: Mandarin, 1993); hereafter cited in text as *Crown*.

18. It is not only girls whose physical and psychic space is vulnerable to invasion by ill-wishing males in children's literature; the episode at the beginning of John Masefield's *The Box of Delights: When the Wolves Were Running* (1935) (Oxford: Windrush, 1987), in which Kay, a small boy, is lured into gambling by cardsharpers posing as priests on a train brings together similar threatening elements. But in this case Kay's fear is of moral degradation and fiscal loss rather than sexual or other physical intimidation.

19. Joan Aiken, *Midnight Is a Place* (London: Cape, 1974).

20. Pat O'Shea, *The Hounds of the Mórrígan* (Oxford: Oxford University Press, 1985).

21. Susan Cooper, *Silver on the Tree* (1977) (Harmondsworth, England: Puffin Books, 1987); hereafter cited in text as *Silver*.

22. Philip Pullman, *The Amber Spyglass* (London: Scholastic, 2000), 516. Pullman's His Dark Materials Trilogy consists of *The Golden Compass* (originally *Northern Lights* [London: Scholastic, 1995]) (New York: Alfred A. Knopf, 1996), *The Subtle Knife* (New York: Alfred A. Knopf, 1997), and *The Amber Spyglass* (New York: Alfred A. Knopf, 2000).

23. Kevin Hetherington, *The Badlands of Modernity: Heterotopia and Social Ordering* (London: Routledge, 1997), 12–13; hereafter cited in text.

Works Cited

Aiken, Joan. *The Wolves of Willoughby Chase*. 1962. London: Red Fox, 1992.

———. *Midnight Is a Place*. London: Cape, 1974.

Carroll, Lewis. *Through the Looking-Glass and What Alice Found There*. 1871. In *The Annotated Alice*, ed. Martin Gardner. 1965. Harmondsworth, England: Penguin Books, 1970.

Cooper, Susan. *Silver on the Tree*. 1977. The Dark Is Rising series. 1984. Harmondsworth, England: Puffin Books, 1987.

Foucault, Michel. "Of Other Spaces," trans. Jay Miskowiec, *Diacritics*, 16 (1986): 22–27.

Garner, Alan. *The Weirdstone of Brisingamen*. 1960. Glasgow: Collins, 1975.

van Gennep, Arnold. *The Rites of Passage*, trans. Monika B. Vizedom and Gabrielle L. Caffee. 1913. London: Routledge & Kegan Paul, 1960.

Grahame, Kenneth. *The Wind in the Willows*. 1908. Oxford: Oxford University Press, 1983.

Hetherington, Kevin. *The Badlands of Modernity: Heterotopia and Social Ordering*. London: Routledge, 1997.

Jones, Diana Wynne. *Fire and Hemlock*. London: Methuen, 1985.

———. *The Crown of Dalemark*. London: Mandarin, 1993.

Lewis, C. S. *The Last Battle: A Story for Children*. 1956. Harmondsworth, England: Penguin Books, 1964.

Masefield, John. *The Box of Delights: When the Wolves Were Running*. 1935. Oxford: Windrush, 1987.

More, Thomas. *Utopia*. Translated by Paul Turner. 1516. Harmondsworth, England: Penguin Books, 1965.

Nesbit, E. *The Phoenix and the Carpet*. 1904. Harmondsworth, England: Puffin Books, 1959.

———. *The Railway Children*. 1906. Oxford: Oxford University Press, 1991.

O'Shea, Pat. *The Hounds of the Mórrígan*. Oxford: Oxford University Press, 1985.

Pullman, Philip. *The Amber Spyglass*. London: Scholastic, 2000.

Rowling, J. K. *Harry Potter and the Philosopher's Stone*. London: Bloomsbury, 1997.

Somerville, Mary. *Physical Geography*. London: John Murray, 1848.

Todorov, Tzvetan. *The Fantastic: A Structural Approach to a Literary Genre*. Translated by Richard Howard. Ithaca: Cornell University Press, 1975.

2

American Boys' Series Books and the Utopia of the Air

FRED ERISMAN

In a volume of essays published in 1930, as the Daniel Guggenheim Fund for the Promotion of Aeronautics was closing its books, Harry F. Guggenheim, president of the Fund, sketched out his vision of an aviation-shaped world. Thanks to the airplane, he wrote, the human race will have "a new freedom, eliminating the geographical barriers of river, sea, mountain and desert between [Man] and his kind, and thus eliminating those prejudices and mis-understandings which have jeopardized human relations in the past."[1] Guggenheim had good reason for his optimism. The Fund, in the five years of its existence, had worked to advance that vision, underwriting develop-ments in aircraft guidance, meteorology, and safety, and paving the way for a national commercial air transport system.

His optimism, however, drew upon sources emotional and intellectual as well as financial and commercial, for he was reflecting a long-standing American zeal for aviation fueled by the Wright Brothers' flight of 1903 and Charles Lindbergh's trans-Atlantic flight of 1927. That pervasive zeal, unique to the United States and dubbed "the winged gospel," anticipated a "great new day in human affairs once airplanes brought about a true air age."[2] In the American popular mind, the airplane would "foster democracy, equal-ity, and freedom . . . improve public taste and spread culture . . . purge the world of war and violence; and even . . . give rise to a new kind of human being" (Corn, 34). It was a zeal of messianic fervor, and its prophecies for America in the coming air age were "extravagant and utopian" (30–31).

Nowhere is this utopian enthusiasm more apparent than in the thirty-some series of aviation-related novels for American boys, published between 1910 and 1945. Comprising more than two hundred titles, these books convey to their young readers a powerful social vision. Like other series books of the times, written for girls as well as boys (the *Tom Swift* books [1910–1935; 38 volumes], for example, or the *Outdoor Girls* series

[1913–1933; 23 vols.]), they reinforce conventional cultural values and attitudes, emphasizing honesty, fair play, conscientiousness, and reliability. Both boys' and girls' series, moreover, establish desirable role models for their readers, giving them pictures of responsible young people growing up to find acceptance and a productive place in an adult society. Unlike the other series, however, the aviation stories present these values to their largely male readership within the greater milieu of aviation, creating the possibility of a world in which the mastery of all that flight offers and requires leads to a mastery of the ills of society.[3]

The aviation series books fall squarely into the pattern of American technological utopianism established by such writers as Edward Bellamy and King C. Gillette. These and other authors envisioned a time when the ideal society would be "brought about primarily through technological changes rather than through a combination of political, social, cultural, and technological changes."[4] Thus, Bellamy, in *Looking Backward* (1888), and Gillette, in *The Human Drift* (1894), offered visions of urban, industrialized societies with technical mastery at their core. Both saw their societies as readily rewarding individual achievement, with advancement the result of education, responsibility, initiative, and ability, and both gave plausible, persuasive pictures of societies that had "facilely tamed . . . the dynamism of industrial-scientific civilization" (Segal, 25–32).[5]

From these and similar utopian visions, then, the American public developed an ingrained sense that technological progress was "equivalent to progress itself" (Segal, 74), and the stage was set for the utopia of the air. As Joseph Corn points out, "[h]istorically accustomed to think of machines as engines of beneficial social change, conditioned by religion to confuse mechanical flight with spiritual transformation, the generations of Americans that responded to the airplane after 1908 accepted eagerly the promises of the winged gospel" (Corn, 50). Within the utopia of the air, the future holds no limits for either aviation or the United States. In that future, the merits of aviation will awaken the merits of the boys who read of it, making them "the men whose destiny it would be to lead the country toward the day when flying had taken its rightful place in the world,"[6] and leading these young men to produce a better world for all.[7]

Although that world will be a decisively technological one, it is a technology deeply engaged with, and tempered by, humanity. Flight will require the individual to forge an intuitive, deeply emotional bond with the machine. Focusing on the aircraft's instruments, trusting their information rather than that of his own senses, the flier will ultimately come to depend on the airplane as readily as he depends on himself. "Do you blame 'Slim' Lindbergh for always referring to his ship and himself as 'WE'?" John Prentice Langley asks.[8] R. Sidney Bowen makes the bonding even more profound ("There are no words in any language that can adequately describe the feeling a pilot holds in his heart for his plane"), and, for Thomson Burtis's Rex Lee, "an air-plane was like a Sweetheart."[9]

The interdependence of man and machine becomes even clearer as instrument technology advances. "The lighted faces of the dials on the instrument board were the faces of friends," thinks Andy Lane, in 1930; "when anything went wrong, these instruments would give him their messages of warning so that he might instantly take steps to correct the trouble."[10] The airman's reliance on his instruments, in fact, extends even to combat, as Lucky Terrell discovers when a sensor alerts him to an enemy threat: "[He] could have kicked himself. Here he had been depending upon his own skill, when science had devised an instrument far superior to human ability."[11] Fliers, in short, come to recognize that, in many respects, the machine can do a better job than the human, and the man-machine symbiosis becomes a crucial part of the utopia of the air.

That symbiosis, however, only enhances the beneficial effects that flight and flying have on the human individual. Aviators are persons set apart ("We are airmen," says Slim Tyler, "and nothing can make us forget it"),[12] and their distinctiveness is a direct result of their involvement with aviation. They come to resemble, in fact, like the meritocrats of the larger American techno-logical utopias, "the technological equivalents of Plato's philosopher-kings" (Segal, 29), a physical, intellectual, and emotional elite poised to shape soci-ety, and they take their diverse responsibilities seriously.

Some of the flier's distinctive elitism is purely physical, an acquired adaptation to the undeniable hazards of flight. "Aviators must necessarily be built on the order of athletes," John Luther Langworthy writes in 1912, "for their very lives may depend on instantaneous action and speedy thought that springs from intuition."[13] But, adding to that physical development, he con-tinues, is a constant alertness, in which "the eyes are almost constantly searching the heavens, perhaps for a glimpse of . . . things that must always be of intense interest to an aviator."[14] Fliers throughout the books radiate alertness and capability, and their distinction is apparent to even a casual observer.

Complementing his physical prowess is the airman's intellectual prowess, for flying is as dependent on mental competence as it is on physical ability. Thus, the aviation mindset requires conscientiousness, after the model of Charles A. Lindbergh, and the books repeatedly speak to the virtues of the trait. Ted Scott readies his aircraft for a trans-Pacific flight "with the extreme caution that had made his name proverbial and which had brought him through so many tight places."[15] And, as late as 1932, Van Powell explic-itly invokes Lindbergh: "Lindbergh had the right idea. His motto was 'pre-paredness.' He took account of every possible factor before he took off. He got everything worked out as closely as human skill, perfect instruments and precision would allow. . . . Consequently, he got there!"[16] In the world of flying, only the careful survive; the airman's mind, the books make clear, must be methodical and painstaking.

The second intellectual requirement is the greater, for it is education— the acquisition of knowledge, whether general or specialized. In the utopia of the air, the citizenry is an educated one. The broader the education, the better-equipped the person, and at the top of the scale stand, once more, "the most manly, most steady, best educated general class of men in industry— pilots!"[17] Reaching that pinnacle, however, is another matter, for it requires discipline as well as obedience, self-education as well as structured education, and practical as well as formal education.

Much of the flier's education, not surprisingly, is technical. Billy Smith, working on his own, studies aircraft construction and maintenance before moving on to "the theory of flight and aeronautics; of radio, both sending and receiving in the Morse and international codes, and of aerial navigation."[18] Larry Turner, like Billy "already 'well up' on all that books could tell about engines," goes on to get "the practical personal experience that is the only real teacher"—lessons that are "more than [he] had ever dreamed there would be to keep in mind," but become "simple, second nature as soon as the flying hours piled up."[19]

The flier's lessons instill perspective and breadth as well as details, for they remind the student that he is the beneficiary of a long, accretive line of historical, scientific, and technological development. One of Gordon Stuart's seasoned fliers spells this out explicitly to his Boy Scout associates: "Every invention has been worked to a finish by a chain of people feeling their way in that direction. . . . Every big bug you hear of in any line of invention is standing on the top of the brains of folks you don't see."[20] The flier benefits from the endeavors of others, and he, in turn, assumes the obligation to add his own broad efforts to that continuity so that the future, in its turn, will benefit as well.

Aviation's emphasis on a wide-ranging education leads to education for the larger society as well as for the individual. While a reception at the Zeppelin works in Friedrichshafen, Germany, forcibly reminds David Ellison that "an aviator ought to be able to speak something besides the good old mother tongue," Ted Scott plans a book to "tell America what she ought to know . . . to advance the cause of flying," and emphatically advocates a midocean, floating airstrip staffed by researchers, which "could be made to add immensely to the world's general knowledge."[21] An aviator's education never stops. He accepts an obligation to share that education, and individual and society alike benefit from the process.

Completing the flier's elite standing is his emotional complexity. Physically sound and broadly intellectual though he may be, it is the aviator's emotional adaptation to flight that at last lifts him out of the ordinary and transforms him into the true "airman" of the aviation utopia. Once having undergone that transformation, the individual does not fall back. He is of the elite; he recognizes the attributes that his position has given him; and he accepts the responsibilities that accompany those attributes. He and his technological kinsmen are to be the shapers of the society to come.

The airman knows, from the outset, that he is one of a special breed, and that breed is bound by bonds exceeding any found in mundane society. John Prentice Langley makes the case explicitly, writing that "[t]he love of aviation, with its amazing victories and dangers, draws men into a close comradeship, such as nothing else on earth may."[22] Such comradeship, in turn, leads to trust—not just trust in technology, but trust in enlightened humankind as well. A society of competent, intelligent persons working in a complex endeavor necessarily requires that each trust the others, for from this mutuality will come a common achievement. Andy Lane, preparing to test an experimental automatic pilot, accepts and expects such mutuality: "So perfectly organized was the crew that each member knew his duties and performed them automatically, thoroughly, and without unnecessary conversation. Each knew he could trust the others."[23]

But trust carries its own responsibilities. Membership in a collaborative, interdependent group means that each individual plays a necessary role in the operations of that group. Flying, even in the most technically sophisticated craft and with the most competent of crews, has inescapable hazards, and any failing on the part of a single person may well bring disaster to all. R. Sidney Bowen's "Red" Randall, newly assigned to a PBY flying boat in the Aleutians, is a case in point: "Twenty-four hours had not passed before Randall and his crew were like old friends who had been flying as a single team for years. Each man realized that his particular job was absolutely essential, and the fate of his five pals could very easily rest on his shoulders at any minute."[24] The responsibilities of flying are many, and they extend to more than the merely personal.

This highly developed sense of individual and mutual responsibility is possible because the act of flying is a cleansing one. Emotionally as well as physically detached from earthly concerns as he courses the air, the airman sloughs the petty rivalries and grievances of mundane life and his truer, cleaner self emerges. Part of that purification, to be sure, involves sacrifices. While the world of flight, in and of itself, does not require celibacy, for example, it is a world of male-to-male associations, and requires that relations with the opposite sex be kept in their proper perspective. Thus, Rex Lee's feeling for a female friend is one of "frank comradeship," for, in the airman's scale of values, flying comes first: "Girls didn't interest him as girls. It was as though his first and only love was the air, and . . . for a long time to come it would have first place in his heart" (*Air Mail*, 211–12). Ultimately, however, the sacrifices will be worthwhile. The attributes of flight will work their magic. Earthly jealousies and flaws will be purged, and the true airman will come forth like a butterfly from a cocoon. Bill Sherman, flying to Fort Sill, discovers that, in the air, "[f]ear fell from him. . . . He felt as uplifted in soul as he was in body. Somehow he longed more than ever to be a good boy; to harbor good thoughts; to do good deeds."[25] And Ted Scott, for his part, finds that purity and delight go together: "He felt as if everything that shackled him on the ground was snapped the moment he soared into the ether. Flying with him was not merely a vocation, it was an unspeakable delight. All the soil and stain of earth seemed stripped away in the clean, cool upper air."[26] Flying, the books imply, achieves what ordinary progress cannot, and the soiled, stained individuals of earthbound existence are replaced by purer, cleaner, exalted ones.

Purification is good, but it is only a stage leading to a greater transcendence. For the true airman, the books repeatedly say, there comes a moment of epiphanic revelation when his distinctiveness bursts upon him. In that moment he grasps, spontaneously, the wholeness of existence, the degree to which he is a person indeed set apart, and the role he is to play in the betterment of the world. Its potential for transcendence gives flight and flying a near-spiritual quality, and it comes as no surprise that Rex Lee views his dreams of flying "like a religion" (*Air Mail*, 74).

Flight, indeed, evokes something close to a religious ecstasy in its adherents. Don Craig, Boy Scout and aviation enthusiast, finds in night flying a sublime detachment, "as if they had floated off into another world; a spirit world, perhaps,"[27] while Buck Welke, an ex-military flier, undergoes a Whitmanesque identification with the world below: "The feeling is something it's almost impossible to put in plain, everyday words. . . . When you get up three or four thousand feet and travel with your compass and map, you feel as if you owned the vast heavens and that the earth was your plaything."[28] Welke, as an airman in flight, is plainly in an ecstatic state, with the universe at his command.

Buck's ecstasy, however, pales alongside that of Ted Scott, for, whereas Buck confines his feelings to those of the corporeal world, Ted becomes a wholly spiritualized entity: "Here was where he belonged, in the broad, limitless reaches of the air. He felt akin to the eagle. All care dropped away from him. Earth seemed far away. He was brother to the sun and moon and stars. He was cradled in immensity. The clay of the flesh seemed stripped from him. He felt as though he were a disembodied spirit. He was pervaded with a compassionate pity for the great mass of humanity doomed to walk the earth" (*Pacific*, 54). Flight, in short, exalts the spirit, liberates the flesh, links the one to the all, and makes the human more humane. It is a notable achievement, and one wholly appropriate to the utopia of the air.

The benefits accruing to the individual through the agency of flight influence the larger society as well. The world will become—or, at least, *can* become—one shaped by flight and the airplane. The nature of the cities and the landscape will change. Patterns of work and recreation will take new shapes and directions as airplanes, associated aircraft technology, and their accompanying merits devolve to the general public, and American attitudes toward the world and progress will be altered, expanded, and bettered as the qualities of flight are assimilated into society. The books' belief in aviation as a world-shaping force is overt, and the effects of that force are unquestionably utopian.

In the flight-centered world, there will be no escaping the presence of aircraft. Machines will fill the skies, of course, but their mechanical requirements—take-off and landing areas, maintenance facilities, storage hangars, and the like—will appear on the ground. But these facilities will be anything but unsightly; they will, instead, evoke the progressive, forward-looking spirit of flight for all who encounter them.[29] Andy Bird, for example, enthuses as early as 1912 about "the time coming when the town will be a regular aviation center, with aerodromes and hangars dotting the landscape. And we're the pioneers of the great uplift movement!" (*First Voyage*, 27). Tangible as well as spiritual, the great uplift movement of flight will be apparent to all.

Everywhere one looks, there will be artifacts of flight. Jimmy Donnelly looks at the flashing beacons marking the transcontinental airmail routes and finds in them "a powerful appeal, a suggestion of romance, that thrilled [him] through and through."[30] Ted Scott notes that a "big business man had the top of the main building of his plant arranged so that his private plane could take off and land" (prompting a friend to speculate that "a host of others [will] follow his example"), while Eustace Adams projects a midocean landing strip, "a perfectly flat surface of steel, high above the tumbling waves . . . nearly a thousand feet long and five hundred feet wide," to provide a stopping-point for transoceanic flights.[31]

Homes and cities alike will evolve to accommodate the airplane even as the airplane evolves to accommodate them. Ted Scott looks to "folding wings that will enable the plane to take up no more room in the garage than a car,"[32] while another enthusiast sees the city as wholly adapted to flight: "Airplane terminals are built right upon the roofs of high down-town buildings; every little home has its private landing field upon its own rooftop. . . . Suddenly you open up a new world in aviation" (*Dirigible*, 155–56). Aviation will be a part of day-to-day life, and reminders of its powerful presence will be visible everywhere.

That presence is equally apparent in the social patterns of the aviation-based society, for aircraft and flight will change the way Americans live and work. Adult adherents of the winged gospel see this clearly: "It was . . . the way of life that flying would make possible which sent them into rapture" (Corn, 91–92). The boys' books, if anything, are even more explicit. Rex Lee confidently believes that "stately craft [will] sweep the sky, and a proportion of the business of the world go on in the limitless heavens."[33] Jimmy Don-nelly pilots a Wall Street financier from his suburban estate to downtown Manhattan in a Loening amphibian, and as the magnate becomes accustomed to the ease and speed of the process, "he practically abandoned all other methods of transportation."[34]

It remains, though, for Ted Scott once again to make the fullest state-ment of life in the new world of the air, as airplanes become as numerous as automobiles, with effects as profound as those of the car. Not only, he says, will it "be thought a disgrace, or at least a sign of poverty, not to own an air-plane" (*Lost*, 45), but also "[t]he sky will soon be dotted with airplanes, as the roads are now dotted with cars. Dad will step out of the back door after breakfast, jump into the plane and be whisked to his office in a jiffy. Mother and the girls will have one of their own for going shopping. The big office buildings and department stores will have their roofs fitted up to receive and store the planes while their owners are in the buildings."[35] The Sunday after-noon drive will be replaced by the Sunday afternoon flight, and families will "fly over two or three states, land in some pleasant field for a picnic supper, come back at dark, put the machine into the garage, go into the house, wind up the clock, put out the cat, and climb into bed."[36] Whether for work or for recreation, for man or for woman, the airplane will be integral to American life.

Underlying the enlightenment, however, is a still greater sense—a belief that the world is perfectible, and that progressive aviation will contribute to that perfection. Progress, for the boys' books, is inevitable and unending. "The fantastic things of today are the realities of tomorrow," the Secretary of Government Aviation tells Ted Scott; "Nine-tenths of the things that are being done today would have been called fantastic twenty years ago" (*Hero*, 118–19). An academic, Princeton Professor Trigg, sees those advances in the context of historic human endeavor: "In the modern aviator there lives the spirit of the adventurers of all time; a gallant, intrepid and invincible army that comes marching down the gray ages to be reincarnated in the greatest of all the cavaliers of chance. . . . They have fought the dragons of every age and clime, wrestling with the earth for jewels and gold, building glittering cities in desert places, throwing fairy bridges from crag to crag. Now, spurn-ing the reclaimed earth, they have taken their indomitable courage and their boundless enthusiasm . . . into the limitless sea of the air" (*Dirigible*, 76–77).

Its spirit of progress, Ted Scott concludes, is what has led—and will con-tinue to lead—aviation and aviators to their pinnacle. For him, the successes of aviation prove "the superiority of mind over matter. Any success of that kind gives the human race a new confidence in itself, spurs it on to greater endeav-ors. Why, if it hadn't been for that spirit, we'd still be in a state of barbarism."[37] These endeavors will benefit all humanity, but leading them will be the United States, fueled and shaped by the possibilities of aviation, establishing for all time that "young, virile, energetic America is the hope of the world, a sort of twentieth-century paradise."[38] In their vision of an air-minded America leading the world to a new perfection, the boys' books make clear to their young, male readers that, with the right preparation (i.e., aviation), the society's future leaders can make of it still more than has already been made. It is a vision utopian in the very best of senses.

The aviation series, as a genre, project a remarkably consistent view of aviation and its potential for social change. In so doing, they are part of a larger, contemporaneous movement propounding technology as an agent of progress. Directed toward children and adults alike, the movement appears in such diverse works as the Tom Swift and Young Engineers series for young readers and Charles A. Beard's adult-oriented essay collection, *Toward Civilization* (1930), which speaks to the value systems inherent in engineering.[39] Like these more general works, the aviation series promote the prevalence of technology (in this case, specifically aviation technology) as the stimulus for progress, and, more important, they seek to further the consciousness of that specific technology and its potential in the minds of the young, male Americans who will become the citizens of the future.

In so doing, the series offer aviation as an ideology—that is, a preexisting, "coherent view of reality"—and use that ideology "as an illumination rather than distortion of reality" (Segal, 4–5). The reality they illuminate is one already attuned to aviation: the National Advisory Committee for Aeronautics (NACA) had been established in 1915, the Kelly Act of 1925 paved the way for a national air transport system, the Air Commerce Act of 1926 provided for an aeronautical regulatory agency within the Federal government, and the Daniel Guggenheim Fund for the Promotion of Aeronautics made its first grants in mid-1926.[40] Whereas the real-world efforts are piecemeal and sporadic, though, the aviation series books present a coherent, all-inclusive vision of the coming air age.

It is this inclusiveness that at last confirms them as utopian. Like the technological utopias that Howard Segal details, the series books offer "blueprints of their authors' version of utopia," complete with descriptions of "its physical appearance, its institutions, its values, and its inhabitants" (Segal, 6). They look to a time when aviation technology is accessible to all. They look to a time when the physical world will be changed for the better by the workings of that technology, and the very institutions and operations of society will be shaped by it. Most important of all, they look to a time when mankind itself will be liberated and exalted through the transcendence offered by that technology. They present a vision of the future to generations of young American men, offering the implicit (and often explicit) message that, through the mastery of flight technology and the sociocultural adaptations that will necessarily follow, this future can be attained. They document an important stage in the shaping of a nation's progressive vision of itself and its future, and their tragedy is that reality (the Great Depression, World War II, and the Cold War) has compelled the United States and the world to fall so desperately short of their dream.

Acknowledgments

Research for this essay was funded in part by Faculty Research Grants from the Texas Christian University Research and Creative Activities Fund, and was conducted in the Series Books Collection of the Children's Literature Research Collections, University of Minnesota, Twin Cities.

Notes

1. Harry F. Guggenheim, *The Seven Skies* (New York: Putnam, 1930), 12.
2. Joseph J. Corn, *The Winged Gospel: America's Romance With Aviation, 1900–1950* (New York: Oxford University Press, 1977), 44, 27; hereafter cited in text.
3. The aviation series have yet to receive extensive attention as a genre, although they get modest mention in Francis J. Molson, "American Technological Fiction for Youth: 1900–1940," in *Young Adult Science Fiction*, ed. C. W. Sullivan III (Westport, Conn.: Greenwood Press, 1999): 7–20. Individual series (*Andy Lane, Rex Lee,* and *Dave Dawson/Red Randall*) are examined by David K. Vaughan and Paul Holsinger, respectively. See Vaughan, "Eustace Adams' Andy Lane Series," *Dime Novel Roundup* 57 (1988): 52–60; 68–73, and "Thomson Burtis' Rex Lee Aviation Stories," *Dime Novel Roundup* 59 (1990): 2–7. See also M. Paul Holsinger, "For Freedom and the American Way," *Newsboy* 32 (1994): 9–16. Fred Erisman undertakes more synthetic analyses of the series' themes and value systems in "American Boys' Aviation Books and the Humanizing of Technology," *Social Science Journal* 29 (1992): 119–27, and "Boys' Books and the Popularizing of American Aviation," *1998 National Aerospace Conference Proceedings* (Dayton, Ohio: Wright State University, 1998), 8–16. Deidre Johnson examines the contributions of Edward Stratemeyer and offers a helpful context for the series-book genre as a whole in *Edward Stratemeyer and the Stratemeyer Syndicate* (New York: Twayne, 1993). Vaughan considers three of the only eight known aviation series for girls in "Girl Fliers in a World of Guys: Three 1930s Girls' Juvenile Aviation Series," *Dime Novel Roundup* 68 (1999): 16–27.
4. Howard P. Segal, *Technological Utopianism in American Culture* (Chicago: University of Chicago Press, 1985), 74; hereafter cited in text.
5. See also Frank E. Manuel and Fritzie P. Manuel, *Utopian Thought in the Western World* (Cambridge: Belknap Press of Harvard University Press, 1979), 762.
6. Thomson Burtis, *Rex Lee, Ace of the Air Mail* (New York: Grosset & Dunlap, 1929), 212; hereafter cited in text as *Air Mail*.
7. Although the aviation series, like the other boys' series of the time, conventionally relegate women to the roles of mothers and sweethearts, the handful

of contemporaneous girls' aviation books suggests that the benefits of aviation are nearly as accessible to women as they are to men. Vaughan points out that these series present girl fliers as "practical, capable, determined, hard-working, idealistic, and possessed of above-average amounts of resourcefulness and initiative," and make clear that "the field of aviation was open to girls who had the desire and determination to persevere" (Vaughan, 1999, 17, 25). Thus, though the numerically dominant boys' series portray the utopia of the air as a generally male preserve, the girls' series, in a minority report, maintain that it can be an equal-opportunity society. A full study of the considerable contributions of women to real-world aviation has yet to be made.

8. John Prentice Langley, *Spanning the Pacific or A Non-stop Hop to Japan* (New York: Barse, 1927), 45–46.

9. R. Sidney Bowen, *David Dawson at Casablanca* (Akron, Ohio: Saalfield, 1944), 176; Burtis, *Rex Lee, Ace of the Air Mail* (New York: Grosset & Dunlap, 1929), 74.

10. Eustace L. Adams, *The Flying Windmill* (New York: Grosset & Dunlap, 1930), 71–72.

11. Canfield Cook, *Secret Mission* (New York: Grosset & Dunlap, 1943), 43.

12. Richard H. Stone, *An Air Cargo of Gold or Slim Tyler, Special Bank Messenger* (New York: Cupples & Leon, 1930), 114.

13. John Luther Langworthy, *The Aeroplane Boys or The Young Sky Pilot's First Voyage* (Chicago: M. A. Donohue, 1912), 90; hereafter cited in text as *First Voyage*.

14. Langworthy, *The Aeroplane Boys Flight, or, A Hydroplane Roundup* (Chicago: M. A. Donohue, 1914), 156.

15. Franklin W. Dixon, *Across the Pacific or Ted Scott's Hop to Australia* (New York: Grosset & Dunlap, 1928), 53; hereafter cited in text as *Pacific*.

16. Van Powell, *The Vanishing Air Liner* (Akron, Ohio: Saalfield, 1932), 228–29.

17. Powell, *The Mystery Crash* (Akron, Ohio: Saalfield, 1932), 189.

18. Noel Sainsbury Jr., *Billy Smith Exploring Ace or By Airplane to New Guinea* (New York: Cupples & Leon, 1928), 17–18.

19. Powell, *The Haunted Hangar* (Akron, Ohio: Saalfield, 1932), 104, 108–9.

20. Gordon Stuart, *The Boy Scouts of the Air at Cape Peril* (Chicago: Reilly & Lee, 1921), 157.

21. Hugh McAlister, *The Flight of the Silver Ship: Around the World Aboard a Great Dirigible* (Akron, Ohio: Saalfield, 1930), 191; hereafter cited in text as *Dirigible*, and Dixon, *Rescued in the Clouds or Ted Scott, Hero of the Air* (New York: Grosset & Dunlap, 1927), 72; 122; hereafter cited in text as *Hero*.

22. Langley, *The "Pathfinder's" Great Flight or Cloud Chasers Over Amazon Jungles* (New York: Barse, 1928), 70.

23. Adams, *The Plane Without a Pilot* (New York: Grosset & Dunlap, 1930), 146.

24. Bowen, *Red Randall in the Aleutians* (New York: Grosset & Dunlap, 1945), 23.

25. Captain Frank Cobb, *Battling the Clouds, or For a Comrade's Honor* (Akron, Ohio: Saalfield, 1927), 134.

26. Dixon, *Lost at the South Pole or Ted Scott in Blizzard Land* (New York: Grosset & Dunlap, 1930), 10.

27. Irving Crump, *The Cloud Patrol* (New York: Grosset & Dunlap, 1929), 110.
28. Stuart, *The Boy Scouts of the Air in the Dismal Swamp* (Chicago: Reilly & Britton, 1914), 96–97.
29. Some examples of this vision appear in Forgey, who reproduces illustrations from the 1929 "First National Contest for Designs of Modern Airports held in the United States." See Benjamin Forgey, "The Greatest Airports Never Built," *Air & Space* 6 (October/November 1991): 82–86.
30. Lewis E. Theiss, *The Search for the Lost Mail Plane* (Boston: W. A. Wilde, 1928), 47.
31. Dixon, *The Lone Eagle of the Border or Ted Scott and the Diamond Smugglers* (New York: Grosset & Dunlap, 1929), 95, and Adams, *Pirates of the Air* (New York: Grosset & Dunlap, 1929), 49.
32. Dixon, *The Search for the Lost Flyers or Ted Scott over the West Indies* (New York: Grosset & Dunlap, 1928), 45; hereafter cited as *Lost*.
33. Burtis, *Rex Lee, Ranger of the Sky* (New York: Grosset & Dunlap, 1928), 165.
34. Theiss, *The Pursuit of the Flying Smugglers* (Boston: W. A. Wilde, 1931), 123.
35. Dixon, *Flying to the Rescue or Ted Scott and the Big Dirigible* (New York: Grosset & Dunlap, 1930), 3–4.
36. Dixon, *The Search for the Lost Flyers or Ted Scott Over the West Indies* (New York: Grosset & Dunlap, 1928), 44.
37. Dixon, *Danger Trails of the Sky or Ted Scott's Great Mountain Climb* (New York: Grosset & Dunlap, 1931), 2.
38. Dixon, *Hunting the Sky Spies or Testing the Invisible Plane* (New York: Grosset & Dunlap, 1941), 144.
39. Cecelia Tichi, *Shifting Gears: Technology, Literature, Culture in Modernist America* (Chapel Hill: University of North Carolina Press, 1987), 100–102. See also John M. Jordan, *Machine-Age Ideology: Social Engineering & American Liberalism 1911–1939* (Chapel Hill: University of North Carolina Press, 1994), 217–18.
40. Ruth Schwartz Cowan, *A Social History of American Technology* (New York: Oxford University Press, 1997), 252–53; Richard P. Hallion, *Legacy of Flight: The Guggenheim Contribution to American Aviation* (Seattle: University of Washington Press, 1977), 6, 11, 49–50.

Works Cited

Adams, Eustace L. *Pirates of the Air*. New York: Grosset & Dunlap, 1929.
———. *The Flying Windmill*. New York: Grosset & Dunlap, 1930.
———. *The Plane Without a Pilot*. New York: Grosset & Dunlap, 1930.
Bellamy, Edward. *Looking Backward, 2000–1887*. Boston: Ticknor and Company, 1888.
Bowen, R. Sidney. *Dave Dawson at Casablanca*. Akron, Ohio: Saalfield, 1944.
———. *Red Randall in the Aleutians*. New York: Grosset & Dunlap, 1945.
Burtis, Thomson. *Rex Lee, Ranger of the Sky*. New York: Grosset & Dunlap, 1928.
———. *Rex Lee, Ace of the Air Mail*. New York: Grosset & Dunlap, 1929.
Cobb, Captain Frank. *Battling the Clouds, or For a Comrade's Honor*. Akron, Ohio: Saalfield, 1927.

Cook, Canfield. *Secret Mission*. New York: Grosset & Dunlap, 1943.

Corn, Joseph J. *The Winged Gospel: America's Romance with Aviation, 1900–1950*. New York: Oxford University Press, 1983.

Cowan, Ruth Schwartz. *A Social History of American Technology*. New York: Oxford University Press, 1997.

Crump, Irving. *The Cloud Patrol*. New York: Grosset & Dunlap, 1929.

Dixon, Franklin W. *First Stop Honolulu or Ted Scott over the Pacific*. New York: Grosset & Dunlap, 1927.

———. *Rescued in the Clouds or Ted Scott, Hero of the Air*. New York: Grosset & Dunlap, 1927.

———. *Across the Pacific or Ted Scott's Hop to Australia*. New York: Grosset & Dunlap, 1928.

———. *The Search for the Lost Flyers or Ted Scott over the West Indies*. New York: Grosset & Dunlap, 1928.

———. *The Lone Eagle of the Border or Ted Scott and the Diamond Smugglers*. New York: Grosset & Dunlap, 1929.

———. *Flying to the Rescue or Ted Scott and the Big Dirigible*. New York: Grosset & Dunlap, 1930.

———. *Lost at the South Pole or Ted Scott in Blizzard Land*. New York: Grosset & Dunlap, 1930.

———. *Danger Trails of the Sky or Ted Scott's Great Mountain Climb*. New York: Grosset & Dunlap, 1931.

———. *Hunting the Sky Spies or Testing the Invisible Plane*. New York: Grosset & Dunlap, 1941.

Erisman, Fred. "American Boys' Aviation Books and the Humanizing of Technology." *Social Science Journal* 29 (1992): 119–27.

———. "Boys' Books and the Popularizing of American Aviation." *1998 National Aerospace Conference Proceedings*, 8–16. Dayton, Ohio: Wright State University, 1998.

Forgey, Benjamin. "The Greatest Airports Never Built." *Air & Space* 6 (October/November 1991): 82–86.

Gillette, King C. *The Human Drift*. Boston: New Era Publishing Co., 1894.

Guggenheim, Harry F. *The Seven Skies*. New York: Putnam, 1930.

Hallion, Richard P. *Legacy of Flight: The Guggenheim Contribution to American Aviation*. Seattle: University of Washington Press, 1977.

Holsinger, M. Paul. "For Freedom and the American Way." *Newsboy* 32 (1994): 9–16.

Johnson, Deidre. *Edward Stratemeyer and the Stratemeyer Syndicate*. Twayne's United States Authors Series 627. New York: Twayne, 1993.

Jordan, John M. *Machine-Age Ideology: Social Engineering & American Liberalism, 1911–1939*. Chapel Hill: University of North Carolina Press, 1994.

Langley, John Prentice. *Spanning the Pacific or A Non-stop Hop to Japan*. New York: Barse, 1927.

———. *The "Pathfinder's" Great Flight or Cloud Chasers Over Amazon Jungles*. New York: Barse, 1928.

Langworthy, John Luther. *The Aeroplane Boys or The Young Sky Pilot's First Voyage*. Chicago: M. A. Donohue, 1912.

————. *The Aeroplane Boys Flight, or, A Hydroplane Roundup*. Chicago: M. A. Donohue, 1914.

Manuel, Frank E., and Fritzie P. Manuel. *Utopian Thought in the Western World*. Cambridge: Belknap Press of Harvard University Press, 1979.

McAlister, Hugh. *The Flight of the Silver Ship: Around the World Aboard a Giant Dirigible*. Akron, Ohio: Saalfield, 1930.

Molson, Francis J. "American Technological Fiction for Youth: 1900–1940." *Young Adult Science Fiction*. Ed. C. W. Sullivan III, 7–20. Westport, Conn.: Greenwood Press, 1999.

Powell, Van. *The Haunted Hangar*. Akron, Ohio: Saalfield, 1932.

————. *The Mystery Crash*. Akron, Ohio: Saalfield, 1932.

————. *The Vanishing Air Liner*. Akron, Ohio: Saalfield, 1932.

Sainsbury, Noel Jr. *Billy Smith Exploring Ace or By Airplane to New Guinea*. New York: Cupples & Leon, 1928.

Segal, Howard P. *Technological Utopianism in American Culture*. Chicago: University of Chicago Press, 1985.

Stone, Richard H. *An Air Cargo of Gold or Slim Tyler, Special Bank Messenger*. New York: Cupples & Leon, 1930.

Stuart, Gordon. *The Boy Scouts of the Air in the Dismal Swamp*. Chicago: Reilly & Britton, 1914.

————. *The Boy Scouts of the Air at Cape Peril*. Chicago: Reilly & Lee, 1921.

Theiss, Lewis E. *The Search for the Lost Mail Plane*. Boston: W. A. Wilde, 1928.

————. *The Pursuit of the Flying Smugglers*. Boston: W. A. Wilde, 1931.

Tichi, Cecelia. *Shifting Gears: Technology, Literature, Culture in Modernist America*. Chapel Hill: University of North Carolina Press, 1987.

Vaughan, David K. "Eustace Adams' Andy Lane Series." *Dime Novel Roundup* 57 (1988): 52–60, 68–73.

————. "Thomson Burtis' Rex Lee Aviation Stories." *Dime Novel Roundup* 59 (1990): 2–7.

————. "Girl Fliers in a World of Guys: Three 1930s Girls' Juvenile Aviation Series." *Dime Novel Roundup* 68 (1999): 16–27.

3

Travels through Dystopia: H. G. Wells and *The Island of Dr. Moreau*

ALBERTO MANGUEL

It was summer in Buenos Aires. I was thirteen. My best friend, Lenny Fagin, had given me for my birthday a green-bound Everyman copy of H. G. Wells's *The Island of Dr. Moreau*. That was a lucky summer: in the quiet country house we had rented for the holidays I discovered Nicholas Blake's *The Beast Must Die*, the stories of Horacio Quiroga, Ray Bradbury's *The Martian Chronicles*; now Wells was to be added to my desert-island shelf. I knew nothing of either the book or the author; I shared with the protagonist—"Edward Prendick, a private gentleman"—the uncertainty of what would happen next; I loved the device (which I didn't know was a device) of reading what was meant to be Prendick's own narrative, "found among his papers" after his death.

Fellow enthusiasts, jacket blurbs, teachers, and histories of literature destroy much of our reading pleasure by ratting on the plot; I can barely remember what it was like not to know that Dr. Jekyll and Mr. Hyde were one or that Crusoe would meet the flatfooted Friday. For a few blissful days I was like Prendick. I knew nothing of the island's history, I dreaded the strange Dr. Moreau, I wrongly suspected the beastly inhabitants of having once been normal human beings, I failed to guess what hideous experiments were going on in the House of Pain. When revelation came, halfway through the book, it proved to be much more dreadful than what I had imagined, and I read on, scared and grateful, to the apocalyptic end.

Aristotle, in the second book of the *Politics*, discussing the six types of political systems that he had imagined for six different kinds of citizens, noted that these systems required a concrete setting of symbolic value in which to develop. The first man to realize this, said Aristotle, was the architect Hippodamus of Miletus, a contemporary of Pericles who, even though he knew nothing of politics, was able to draw up the map of an ideal city. Hippodamus's city—or Aristotle's city, since a distance of twenty centuries allows us to confuse an author with his sources—was, apparently, a reflection of the Greek demographical ideal: a limited number of citizens divided by the role they played within society. It was patriarchal, since women had no ruling powers; democratic, in the sense that the affairs of the state were publicly debated; military, but not expansionist, since the ideal state was by definition a limited space; designed for the happiness not of all humanity but of the select citizens whom the fates had caused to be born on this soil, and therefore justified in using slaves to work under them. To serve these metropolitan ideals, the city was divided into a number of different sections—merchants, magistrates, and so on—grouped around the central agora. Each section was in turn organized in a grid of squares or blocks of houses that is still the model of our cities today. Seeing this pattern, an outsider could surmise the purpose of Aristotle's city: a social entity limited unto itself, segregationist and conservative, destined for a happy few. At the beginning of the Western notion of a perfect city is the idea of privilege.

The most famous of ancient ideal cities, Atlantis, exemplifies the same concept. According to Plato, the city of Atlantis rose in the center of a plateau, surrounded by concentric rings of earthworks separated from one another by deep canals. The central nucleus or first ring was protected by a wall 900 meters in circumference, and contained the seats of power: the fortress, the Royal Palace, and the Temple of Poseidon. The first ring was separated from the second one by a canal that served as an interior port, allowing access to the military section: the second ring, with barracks, gymnasium, and racing tracks. Another canal separated the second from the third section, which in turn housed the main port of Atlantis. Finally, yet another canal divided the port from the outer or fourth ring, the merchants' section of the city. Once again, the city was presented as a physical mirror of the social order. In the beginning, the utopian site corresponds exactly with the utopian ideal.

By the time Wells wrote his "scientific romances" (*The Invisible Man, The Time Machine, The First Men on the Moon, The Island of Dr. Moreau*) the utopian ideal had long faded into its shadow image: the place that allows our worst qualities to bloom unhampered, like carnivorous plants. When I was a child, science and magic presented hazy borders, and the marvels advertised daily in the papers of my childhood (Dr. Salk's polio vaccination, the first television sets in Buenos Aires, the early computers, space travel) shared an imaginary bookshelf with Enid Blyton's Wishing Chair and Pinocchio's Land of Laughs. But while many of the wonders spoke of worlds that seemed delightful, many others depicted gloomy realms in which unspeakable deeds went unpunished and the stuff of nightmares roamed undisturbed. These worlds reflected, as in a dark glass, the secret world of adolescence, which Henry James's father described to his sons in these words: "Every man who has reached even his intellectual teens begins to suspect that life is no farce; that it is not genteel comedy even; that it flowers and fructifies on the contrary out of the profoundest tragic depths of the essential dearth in which its subject's roots are plunged. The natural inheritance of everyone who is capable of spiritual life is an unsubdued forest where the wolf howls and the obscene bird of night chatters."

Moreau and his unsubdued island forest terrified me, as it probably did Wells himself. At the age of seven, in an old issue of *Chambers' Journal*, he had read of a man broken on a wheel. That night the boy had a horrible dream in which God Himself was turning the instrument of torture. God, the sleeping boy concluded, being responsible for everything in the world, must also be responsible for all its evil; next morning Wells decided that he could no longer believe in the Almighty. The nightmare probably gave him the character of Moreau; in turn, Moreau gave me a healthy fear of doctors and a general distrust of authority figures.

I've gone back to Moreau's island "where the wolf howls and the obscene bird of night chatters" many times since that distant summer. Though it has lost nothing of its wonderful horror, as I grow older it seems to have become a far more difficult and complex place, crowded with literary allusions. The mad scientist as a Blakean Nobodaddy; the beastly creatures echoing, in reverse, the existential plight of Kafka's metamorphosed Gregor; the island, once as faraway as Prospero's, now mapped by postcolonial explorers who see Moreau as the arch-imperialist—all these are now part of my readings which the story dutifully accepts and almost immediately outgrows.

Wells attempted, in later life, to give a less fanciful, more serious shape to his ideas. For me, however, his attempt didn't pay off: it's the young scribbler that I remember, the author of the "scientific romances" of whom Jules Verne said, indignantly, "But this man makes things up!" I remember, together with the awful god Moreau, the Time Traveller who brings from the future an impossible flower, the poor invisible man whose eyelids won't shut off the light and whose naked skin won't protect him from the cold, the traitor on the coveted moon; I remember (I can't forget) all these necessary inventions that Wells wrote before he was thirty-five. In the next half-century or so he discussed commonsense and history, social reform and the theories of education in earnest books such as *A Modern Utopia, The New Machiavelli, The Outline of History*, and *The Science of Life*. He was still brave and intelligent in difficult times, and honest and sometimes mistaken, but by then the gift for mythmaking had left him almost completely. One or two stories still made their way to the surface—*The Country of the Blind, The Croquet Player*—but by and large the dream-source had apparently dried up. It is almost as if the older man, no longer able to dream, had set out to make books from solid facts, in an effort to recapture what the younger man, inexperienced and untrained, had effortlessly conjured up in intuitions and imaginings—much like this older reader now tries to recall, though he knows it's impossible, something of the rookie thrill of first reading *The Island of Dr. Moreau* and not knowing what was lurking on the following page.

PART II

Community and Socialism

4

Sarah Fielding's Childhood Utopia

SARA GADEKEN

The first English novel for children, Sarah Fielding's *The Governess, or Little Female Academy* (1749), promises to teach its young readers "a Method of being very Happy," offering a story of a group of girls who learn to live in perfect harmony.[1] Children's literature, therefore, begins with a utopian vision. The novel assimilates the utopian genre to the novel of formal realism, setting its utopia not in another place or time but in a girls' boarding school of the sort that her young reader might aspire to attend. The setting ensures narrative continuity and stability, and the familiar location means that the discourse can range over familiar ground: fairy tales, autobiographies, romances, fables, a plot summary of a play, and descriptions of excursions the girls take to a local farm and to the country house of a neighboring nobleman. Instead of focusing on a person or persons or on an imaginary journey, then, Fielding makes place itself the main structural principle of her story.

At the same time, the little girls at Mrs. Teachum's school are, in a certain sense, travelers from another culture. Before they came to school they inhabited the culture of conventional, male-dominated families who have taught their daughters to suppose that happiness consists of outdoing everyone else and then reveling in the envy and frustration that this causes others. Finding themselves self-absorbed and miserable yet unaware that they can change this unhappy state, the girls, like any visitor to utopia, must first recognize their unhappy condition and then examine the assumptions that brought them to this state. The girls' progressive edification is intended to parallel the reader's own conversion to the novel's values.

As a utopian novel, *The Governess* is one of a number of mid-eighteenth century novels by women writers who envision all-female utopian spaces intended to protect gentlewomen from economic and social dangers. Sarah Scott's *Millenium Hall* (1762) is perhaps the best known of these, but the model family in Sarah Fielding's first novel, *David Simple* (1744), and the model community developed by the exemplary Mrs. Bilson in her *History of the Countess of Dellwyn* (1759) are earlier examples.[2] Sarah Fielding and Jane Collier's collaborative work *The Cry* (1754) is an extended commentary on such communities, and some years later Mary Hamilton's *Munster Village* (1778) offers much the same project.[3] These adult novels are logical sequels to *The Governess*, which teaches the little girls the technologies of self that will enable them to be the kind of women who will then inhabit the communities described in the novels addressed to adults.

"Technologies of self" is a term that Michel Foucault applies to religious confession from its inception as a mandated Catholic ritual in 1215 as a way of regulating interiority, of constructing the subject within power relations as individuals submit themselves to the Church or its human representative to make themselves in the arbitrary manner prescribed by the institution. His most extended explanation of the term is found in *The History of Sexuality, Vol. I*.[4] Felicity Nussbaum follows Foucault when she argues in *The Autobiographical Subject: Gender and Ideology in Eighteenth-Century England* that eighteenth-century autobiography "may be regarded as a technology of the self which rests on the assumption that its truth can be told."[5] *The Governess* seeks to inculcate in its young readers those technologies of self that each must learn in order to become the kind of adult woman who can live happily in the all-female spaces envisioned by Scott, Fielding, and Hamilton.

Although very different in style, each of these novels implicitly assumes a collective utopian theory of social relations that resists the theories of property and social contract, sometimes called possessive individualism, that have dominated Western thinking since the seventeenth century. The most important proponent of these theories is John Locke, whose political writing assumes that the community is essentially derivative, and that the individual is produced within the confines of a consensual social contract through reasoned defense of his property rights against competing claims. In contrast, Fielding, Scott, and Hamilton suppose that an individual is produced by and embedded in her community, and that her capacities will develop within a context of nonconsensual relations, a culture and a family that she does not choose. They draw on earlier social forms that reject the assumption that individuals are necessarily propertied, self-reliant, and autonomous, for such assumptions ignore the material realities of eighteenth-century women's lives.

Because it is written for children, *The Governess* sets out its argument simply. The story is too slight to support a systematic critique of social-contract theory or a general assessment of the relationship between political and social theory. In uncomplicated language appropriate for children, the novel expresses the social nature of identity and relationships in a way that conceives of value as rooted in communal practice, and argues that the community should be constructed and guided by values that emphasize communal rather than individual good.

I

Locke's theory, against which Fielding's novel should be read, is intended to reject divine right and patriarchy as formal models of political society. He therefore assumes the existence of independent human beings bound together by mutual interest who can and do create all their relationships and obligations. Such human beings are free in the sense that they do not depend on the will of others. Property is constitutive of the individual:

> [E]very Man has a Property in his own Person. This no Body has any Right to but himself. The Labour of his Body and the Work of his Hands, we may say, are properly his. Whatsoever then he removes out of the State that Nature hath provided, and left it in, he hath mixed his Labour with, and joyned to it something that is his own, and thereby makes it his Property. It being by him removed from the common state Nature placed it in, it hath by this labour something annexed to it, that excludes the common rights of other Men.[6]

This view, as C. B. Macpherson points out in his study of possessive individualism, directly opposes an earlier tradition that "property and labour were social functions, and that ownership of property involved social obligations."[7] In contrast, Locke considers that the individual's primary obligation is to himself and that he must continually protect his property against the interests of others. At the same time, however, individuals are bound together in a social contract, "by agreeing with other men to join and unite into a community for their comfortable, safe, and peaceable living amongst another, in a secure enjoyment of their properties, and a greater security against any that are not of it" (Locke, 169).

In this model, each individual sees the world from the perspective of his own self-interest as, within the framework of the social contract, he negotiates with others to ensure that his property rights are not infringed. Associations are assumed to be consensual and based on a reasoned assertion of self-interest unqualified by compassion. The virtues necessary for such individuals are vigor and industry, and much of the educational writing of this period assumes the validity of Locke's model and attempts to instill these virtues in young readers.

Locke argues that an individual should guide his life according to the precepts of reason, "which is that law [that] teaches all mankind who will but consult it" (Locke, 123). Children should be taught to develop their reason and to distrust or deny their feelings, or "passions," to use the common eighteenth-century term. According to James Nelson in *An Essay on the Government of Children* (1756), educators and parents "have two principal Points to aim at, for their own and Children's Happiness; and indeed for the Happiness of all Posterity; *viz.* weakening their [children's] Passions, and strengthening their Reason."[8] Fortitude, in Nelson's view, is the virtue that will prepare men for the active state. Locke's theory supposes, then, unequal relationships among individuals with competing or antagonistic interests. These individuals are connected by contract and, within this contract, each continually adjudicates private claims of self-interest against the claims of others.

This notion of the reasoned, propertied, independent individual vigorously defending his rights, however, bears little relation to the lived reality of eighteenth-century women's lives. In her study of social-contract theory, Carole Pateman contends that such theory supposes a prior distinction between the two genders, one whose members are rational and property-owning and the other whose members are irrational and, in a sense, themselves property: "Only masculine beings are endowed with the attributes and capacities necessary to enter into contracts, the most important of which is ownership of property in the person; only men, that is to say, are 'individuals.' "[9] Ownership of property is as gendered a concept as any other at this time. Susan Staves, in her work on property rights of eighteenth-century married women, also notes women's different relationship to property: "In the property regimes of patriarchy, descent and inheritance are reckoned in the male line; women function as procreators and as transmitters of inheritance from male to male."[10] Her study of the legal status of pin money offers an excellent example of this difference. Pin money can be used to buy clothes and ornaments, which then become the property of the woman who buys them, but if she buys real estate with her pin money, she cannot will or devise it (Staves, 147–48). A woman's real property cannot become capital accumulation even when her labor is mixed with it. Her "labor and the work of her hands," in Locke's words, do not belong to her in the way that those of a man belongs to him, and therefore, property cannot be constitutive of the individual woman in the way Locke describes.

The Governess, by drawing on earlier notions of the relations of self and community, is able to offer a more appropriate model of selfhood for women, who possess little property, who do not have property rights in themselves in the way that men do, and who are reticent to claim self-reliance and independence. It supposes compassion and goodwill among peers rather than hierarchically structured patterns of competition, and it relies on consensus-building to resolve problems rather than on appealing to priorities of rights. A woman in this model is expected to turn to others when she is in need, and her identity depends on being a part of a community of equals whose interests coincide. Members move quickly to eradicate conflict, for conflict calls into question their fundamental conviction that the good of the individual and the good of the community are identical. The privileged virtues in these communities are truth, trust, and comity—the last not a word that the novel employs, but one which expresses its confidence that a willingness to treat others with compassion and respect is the basis of community. Like participants in the social-contract model, members must learn to control their imaginations with right applications of reason, but unlike that model they must also cultivate their imaginations in order to establish the sympathetic bond that is the basis of the community. The selfhood that *The Governess* strives to inculcate sees the individual not as independent but part of a larger whole.

II

The opening pages of *The Governess* directly challenge Locke's notion of a unified self constructed in the course of defending property rights. A vigorous emphasis on such rights, it argues, produces chaos and destruction. The little girls, given a basket of apples for a special treat, engage in a robust fist fight over the largest apple—not over who actually should possess the apple, since the oldest scholar, Jenny Peace, who is their peer and mentor, throws it over the wall before the fight begins—but over who had the "most Right" to possess it (*Governess*, 4). In this rewritten Eden story, no one actually has any better claim to the apple than anyone else. Yet "[e]ach gave her Reasons why she had the best Title to it: The youngest pleaded her Youth, and the eldest her Age; one insisted on her Goodness, another from her Meekness claimed a Title to Preference; and one, in confidence of her Strength, said positively, she would have it" (3). Each fights vigorously for her nonexistent right to the now unavailable yet inexplicably still desirable apple until "their anger by degrees became so high, that Words could not vent half their Rage; and they fell to pulling of Caps, tearing of Hair, and dragging the Cloaths off one another's Backs" (4). In a mock epic battle, the girls tear at each other until each "held in her Right-hand, fast clenched, some Marks of Victory; for they were beat and beaten by Turns. One of them held a little Lock of Hair. . . . [a]nother grasped a Piece of a Cap. . . . [a] third clenched a Piece of an Apron; a fourth, of a Frock" (4–5). This scene attacks Locke's notion that the self is produced in the process of a reasoned defense of property rights in the person; here, selves are dismembered by such a defense. Moreover, the rights asserted are entirely imaginary, and the ease and speed with which each girl invents a special right for herself demonstrates the absurdity of thinking that rights are natural rather than self-created and self-serving.

Rather than assert her imagined rights against the rights of others, each girl must learn to subordinate her desires to the good of all. The process by which Jenny Peace teaches this lesson and restores peace to the shattered community exposes many of the veiled power relations, assumptions, and values that inform Fielding's utopian vision. At no time does Jenny claim direct authority over the younger girls. Instead, she offers to teach the next oldest scholar, Sukey Jennet, a "Method of being very happy" (*Governess*, 8). She begins with a reasoned appeal to Sukey's self-interest: if she had yielded the apple to another, "you would have proved your Sense; for you would have shewn, that you had too much Understanding to fight about a Trifle. Then your Cloathes had been whole, your Hair not torn from your Head, your Mistress had not been angry, nor had your Fruit been taken away from you" (7). In Jenny's view, the powerless should not, for the sake of their self-esteem, see themselves as powerless but instead as having the moral strength to choose not to retaliate. A refusal to fight, according to Jenny, is not an admission of weakness but a deliberate recognition that one's interests are better served by this choice.

This reasoned argument exemplifies the community's professed belief that even a child can and should regulate her life by reason. However, Sukey, sharp as well as stubborn, finds a vulnerable point in Jenny's logic: "if I could but hurt my Enemies, without being hurt myself, it would be the greatest Pleasure I could have in the World" (*Governess*, 7). Pleasure is a matter of definition, Sukey argues, and her own idea of what is pleasant differs from Jenny's. The greatest pleasure, she asserts, would be to have more power than anyone else and to exert that power over others.

Jenny's response demonstrates that reason is not really the principal value in this community, in spite of the many professions to the contrary. She refuses to cooperate in Sukey's argument by engaging in a debate over legitimate and illegitimate pleasure. Instead, Jenny abandons reason and invokes shame: "Oh fy, Miss *Sukey*! What you have now said is wicked. Don't you consider what you say every Day in your Prayers?" (*Governess*, 8). She invokes a common though unspoken community agreement on appropriate behavior and suggests that Sukey herself knows that her behavior is wrong. Sukey eventually succumbs to Jenny's urging and "did indeed stammer out some Words, which implied a Confession of her Fault; but they were spoke so low they could hardly be heard: Only Miss *Jenny*, who always chose to look at the fairest Side of her Companions Actions, by Miss *Sukey's* Look and Manner, guessed her Meaning" (9). Jenny can guess the meaning because she has provided the meaning. As Mrs. Teachum's surrogate, she articulates the knowledges produced by this community.

Jenny's appeal to communal standards of right and wrong differs both from Locke, who contends that an individual discerns these by reason, and from Locke's pupil Anthony Shaftesbury, who contends that a sense of right and wrong is a first principle implanted in individual human hearts: "No sooner are actions viewed, no sooner the human affections and passions discerned . . . then straight an inward eye distinguishes, and sees the fair and shapely, the amiable and admirable, apart from the deformed, the foul, the odious, or the despicable."[11] In contrast, in *The Governess* the final distinction between right and wrong rests not with the individual but the community, an unspoken but tacitly understood consensus to which an individual contributes but to which she also appeals. By abandoning reason when it does not serve her purpose, Jenny reveals it to be a community construct that depends on cooperation with a set of shared assumptions. When these assumptions are questioned, she invokes shame, not logic, to bring the miscreant to order.

This exchange, particularly in Jenny's refusal to assert overt authority over Sukey, reveals one of the serious flaws in this little utopia—its lack of a coherent theory of authority. Social-contract theory supposes that authority is negotiated among independent individuals intent on protecting their self-interest. In contrast, Jenny insists that in her community no authority operates at all, because each member voluntarily regulates her behavior out of a sincere regard for the community's well-being. This requires each member to internalize authority. The community shapes the individual through the influence of external means that are first rendered invisible and then gradually internalized. Individuals, unaware of the control being exerted, believe that what they do is controlled entirely by their own desires. The individual's own desires for herself come to coincide with what the community wants for the individual. That the best interests of the individual and the best interests of the community should differ, or worse, that they should actually conflict, is unthought-of, if not unthinkable, in this children's utopia.

As a result, although Jenny insists that the girls learn obedience, she does not mean obedience to an external authority figure, something that the narrator regards with deep suspicion. When, for example, Mrs. Teachum requires the girls to "embrace one another, and promise to be Friends for the future; which, in Obedience to her Commands, they were forced to comply with . . . there remained a Grudge, and Ill-will in their Bosoms . . . and they contrived all the sly Tricks they could think on to vex and teaze each other" (*Governess*, 6). Unless individuals internalize their community's regulations, *The Governess* warns, they may disguise their true feelings under a façade of generosity when an authority figure is present but will act them out whenever that figure is absent. True obedience, then, does not mean adherence to a set of clearly articulated regulations enforced externally by a clearly defined authority. Instead, obedience is a subtle matter of discerning the unspoken will of the community.

To teach the little girls to be such discerning women, *The Governess* appropriates the seventeenth-century tradition of women's autobiographical writing, for "there is nothing more likely to amend the future Part of any one's Life, than the recollecting and confessing the Faults of the past" (*Governess*, 12). The pupils meet each day in the garden to tell each other stories that are a part of a complex web of self-representation, and Jenny Peace acts as the moral arbitrator through which these stories can be understood. Each child tells a narrative about herself that outlines and frames her identity, operating as a language of self-definition within which the girls become speaking subjects. These stories place each teller within the community, because she tells her own story according to her community's predetermined pattern of narrative, conforming to prescribed notions and generic patterns of life experience as she tailors her identity to fit her culture's patterns of perceiving and organizing experience. Through her own story, Jenny prescribes the pattern through which her schoolmates organize their experiences and construct their identities.

Jenny's story, although it purportedly teaches self-control and devotion to duty, more importantly teaches the girls to desire the approbation of their peers: "if you do not keep Command enough of yourself . . . you will be unfit for all the social Offices of Life, and be despised by all those whose Regard and Love is worth your seeking" (*Governess*, 17). Rather than adhering to a set of clearly articulated rules regulating property rights, the children in *The Governess* have a duty to seek community approval, the highest reward for correct behavior, and to consider withdrawal of such approval as the severest of punishments. After Jenny finishes, each of the girls tells her own story according to the pattern that Jenny sets—she identifies a wrong desire in herself, recognizes its source, and agrees that by eradicating it she will win the approval of her classmates, now the highest object of her desire. After the little girls tell their stories, their "Hearts [became] so open to each other, that they had not a Thought they endeavoured to conceal" (95). This loving openness, based on absolute trust, is the heart of Fielding's utopian vision.

Since the community demands this kind of trust, its perpetuation necessitates a perfect reliance on members' truthfulness, which is presented as clear and unproblematic. Lying is wrong even when, or perhaps especially when, a lie might appear to benefit another member of the community: "Lying for each other, or Praising each other when it was not deserved, was not only a Fault, but a very great Crime [demonstrating] not Love, but Hatred; as it was encouraging each other in Folly and Wickedness" (*Governess*, 16). Lying to protect a friend injures the friend but also the entire community, for each member is responsible not only for her own moral life but for the moral well-being of all or, more accurately, her own moral well-being is inseparable from that of the others.

The importance of truthfulness is forcefully impressed on the little girls when they hear shrieks from a neighboring garden and find a middle-aged woman beating an eight-year-old girl. Although the girls successfully persuade the woman to forbear, nonetheless when she assures them that the child is a liar and that the beating is intended "to break her of this horrid Custom," the girls approve of the woman's motives even as they sympathize with the child (*Governess*, 41). A less approving narrator might have noted the violence or pointed out that the beaten child has no sympathetic community to which to appeal or from which to learn, and that the girls themselves have no power to take the child into their community in order to teach her better ways. This scene of a woman's violence against a helpless member of her own sex is troubling to the modern reader.

In late-eighteenth-century writing directed toward boys, the emphasis on truth takes a slightly different turn. Locke insists that a child "should be brought up in the greatest abhorrence of [lying] imaginable . . . a premeditated *lie* must always be looked upon as obstinacy and never be permitted to escape unpunished."[12] But in many stories from the late eighteenth and early nineteenth century, boys are also warned never to be tale-bearers, even if this compromises their dedication to the truth. Maria Edgeworth's hero Hardy, in *Tarlton* (1809),[13] exhibits both the strength of character and the sturdy individualism beloved by the social-contract model when he refuses to tell his schoolmaster which of his schoolmates tried to poison a dog: "I would never try to get myself off by betraying my companions" (Edgeworth, 83). In Maria Budden's *Always Happy* (1815), as Felix departs for school his father warns him not to expose his "schoolmates' thoughts nor cause their punishment; it will be enough for you to guard your own conduct and not disgrace yourself by becoming a spy on others."[14] The emphasis in both stories is the personal superiority of the boy who will not betray his classmates, which to Fielding means encouraging them in weakness or folly. The boy's first duty is to himself—to be the best possible person. He is not responsible for the moral improvement of his friends but only for his own. Moreover, unlike the girls, who must be sensitive to an unspoken set of community assumptions, the boys can appeal from one clearly articulated rule ("always tell the truth") to another ("never be a sneak").

Dedication to truth does not, however, require the girls to abandon imagination, a crucial element in the development of their community, for this story sees truth and imagination not as opposed to but as dependent on each other. Imagination enables one to discover truth by developing the ability to discern what another person is feeling. Adam Smith explains in *The Theory of Moral Sentiments* (1759): "As we have no immediate experience of what other men feel, we can form no idea of the manner in which they are affected, but by conceiving what we ourselves should feel in the like situation . . . it is by the imagination only that we can form any conception of what are his sensations."[15] The girls must develop their imaginations so that each can understand what her companions are feeling and respond appropriately. To encourage this, the girls tell each other fairy tales, and later in the century *The Governess* will be severely condemned for this perceived lapse from absolute truthfulness.

Such condemnation comes from two educational factions that are often thought to be very different but which in fact have many ideas, including this one, in common: on the one hand, the rationalist school represented by Maria and Richard Edgeworth, Anna Barbauld, and Mary Wollstonecraft, and, on the other, the Christian moralist school, which includes Sarah Trimmer and Mary Martha Sherwood. Richard Edgeworth, in the preface to his daughter Maria's *The Parent's Assistant* (1796), attacks Samuel Johnson for approving of children's fairy tales: "Why should the mind be filled with fantastic visions, instead of useful knowledge? It is to be hoped that the magic of Dr. Johnson's name will not have the power to restore the reign of fairies."[16] Reason and truth, Richard Edgeworth contends, prohibit imaginative literature. Christian moralists also condemn fairy tales. Sarah Trimmer, in 1786, condemns all such literature as "fit only to fill the heads of children with confused notions of wonderful and supernatural events, brought about by the agency of imaginary beings."[17] Children should learn only what is factually true.

The Governess finds this attitude priggish, and in the story of little Polly Suckling, Fielding explicitly ridicules the anti-fairy-tale argument. The youngest scholar and pet of the school, little Polly, announces self-importantly that she prefers to hear "some true History, from which they might learn something . . . for Fairy-Tales were fit only for little Children" (*Governess*, 63). But instead of praising Polly's maturity, the wiser Jenny delicately chides her for affectation. Rather than condemning the little one directly, however, Jenny deflects her criticism by telling a story of her own youthful folly. She explains that she herself, when a little girl, had decided that she was too important to see a Raree-Show but only in order to boast of her superiority in being above such trifles. Her discerning mother laughed at her, because "Laughing is the proper Manner of treating Affectation; which of all Things, she said, she would have me carefully avoid" (63). Affected virtue, Jenny explains gently to her listeners, is a form of self-centeredness, the great enemy to the community. Affectation, not imagination, violates the commitment to absolute truth that grounds this community. Although Mrs. Teachum scrupulously explains that fairy tales are not to be taken literally, she nonetheless places a moral value on the genre: "Giants, Magic, Fairies, and all Sorts of supernatural Assistances in a Story, are only introduced to amuse and divert: For a Giant is called so only to express a Man of great Power; and the magic Fillet round the Statue was intended only to shew you, that by Patience you will overcome all Difficulties" (34). Cultivation of the imagination has a legitimate place in the construction of selfhood, according to *The Governess*, and only sanctimonious pretension condemns it.

The fairy tales also help to validate the community's sense of itself as powerful in spite of physical weakness, for in these tales, meekness, compassion, and patience prevail over mere strength. In the story of the Good Giant Benefico and the Evil Giant Barbarico, for example, Barbarico is defeated not by the mighty giant but by two meek and feminized men, the kind-hearted little shepherd Fidus and the gentle and compassionate Mignon, whose countenance is soft and temper sweet (*Governess*, 23–25). The weak can overcome the mighty through courage, kindness, and persistence, and this conviction is important to the community's sense of its own importance.

A longer fairy tale teaches the dangers of false friendship. The Princess Hebe, deprived of her rightful claim to the throne and raised in rural isolation by two women, is nearly destroyed by the wicked fairy Rozella, who pretends to be her friend. The girls sympathize with Hebe: "Miss *Dolly Friendly* said, that *Rozella's* artful manner was enough to have drawn in the wisest Girl into her Snares; and she did not see how it was possible for the Princess *Hebe* to withstand it, especially when she cry'd for fear of parting with her" (*Governess*, 91). The little girls understand the dangers of trusting friends who are not worthy. Yet this story reveals another serious flaw in their community, which, by its very nature, lacks any objective standard by which to recognize and defend against the power of active malevolence. The girls are taught that they can understand what another person would do in any situation by imagining what they themselves would do in the same situation. Since they have learned to act with trust, kindness, and compassion, they assume that these are universal characteristics, and so they are at a loss to deal with malevolence and selfishness when they encounter it. The story points ahead to Fielding's next novel, *The adventures of David Simple . . . volume the last* (1753),[18] in which David Simple continually trusts the false friends who continually betray him.

III

A mistaken application of Lockean ideas to Fielding's pedagogy has led to an entirely unjustified charge that *The Governess* idealizes marriage and seeks only to repress her readers into submissiveness and domesticity. The critics who make these charges see Fielding's insistence that the individual submit to the will of her community as a wish for a conventional wifely submission to a husband. Elizabeth Bergen Brophy, in an important study of eighteenth-century women's literature, condemns *The Governess* for exalting "quiet domesticity above any talent or achievement."[19] She bases this condemnation on the "Fable of the Birds," in which the Dove sings a lullaby to her nestlings about the strength and generosity of their father: "chief the Lord of my Desire/ My Life, myself, my Soul, my Sire" (*Governess*, 120). Similarly, Judith Burdan reads *The Governess* as repressing the girls into domesticity and obedience by destroying their individuality: "[t]heir pasts and their individual differences are homogenized; the girls, who before their confessions are presented as differentiated individuals, are transformed in the end to a set of acceptable behaviors and appearances. . . . [t]he story ends happily when the girls as a group are rendered fit for the adult world of marriage and motherhood."[20] To Burdan, *The Governess* is a repressive tale designed to force young women to accept willingly a domestic prison.

Such criticism is echoed by Arlene Fish Wilner, who cites three embedded narratives as evidence that the novel "explicitly promote[s] the circumscribed aspects of the female role."[21] Wilner argues that Amata, in a fairy tale about a good and a bad giant, is rewarded with marriage to Fidus because of her delicacy and passivity and that Caelia, in a romance story, is rewarded with marriage because she is artless and dispassionate. In a third story, Lady Harriot is so pleased at being reproved by Mr. Camply for being gay and coquettish that she consents to marry him. These examples are evidence, according to Wilner, that the girls are only being taught "what makes a good wife" (Wilner, 315).

The Governess emphatically does not support these readings. There is little to choose between Amata and Fidus in the matter of delicacy and passivity; Fidus is one of Fielding's most feminized heroes, waiting patiently in the giant's dungeon until Mignon, only slightly less passive, rescues him. Caelia wins her husband because she tells the truth, a matter of utmost importance in this community, and the point of Caelia's story is not who is rewarded with a husband (in Fielding's adult texts always a dubious reward) but the importance of female friendship. The condemnation of Lady Harriot for coquetry, like the valorization of the dove that sings to her nestlings rather than compete for a prize, is consistent with Fielding's condemnation of those who seek to attract attention to themselves rather than to focus on the good of others.

Far from preparing its young readers to be obedient wives, *The Governess* explicitly stresses that marriage cannot guarantee women's happiness. Apart from the conventionally romantic forms of the interpolated tales, the only examples of marriage in *The Governess* are Mrs. Teachum, whose husband leaves her destitute, and Lord and Lady X, whose unhappy marriage is about to end. Lord and Lady X live "in the most jarring disputing manner, and took no care to conceal their Quarrels from the World; but at last they have agreed to part by Consent" (*Governess*, 116). The story of Lord and Lady X is especially astounding in that it is told in a book for children, but Fielding is at pains to ensure that even these very young women are aware of the potential dangers of marriage. At no time does any pupil of Mrs. Teachum's speak of marriage or motherhood as one of her goals. No one is ever told that certain kinds of behavior will make her more eligible for marriage, or that marriage, motherhood, and family life bring happiness. On the contrary, except for Jenny Peace, the little girls' stories invariably describe their own families as places where they are taught to be mean, envious, and unhappy, and such bleak pictures of domesticity cannot reasonably be seen as urging young women to marry. Only a Lockean reading, in which obedience is always a potential threat to personal autonomy, could construe these texts this way.

According to Fielding, a woman will most likely realize true happiness not within marriage but within communities of supportive female friends, the basis of Fielding's utopian vision. The traits necessary for such communities, of course, are not entirely dissimilar from the traits necessary for marriage. In either case a woman accedes to an authority outside herself—her husband or her community. In the female community, however, submissiveness is not a relationship of subordination but of equality. When women learn to cultivate other women as steadfast and trustworthy friends, they recognize their mutual dependence. The way to do this, *The Governess* teaches, is to be truthful, to avoid self-approbation, and always to find pleasure in the happiness of others.

The Governess, then, teaches its readers the technologies of self that will enable women to lead happy lives in small communities of supportive female friends. Her vision has serious flaws, for it lacks a coherent theory of authority, it has no way to resolve conflicts within the community and so must deny their existence, and it cannot recognize and defend the community from outside dangers. Nonetheless, by rejecting the unequal, competitive model of possessive individualism that Locke envisions, and appealing instead to an earlier idea of self defined by community, Fielding assures her young female readers that other and more appropriate versions of selfhood are available to them. They can realize these visions through their own efforts, Fielding promises; they are capable of and responsible for creating their own utopia.

Notes

1. Sarah Fielding, *The Governess, or Little Female Academy* (1749) (London: Pandora, 1987), 8; hereafter cited in the text as *Governess*.
2. Sarah Scott, *A Description of Millenium Hall and the Country Adjacent* (1762) (London: Virago, 1986); Sarah Fielding's *The Adventures of David Simple* (1744), ed. Malcolm Kelsall (Oxford: Oxford University Press, 1987); and Sarah Fielding, *The History of the Countess of Dellwyn* (1759) (New York: Garland Publishing, 1974).
3. Sarah Fielding and Jane Collier, *The Cry: A New Dramatic Fable, etc.*, 3 vols. (London: R. & J. Dodsley, 1754) and Mary Hamilton, *Munster Village* (1778) (New York: Pandora, 1987).
4. Michel Foucault, *The History of Sexuality, Vol. I.: An Introduction*, trans. Robert Hurley (New York: Vintage Books, 1980), 58. See also *Technologies of the Self: A Seminar with Michel Foucault*, eds. Luther H. Martin, Huck Gutman, and Patrick H. Hutton (Amherst: University of Massachusetts Press, 1988).
5. Felicity Nussbaum, *The Autobiographical Subject: Gender and Ideology in Eighteenth-Century England* (Baltimore: Johns Hopkins University Press, 1989), xv.
6. John Locke, *Two Treatises on Government with a Supplemental* Patriarcha *by Robert Filmer* (New York: Hafner Press, 1947), 52; hereafter cited in text.

7. C. B. Macpherson, *The Political Theory of Possessive Individualism* (Oxford: Clarendon Press, 1962), 221.
8. James Nelson, *An essay on the government of children, under three general hands: viz. health, manners and education* (1756) (Dublin: W. Williamson, 1763), 17.
9. Carole Patemen, *The Sexual Contract* (Stanford: Stanford University Press, 1988), 5–6.
10. Susan Staves, *Married Women's Separate Property in England, 1660–1833* (Cambridge: Harvard University Press, 1990), 4; hereafter cited in text.
11. Anthony, Lord Shaftesbury, *Characteristics of Men, Manners, Opinions, Times*, 2 vols., ed. J. M. Robertson (Indianapolis: Bobbs-Merrill, 1964), 1. 260.
12. John Locke, *Some Thoughts Concerning Education* (1695), ed. Ruth W. Grant and Nathan Tarcov (Indianapolis: Hackett, 1996), 101.
13. Maria Edgeworth, "Tarlton," in *The Parent's Assistant* (Georgetown, D.C.: Joseph Milligan, 1809), 83.
14. Maria Budden, *Always Happy* (1815) (New York: William B. Gilley, 1816), 48.
15. Adam Smith, *The Theory of Moral Sentiments* (1759), ed. D. D. Raphael and A. L. Macfie (Oxford: Clarendon Press, 1976), 9.
16. Maria Edgeworth, *The Parent's Assistant* (1809), ed. Christina Edgeworth Colvin (New York: Garland, 1976), xi.
17. Sarah Trimmer, *Fabulous Histories Designed for the Amusement and Instruction of Young People* (1786) (Philadelphia: Clark and Raser, 1806), xi.
18. Sarah Fielding, *The adventures of David Simple . . . and The adventures of David Simple, volume the last: in which his history is concluded* (1744 and 1753), ed. Peter Sabor (Lexington, Ky.: University Press of Kentucky, 1998).
19. Elizabeth Bergen Brophy, *Women's Lives and the 18th Century English Novel* (Tampa: South Florida University Press, 1991), 56.
20. Judith Burdan, "Girls *Must* be Seen *and* Heard: Domestic Surveillance in Sarah Fielding's *The Governess*," *Children's Literature Association Quarterly* 19 (Spring 1994), 12.
21. Arlene Fish Wilner, "Education and Ideology in Sarah Fielding's *The Governess*," in *Studies in Eighteenth-Century Culture*, ed. Carla H. Hay and Syndy M. Conger (Baltimore: The Johns Hopkins University Press, 1995), 314; hereafter cited in text.

Works Cited

Brophy, Elizabeth Bergen. *Women's Lives and the 18th Century English Novel*. Tampa: South Florida University Press, 1991.
Budden, Maria. *Always Happy*. 1815. New York: William B. Gilley, 1816.
Burdan, Judith. "Girls *Must* Be Seen *and* Heard: Domestic Surveillance in Sarah Fielding's *The Governess*." *Children's Literature Association Quarterly* 19 (Spring 1994): 8–13.
Edgeworth, Maria. "Tarlton." In *The Parent's Assistant*, 81–94. Georgetown, D.C.: Joseph Milligan, 1809.

Edgeworth, Richard. "Introduction." In *The Parent's Assistant*, ed. Christina Edgeworth Colvin, iv–xx. New York: Garland, 1976.

Fielding, Sarah. *The Adventures of David Simple*. 1744. Edited by Malcolm Kelsall. Oxford: Oxford University Press, 1982.

———. *The Adventures of David Simple . . . and The adventures of David Simple, volume the last: in which his history is concluded*. 1744 and 1753. Edited by Peter Sabor. Lexington, Ky.: University Press of Kentucky, 1998.

———. *The Governess, or Little Female Academy*. 1749. London: Pandora, 1987.

———. *The History of the Countess of Dellwyn*. 1759. New York: Garland Publishing, 1974.

Fielding, Sarah and Jane Collier, *The Cry: A New Dramatic Fable, etc.* 3 vols. London: R. & J. Dodsley, 1754.

Foucault, Michel. *The History of Sexuality, Vol. I: An Introduction*. Translated by Robert Hurley. New York: Vintage Books, 1980.

Hamilton, Mary. *Munster Village*. 1778. New York: Pandora, 1987.

Locke, John. *Two Treatises on Government with a Supplement* Patriarcha *by Robert Filmer*. New York: Hafner Press, 1947.

———. *Some Thoughts Concerning Education*. 1695. Edited by Ruth W. Grant and Nathan Tarcov. Indianapolis: Hackett, 1996.

Macpherson, C. B. *The Political Theory of Possessive Individualism*. Oxford: Clarendon Press, 1962.

Martin, Luther H., Huck Gutman, and Patrick H. Hutton, eds. *Technologies of the Self: A Seminar with Michel Foucault*. Amherst, Mass.: University of Massachusetts Press, 1988.

Nelson, James. *An essay on the government of children, under three general hands: viz. health, manners and education*. 1756. Dublin: W. Williamson, 1763.

Nussbaum, Felicity. *The Autobiographical Subject: Gender and Ideology in Eighteenth-Century England*. Baltimore: The Johns Hopkins University Press, 1989.

Patemen, Carole. *The Sexual Contract*. Stanford: Stanford University Press, 1988.

Scott, Sarah. *Millenium Hall*. 1762. London: Virago, 1986.

Shaftesbury, Anthony. *Characteristics of Men, Manners, Opinions, Times*. 1711. 2 vols. Edited by J. M. Robertson. Indianapolis: Bobbs-Merrill, 1964.

Smith, Adam. *The Theory of Moral Sentiments*. Edited by D. D. Raphael and A. L. Macfie. Oxford: Clarendon Press, 1976.

Staves, Susan. *Married Women's Separate Property in England, 1660–1833*. Cambridge: Harvard University Press, 1990.

Trimmer, Sarah. *Fabulous Histories Designed for the Amusement and Instruction of Young People*. 1786. Philadelphia: Clark and Raser, 1806.

Wilner, Arlene Fish. "Education and Ideology in Sarah Fielding's *The Governess*." *Studies in Eighteenth-Century Culture*. Edited by Carla H. Hay and Syndy M. Conger, 307–27. Baltimore: The Johns Hopkins University Press, 1995.

5

Tinklers and Time Machines: Time Travel in the Social Fantasy of E. Nesbit and H. G. Wells

CATHRINE FRANK

In E. Nesbit's *The Story of the Amulet* (1906), Cyril, Robert, Anthea and Jane repeatedly journey to the past in search of the missing half of a magic amulet that will bring them their "heart's desire."[1] After several failed adventures, Cyril proposes they travel to a future time after the amulet will have been recovered and when they thus will be able to remember how they first discovered the missing piece. In this later London, they find not only the amulet but a world of greenery and goodwill, where dirty pigeons are "birds of new silver" (*Amulet*, 231), men and women jointly care for their children, no one looks worried, and work and school alike are both honorable and fun.

There they encounter Wells, the little "expelleder" sent home from school for littering (*Amulet*, 233), whose mother tells the children he is named "after the great reformer. . . . He lived in the dark ages, and he saw that what you ought to do is to find out what you want and then try to get it. Up to then people had always tried to tinker with what they'd got. We've got a great many of the things he thought of" (*Amulet*, 239). Nesbit's imaginary London is free from the social extremes of beggary and aristocracy and their accompaniments, squalor and luxury. The freedoms, comfort, and general welfare it does have are the results of a break from tradition, from the "tinkering" with existing conditions with no alteration of their underlying assumptions, which the real Wells had challenged in *A Modern Utopia* (1905).[2]

Throughout *A Modern Utopia*, Wells insists that in order to conceive an ideal society, there must be a break with the past: "We must turn our backs for a space upon the insistent examination of the thing that is," he writes, "and face towards the freer air, the ampler spaces of the thing that perhaps might be, to the projection of a State or city 'worth while,' *to designing upon the sheet of our imaginations* the picture of a life conceivably possible, and yet better worth living than our own" (emphasis mine, *Modern*, 17). We must abjure the postulates of "tradition" and work from a new "assumption of emancipation" that gives individuals "the power to resist the causation of the past, and to evade, initiate, endeavour, and overcome" (19–20). Moreover, this break requires a new form of expression. Evaluating the trajectory of his utopian writings in the preface, Wells explains that in this latest work he returned from objective speculations to the more liberating mode of imaginative writing that gives movement to an otherwise static presentation of an ideal and allows that ideal to be truly new, unhinged from past and present, in the first place (6).

Nesbit's pointed reference to Wells in *The Story of the Amulet* marks a congruence not only of their political principles but of their literary methods as well. For each the expression of ideals in action is both immanent in their choice of imaginative fiction as a medium for social criticism and explicit in their use of travel, in these examples for the projection of future worlds. Indeed, Wells proposes that travel should be a staple in his future world because it gives individual imagination greater scope (*Modern*, 52); still more striking is the observation that his narrator's presence there is the result of "some strange transition in space or time" (*Modern*, 59). Similarly, Nesbit's Psammead explains to the children that they can move through time because both it and space are only "forms of thought" (*Amulet*, 46). Thus liberated from the strict geographies of place and present, both authors are free in their fiction to imagine other worlds which, divorced from the real present, teach their readers a better way to be.

Judith Barisonzi notes that it is not until the appearance of the Arden books, however, that Nesbit fully deploys this temporal thematic and narrative device in the interests of political commentary.[3] But if *Amulet* is Nesbit's first full-scale use of time travel, *A Modern Utopia* is not Wells's. That is, if *The House of Arden* (1908)[4] and *Harding's Luck* (1909)[5] are indebted to Wells, part of the project of exploring their utopian dimension must involve a leap backward to Wells's first novel *The Time Machine* (1895),[6] in which his contemporary views of human and cultural decay are pursued to their alarming conclusion. Like other fin de siècle novels, the Arden books and *Time Machine* engage late-Victorian ideas of disrupted chronology; they are conscious of Darwinian evolution and of the degeneration Max Nordau foretells. Unlike realistic adult fiction, however, these novels pair their real social concerns with fantastic modes of expression that render them innovative in both adult and children's genres.

In this essay I argue that both Nesbit's and Wells's narrative use of time travel firmly though ironically situates them between two eras. Their emphasis on the realistic characters' temporal movement out of contemporary England links their dissatisfaction with fictional realism to their participation in the Fabian Society and its political disapproval of real turn-of-the-century social conditions. Moreover, the idea of permeable Time addresses the concerns of two centuries: one discomfited by challenges to its erstwhile belief in inviolable progress, and another which responds variously to that challenge through more vigorous positivism or nostalgia. Thus, both Nesbit's and Wells's sense of transition becomes the springboard for their politicized use of the time-travel motif in their fiction. Where Wells's introduction of science and fantasy into adult fiction inaugurates a new genre altogether, Nesbit's modernization of the Victorian fairy tale (achieved, in contrast to Wells, through the inclusion in her fantasy of the real or familiar) produces a new type of children's literature.

1. Fabian Fantasies and Socialist Utopias

The ideal communities imagined in Wells's and Nesbit's novels place them within the shared contexts of a utopian literary tradition and nineteenth-century socialism. As many critics of utopia have noted, to define it in terms of form, in this case in terms of literature, is to limit the definition too rigorously. However, Nesbit's writing for children and Wells's science fiction are both so didactic in nature that they seem to belong to what Ruth Levitas identifies as a "largely, but not exclusively, Marxist tradition [that] has defined utopia in terms of its function—either a negative function of preventing social change or a positive function of facilitating it, either directly or through the process of the 'education of desire.' "[7] In this sense, writing for children, because it seeks at the very least to educate its readers into better ways of being, is utopian writing that shares a political vision with Wells's adult-oriented fantastic fictions.

In the nineteenth century, utopianism came to mean socialism.[8] And at the turn of the century in Britain, socialism meant the Fabian Society of which both Wells and Nesbit were members. The Society began in 1884 as an offshoot of the more idealistic Fellowship of the New Life. In Hubert Bland's 1908 reflection on his own political development, "The Faith I Hold," he nostalgically portrays the group as a retreat from the "stupid, vulgar, grimy age" of late Victorianism: "[w]e turned away from it to a little world within a world, a world of poetry, of pictures, of music, of old romance, of strangely designed wall-papers, and of sad-coloured velveteen."[9] But Bland's sentimental portrayal of the new Society, named for Fabian Cuncator, who followed deliberation with decisive action, muted its political ardor. Its ideological antecedents lay in Henry Hyndeman's Social Democratic Federation, Henry George's studies in economics and in Thomas Davidson's reflective idealism. Departing from the latter's emphasis on spirituality, the Fabians nonetheless maintained at least one of the Fellowship's founding principles: "The supplanting of the spirit of self-seeking by that unselfish regard for the general good" (Briggs, 64). It is this opposition to capitalism and private wealth that gave the group what George Mariz identifies as its nearest approach to a political platform from which they "argued for the establishment of a minimum wage, workers' unemployment insurance, old age pensions, poor law reform and housing reform" (Briggs, 88).

But unlike more staunchly Marxist advocates for revolution, the Fabian opposition to capitalism took a "gradualist 'permeation' of existing political institutions" as the road to reform (Claeys, 234). According to Mariz, the group's secretary Edward Pease characterized it as "something of a club" in which all members "believed in an intellectual approach to problems, with research and analysis of individual matters as a key to understanding social, economic and political subjects."[10] In this vein, they refrained from piggy-backing on a specific partisan agenda, opting instead to insinuate themselves into the mentalities of all the groups and, through this process of subversion, change the minds of the country's lawmakers. Indeed, the Society's apparently mild methods caused some to doubt their zeal. Portrayed by Pease as a tolerant group, the "Old Gang" Fabians were accused by fledgling Fabians, of whom Wells was one, of "parochialism and exclusiveness" (84). Moreover, their renowned "caution" and "thoughtfulness" (85) and their unwillingness even to formulate a clear statement of purpose, made them, in the eyes of more radical members, too tame to effect real political change (84).

In terms of Wells's involvement with the organization, he was already a regular correspondent with and friend of the Blands when Shaw and Graham Wallas sponsored his membership in the Society in 1903, believing that his unconventional character would add to the club's eclecticism. Drawing from one of Wells's early lectures on socialism, Mariz observes that for Wells, socialism was synonymous with "matters of property holding" (Mariz, 90), and so, taking a moderate stance, he advocated taxes on private property that would then be directed toward public benefit (Mariz, 91). Thus, in matters of substance, Wells and the leading Fabians agreed.[11] This would change. If initially Wells and the Fabians differed only in terms of "style" (Cole, 109) and "method" (Cole, 110), by the time of the famed "incident" with Shaw three years later Wells would be much more insistent on the implementation of views such as "radical equality of the sexes, absolute communism of property and rigid, central control," ideas to be developed in *A Modern Utopia* (Mariz, 92). In fact, in his last address to the Society before making his American tour, a discussion which was resumed shortly after his return in the debate with Shaw, Wells outlines a view of the Fabians as a has-been operation, which was critically at odds with Bland's reflections. Margaret Cole, herself a Fabian, summarizes:

> The Society had had a good past, he [Wells] admitted; but in the present it was no good. It was small, shabbily poor and collectively inactive; it lived in a dismal basement, tested applicants savagely instead of welcoming them in, made them sign a stupidly drafted Basis of Faith, and when they had

signed set them to rubbishy tasks like writing letters to the local press. Most
irritating of [its] defects was the tendency of its members to have private
jokes: their supreme delight was to giggle, and they permeated English
society with their ideas about as much as a mouse may be said to permeate
a cat. (Cole, 110)

Bland's "world within a world" is now a "dismal basement," and Bland's
wife, E. Nesbit, whose support Wells had cultivated to bring his ideas before
the Fabian executive, was no better than a disruptive schoolgirl.

Wells's jabs at Nesbit, though perhaps motivated by personal rancor,
were neither unusual nor limited to the younger sect. Shaw described Nesbit
as Bland's "very pretty wife" who during meetings "made scenes and simu-
lated fainting fits."[12] Julia Briggs observes that she frequently turned meetings into opportunities for self-display, regardless of how much she believed
in the work that was being forwarded (Briggs, 70), and it is perhaps this
inconsistency for which her avowedly political activity is most noteworthy.
On the one hand, she tried to implement Fabian principles by throwing par-
ties for poor children and forming organizations for their relief (Schenkel,
111). She accompanied Marshall Steele on his lecture tour of Working Men's
Clubs, followed liberating trends in hair and dress, and smoked in public. On
the other hand, she sided with Hubert's conservative views of the Women's
Suffrage Movement and dismissed its members as intellectual snobs (Briggs,
69). However, the inconsistency may not be a matter entirely of Nesbit's own
political thinking. Briggs speculates that Wells himself appealed to Nesbit
and the other Fabian Women because he perceived them as having comparatively little opportunity for action within the Society and felt, therefore, that
they would be most sympathetic to his intended reforms. As a case in point,
Nesbit, who was elected to the Pamphlets Committee in 1884 because of her
literary experience, actually had little to do with the drafting of their first
tract, "Why Are the Many Poor?" (Briggs, 65).

If both Nesbit's and Wells's social activism found limited expression in
the real world of Fabian politics, their fictional fantasies offered in contrast
tremendous range. As a "symbolic world between Reality and the Imagination," fiction in general enjoys experimental latitude unmatched by the everyday world of even politically liberal times (Schenkel, 120). Utopian writing
in particular relies on the disparity between real and imagined worlds
because only the latter can satisfy the desires prompted by real-world failings
(Levitas, 8, 191). Similarly, writing for children challenges social realities
through the power of play and its roots in the imagination. Elmar Schenkel
observes that "[t]he children's book since Lewis Carroll proves itself to be an
experimental field for new ideas, which only later develops in adult literature. One can play in the children's book because the genre undergoes less
critical observation, and play is the prerequisite for everything new, be it in

inventions, philosophies, or in the natural sciences" (Schenkel, 120). As the preeminent mode of fantastic exploration in the nineteenth century, children's literature provides the backdrop for fin de siècle fantastic literature for adults, and in both cases it is the author's (and the audience's) opportunity to play that lends the genres their "great utopian potential" to reform the existing social order.[13]

2. Pasts Perfect and Future Tensions

For Nesbit, the children's tale is most often a tale of children. By introducing groups of children, she adds a social dimension to literature of the Golden Age that focused on the individual child, and which would influence twentieth-century writers like C. S. Lewis and Kenneth Grahame (Schenkel, 107). To this basic interest in social relations, her later work on time travel adds the necessity and possibility of reforming them. In *The House of Arden*, for example, Edred and Elfrida Arden journey to the past in search of the family fortune that could restore their father to them. While on their quest, they adopt a plan of centralized subsidization of the working-class members of their community that recalls the narrator's reflections on the nature of private wealth. "When you are a child," she says,

> you always dream of your ship coming home—of having a hundred pounds, or a thousand, or a million pounds to spend as you like. . . . Of course, we buy ourselves a motor-bicycle straight-away, and footballs and bats . . . but when we have done that we begin to buy things for other people. It is a beautiful dream, but too often, by the time it comes true—up to a hundred pounds or a thousand—we forget what we used to mean to do with our money, and spend it all in stocks and shares, and eligible building sites, and fat cigars and fur coats. (*Arden*, 5)

Nesbit idealizes childhood as the purer past of one's adult life in the same way that she valorizes the historical past and the Edenic, pre-industrial South American culture in which the children find their father. Trapped for years in a country whose kings "will die sooner than allow the plain to be infected by the wicked cruelties of modern civilization," Edred Arden, Sr. declares, "If I let in our horrible system of trusts and syndicates, and commercialism and crime, on this golden life, I should know myself to be as great a criminal as though I had thrown a little child to the wild beasts" (*Arden*, 252), much as Wells's childlike Eloi become prey to the working-class Morlock cannibals.

The analogy between the paradisial innocence and vulnerability of childhood to the beastliness of capitalist industrialization assumes physical dimensions in the body of Dickie Harding. Dickie is introduced in *Arden* when Edred and Elfrida, taken aback by their cousin's uncanny knowledge of the Brownie camera and Cricket results from 1908 (*Arden*, 174–75), discover that Dickie is also a fellow time traveler. When they beg him to return to the present and escape danger, Dickie's refusal is vehement:

> I hate your times. They're ugly, they're cruel. . . . They make people work fourteen hours a day for nine shillings a week, so that they never have enough to eat or wear, and no time to sleep or to be happy in. They won't give people food or clothes, or let them work to get them; and then they put the people in prison if they take enough to keep them alive. They let people get horrid diseases, till their jaws drop off, so as to have a particular kind of china. Women have to go out to work instead of looking after their babies, and the little girl that's left in charge drops the baby and it's crippled for life. Oh! I know. I won't go back with you. You might keep me there forever. (*Arden*, 235)

Dickie's story provides the basis for Nesbit's sequel to *Arden*, *Harding's Luck*. He is poor and orphaned and lame, and his sole companion is his "Tinkler," a worn-out rattle given to him by his father on his deathbed. (Like the Mouldiwarp of *Arden* and Wells's time machine, the Tinkler is the magical prop that transports Dickie to the past, where he discovers the familial and physical wholeness he lacks in the present.) In *Harding's Luck*, the reader discovers that Dickie has already absorbed what Edred and Elfrida are trying to learn. In oscillating between his universally admired and protected seventeenth-century self and his dispossessed twentieth-century character, Dickie brings to the present the lessons learned in the past. Despite his desire to remain there, sound in body and with his nurse and parents, Dickie repeatedly returns to the present until he is certain that conditions there have been made better. Yet ultimately Dickie opts to live in the past, for no matter how changed his prospects (he is the real heir to the Arden title), Dickie's lameness is a perpetual symbol of social degeneration. Thus, although he returns to the past, he leaves his Uncle to apply the lessons learned from more collaborative societies to make Arden "the happiest and most prosperous village in England" (*Harding's*, 224).

At the conclusion of *The House of Arden*, Edred and Elfrida Arden find their missing father and repair the present only by having journeyed to the past where they learned to become "brave and kind and wise" (*Arden*, 24). In *Harding's Luck*, their lame cousin Dickie discovers that "things that you learned in dreams would 'stay learnt' " (*Harding's*, 90). In both novels, Nesbit's use of time travel advances the layered lessons that reference to the past is the only way to effect positive change in the present, that violent revolutions are counterproductive (because they always fail) and dangerous, and that the lessons learned in fantasy, like those of dreams, can transfer to and transform the real world. By weaving past and contemporary narratives, she expresses nostalgia for a pre-industrial England, but rather than advocating complete regression, she suggests that the restoration of communal social principles, a nexus of feudalism and socialism, can salvage modern-day England from the increasing atomization that abandons the working-class and mechanizes human relationships. The children venture back first to 1807 and the fear of Napoleonic invasion, then on to the time of the Pretender, and further to Elizabethan and Tudor times, specifically Raleigh's imprisonment in the Tower and the first signs of discord in Henry VIII's marriage to Anne Boleyn. By thus choosing other periods of social and political upheaval as the loci of her criticism, she expresses the Fabian attitudes of sympathy with the impulse to challenge the established order and intolerance of outright revolutionary methods.[14]

Where Nesbit's time travel provides the possibility of redeeming Edwardian social relations, Wells's use of the device provides an apocalyptic warning to late Victorians, prophesying not only irreparable class antagonism but its corollary in physical devolution and ultimate human extinction. Yet Wells, as does Nesbit in the Arden series, comes to an ambivalent conclusion. The Time Traveler's account of his ordeal in the far-distant year 802,701 A.D. revolves primarily around the special and classed antagonism between the Earth's latest inhabitants. The Eloi whom he first meets are completely undifferentiated from one another. Childlike in manner and appearance, they disappoint the Traveler's assumption that the future would be better because further along the line of progression. His introduction to the Morlocks, however, changes disappointment to repugnance for the future world that must chasten any complacent view of the present. Like the regressive Doasyoulikes of Charles Kingsley's *The Water-Babies* (1863),[15] the Morlocks undergo a reverse evolution. While Kingsley's creatures are the product of lassitude, the Morlocks are the working-class. Isolated from the "beautiful futility" of the upper-class Eloi (*Time*, 71), indeed, "liv[ing] in such artificial conditions as practically to be cut off from the natural surface of the earth" (*Time*, 61), they become cannibalistic castoffs of civilization.

Initially worried that he "had built the Time Machine in vain" (*Time*, 29), the Traveler finds some benefit in having overshot the zenith of human development. "I began to realize an odd consequence of the social effort in which we are at present engaged," he says. "[I]t is a logical consequence enough. Strength is the outcome of need; security sets a premium on feebleness. The work of ameliorating the conditions of life—the true civilizing process that makes life more and more secure—had gone steadily on to a climax. One triumph of a united humanity over Nature had followed another. Things that are now mere dreams had become projects deliberately put in hand and carried forward. And the harvest was what I saw!" (43). Wells's vague reference to "dreams" becoming "projects" through the efforts of a "united humanity" itself suggests the Fabian ethos of widespread and consistent social change. His futuristic vantage point, however, exposes the irony that a world, having progressed to its perfected climax, must logically descend. Without the hard-ships of living, society has no stimulant to promote the "human intelligence and vigour" (39) of the strong, no further obstacle to weakness. The result, according to the Traveler's observations, is an enervated society that accords perfectly with Nordau's idea in *Degeneration*, also published in 1895, that societies peak and decline. Where Nordau is certain that the nineteenth cen-tury is already on the brink of the abyss, Wells's future vision would seem at least to leave time for drastic improvement before the inevitable end.

But if this lesson confirms that the Traveler did not build his machine in vain, it is hard to see why not. "The true civilizing process" (*Time*, 43), that "dream of the human intellect" (97), has been nothing but a suicide course, mapping out both our need for improvement in the present and the conse-quence of its achievement. The Traveler's formulation underscores the inevitable futility of arriving at social equanimity precisely because it locates all benefits in an unending process of change. As the narrator observes at the novel's conclusion, after the Traveler has disappeared into an unknown time, "[h]e, I know, . . . saw in the growing pile of civilization only a foolish heap-ing that must inevitably fall back upon and destroy its makers in the end" (114). With the brittle petals of Weena's flowers as his talisman and their suggestion that, even when intellectual superiority passes, "gratitude and a mutual tenderness still lived on in the heart of man" (115), the narrator looks toward the "vast ignorance" (114) that is the future and finds instead a reason to hope. Although the Traveler is usually designated as Wells's ideological representative, the abandonment of the present does not square entirely with his socialism except in so far as it symbolically advocates a complete over-haul of the present capitalist system. This is the total break with the present Wells would advocate in *A Modern Utopia* but, while it may make for good utopianism, it is doubtful socialism. Here the narrator steps in as one who shares the Traveler's disenchantment with the present but perforce remains committed to humanist principles because to do otherwise is to precipitate the Traveler's gloomy forecast of the future.

Like Nesbit's fiction, Wells's lays out social ills, and neither is unequivo-cally successful in rectifying them. In the colloquial sense of the term, they may well be called utopian.[16] However, their implementation of time travel at a minimum asks readers to transport themselves out of their everyday dystopias in order to gain imaginatively a perspective that makes those ills visible. The rising socialism of the late Victorian and Edwardian eras indicates that for many social inequities were becoming increasingly politicized issues, which the tussle between nostalgia and progress accentuated. How to preserve what was good of the past, how to avert the dangers to which dogged alle-giance to structures already outmoded by current demands inevitably would lead, how to resist being beguiled by mechanical and technological innova-tions or how to use those advances to promote new modes of thinking are all questions that engaged intellectuals at the end of the last century, as they do now at the beginning of the new millennium. In writing for a rising generation, Nesbit and Wells played on the obsession with flexible time in order to make the point that times of change require more imaginative approaches than perhaps they were able to pursue within the Fabian Society that in other respects represented or contributed to the development of their ideas. Bland's "world within a world" is for them the fictional realm of fantasy.

3. Traversing Time and Genre

It is no mere coincidence that both Wells's and Nesbit's works respond to the cultural upheaval of the century's change with fictionalized accounts of time travel. As Arthur Waugh observed at the time, fiction writing in general rises out of times of upheaval because it imagines ways to cope with, understand, or contain that volatility.[17] But in a cultural climate fraught by dissatisfaction with the present, anxious and perplexed by the task of improving the situation or, alternatively, weighed down by fears that the future cannot possibly sustain contemporary grandeur, time travel is both a highly idealized and a very pragmatic response. If in the sciences, for instance, Henri Bergson and William James's work on time-theory offered alternative ways of thinking about the relationship of past, present, and future to counteract the anxiety of social transformation,[18] for children's writers and utopianists looking for a better life, "[t]ime travel became the prevalent form of the utopian novel in the last third of the nineteenth century."[19]

Gertrud Lehnert-Rodiek has noted that in some instances fantasy can serve a "reactionary" purpose to "stabiliz[e] the existing social and political system" (Lehnert-Rodiek, 70), which raises the question for both utopian and children's literature alike of what sort of desire travel to an imagined world is meant to satisfy: one that would have lost traditions restored or faltering institutions bolstered? Or one that would see the present overhauled? In their politically reactionary capacity, Wells's and Nesbit's stories about time travel signal the symbolic abandonment of one's temporal position: Dickie returns to the Jacobeans, and the Time Traveler disappears indefinitely. Here time travel, as a fictional motif, permits the idealization of other eras, and while such displacements or distortions may be no more than wishful historiography, they underscore the severity of the writers' mistrust of the real present. In this context, the late-Victorian sensitivity to transition, the state of being no longer here and not yet there, finds its perfect analogy in the literary device premised on such temporal fluidity.

But when used symbolically "to dramatize [the utopianists'] break with the present," time travel's answer to late-Victorian upheaval also has a recuperative dimension precisely when it does not "tak[e] leave of reality."[20] With the present firmly in view, both writers venture into other fantastic times expressly to improve contemporary realities. While Nesbit is less radically inclined than Wells, and her historical interest would seem to place her in a conservative utopian camp (Levitas, 187), her forays into the past point out the way that, for her as for Wells, stability itself is part of the fantasy whose fictional nature poses no obstacle to desire. The salient point is that, for both writers, the use of time travel provides a temporal objectivity necessary to effect cultural reform in the present.

The question that remains though is whether, or how, these authors' generic differences affect their themes or vice versa. As utopian expressions of the "desire for a better way of being and living" (Levitas, 7), distinctions such as child/adult or science fiction/fantasy can divert the attention from their function, whether that purpose be to escape from a negative present, to criticize it or to advocate for change (Levitas, 180). Indeed, as a metaphoric mode, literature, unlike other forms, more readily allows for the coexistence of all these. As Juliet Dusinberre argues, "[t]he only real freedom for adults and for children lies in the recognition of the myths by which society orders its vision of the real and the ideal . . . in times of great change some of the most radical ideas about what the future ought to be like will be located in the books which are written for the new generation" (Dusinberre, 33–34). Her observation that time travel is one of the organizing myths of late-Victorian writing is especially telling considering the doubly inflected meaning of a generational shift. Where the emphasis is on the adult-child split, children's literature does indeed serve as a vehicle for transferring stable cultural values or as the testing ground for new ones. However, this attention to individual developmental stages applies to writing for children at any time during the nineteenth century. Writing at the end of a century that was as self-conscious of change as the Victorian era was, that saw generational shifts embodied in the passage of Victoria's crown to her son and took that shift to signify over-all cultural change, however, heightens the utility of time travel as a way to reclaim lost stability or preempt disaster. In this sense both Nesbit and Wells, despite the age difference in their audiences, were writing with a new generation in mind.

Even so, the idea of writing for a new generation is not universally synonymous with writing about the future. For Nesbit it is the past that provides the best lessons for reforming the present.[21] Gertrud Lehnert-Rodiek generalizes that in fantastic writing for children the protagonists typically travel to a past made especially interesting because its events are no longer accessible except through imagination. Relying on the Romantic conception of children as border figures who are closer to the "source of life," time travel translates symbolically into an association of childhood with the past (Lehnert-Rodiek, 70). Elmar Schenkel seconds this view by framing fantastic children's literature within the highly industrialized late nineteenth century. In this context the return to the past is a return to a time when the grass was literally greener.

Late-Victorian attention to the Romantics' emphasis on the natural world highlights the fin de siècle nostalgia, which in children's literature is especially prone to manipulation. As a "specific form of the relationship with the past and with the transmission of values to a new generation," it pairs the longing for a more natural past with the Romantic conception of childhood as just that sort of Edenic existence" (Schenkel, 105).

In each of these examples, children's fantastic writing is associated with the past. However, this pairing should neither suggest that it is only fantasy which functions through the backward glance nor, as I have suggested, that children are associated only with the past. In the first place, the general Edwardian preoccupation with the past colors much (adult) fiction writing at the time, just as utopias, to the extent that their definition is not limited to perfected worlds, can be perceived to have existed in a bygone era.[22] Second, children can be associated equally cogently with the future. Indeed, the point of the children's genre often is to convey lessons to children that will ideally make them better adults. The decisive factor here, rather, is that childhood is linked to lost (perhaps better) time, which time travel can help recover.

The provision of additional time is one of time travel's chief uses because it gives characters more time for working out their wishes and, in Nesbit's case, moral maturation (Lehnert-Rodiek, 69). But writers at the fin de siècle also looked forward and, in contemplating their own changing generation, framed their desire for extra present-time by imagining themselves as a past-that-will-have-been. Moreover, through the objectivity of "hindsight," the present can be improved. Of especial interest here is that where fantastic writing for a generation of children who will become adults is associated with the past, that fantasy becomes future-oriented science fiction when it is directed toward adults entering a new generation.[23] The ability to move through time is precisely what enables Wells's Time Traveler to witness the results of contemporary societal organization and to warn readers that if they continue as they are, they inevitably will become as beasts and children. Worse yet, they will enact Edred Sr.'s own disastrous prophecy in *Arden* that equates the commercialization of paradise with violent sacrifice. Wells's lesson seems to be that we cannot remain children forever. To live in a regressive future such as the dystopia depicted in *The Time Machine* is to be forever vulnerable unless we as adults radically alter the present.

Thus, Nesbit's Arden books and Wells's *Time Machine*, even though they are directed at different audiences, share didactic, thematic concerns that cross generic boundaries. Indeed, the fantastic and thematic similarities between the novels are such powerful points of entry into the texts that the difference in their audiences is almost a point of secondary interest. That is, Nesbit's time fantasies are predicated in part on Wells's earlier science fiction, but science fiction as it was inaugurated by Wells might well have benefited from the development of the fantastic that took place in children's literature since the 1850s. For example, much of the Traveler's sympathy for the Eloi is derived from their childlike helplessness. In having overshot humanity's "manhood" (*Time*, 114), he finds a future world in regression so that, in some respects, he is journeying into the past. In this case it is the history of industrialization told this time with the threats to Edenic Romanticism clearly marked by threats to the child, which children's writers such as Charles Kingsley and George MacDonald had already employed fantasy to accentuate. The point here is that it is the writers' conception of the fantastic and of its social usefulness that makes their utopias realms where age and generic classifications are elided, which lends Nesbit the adult tone of her stories and allows Wells to pursue his own fantasies.

Notes

1. E. Nesbit, *The Story of the Amulet* (1906) (New York: Books of Wonder, 1997), 32; hereafter cited in text as *Amulet*.
2. H. G. Wells, *A Modern Utopia* (1905) (London: Nelson and Sons, n.d.); hereafter cited in text as *Modern*.
3. Judith Barisonzi, "E. Nesbit," in *DLB* 153 (1995): 216–27.
4. E. Nesbit, *The House of Arden* (1908) (New York: Books of Wonder, 1997); hereafter cited in text as *Arden*.
5. E. Nesbit, *Harding's Luck* (1909) (New York: Books of Wonder, 1997); hereafter cited in text as *Harding's*.
6. H. G. Wells, *The Time Machine* (1895) (New York: Bantam, 1991); hereafter cited in text as *Time*.
7. Ruth Levitas, *The Concept of Utopia* (Syracuse, N.Y.: Syracuse University Press, 1990), 6; hereafter cited in text.
8. Gregory Claeys, "Socialism and Utopia," in *Utopia: The Search for the Ideal Society in the Western World*, ed. Roland Schaer, Gregory Claeys, and Lyman Tower Sargent (New York and Oxford: The New York Public Library/ Oxford University Press, 2000), 206; hereafter cited in text.
9. Quoted in Julia Briggs, *A Woman of Passion: The Life of E. Nesbit* (New York: New Amsterdam, 1987), 63; hereafter cited in text.
10. George Mariz, "The Fabians and the 'Episode of Mr. Wells,'" *Research Studies* 51 (1983): 83–84; hereafter cited in text.
11. Margaret Cole, "H. G. Wells and the Fabian Society," in *Edwardian Radicalism, 1900–1914*, ed. A. J. A. Morris (London: Routledge, 1974), 104; hereafter cited in text.
    Part of the reason there seems to be so little discrepancy between the two factions is that Wells's ideas were themselves strongly middle-class so that the society he envisioned (and, following Cole's comparison, all the Fabians in fact desired) would be little more than an expanded middle class. The bigger and more serious reservation about Wells's arguments is their "highly Malthusian, quasi-imperialist, and racialist" underpinnings (Cole, 108). Cole's purpose in pointing out this dimension of Wells's rhetoric (and she implies that his language is rhetorical as opposed to founded in his ideology

when she says that even he may have forgotten about it at the time of the dispute) is to sniff out the basis for his split with the Fabians. In the end, she discounts the views expressed in the inflammatory series *Anticipations* (1901) as ones that Wells was most likely not trying to sell to the Fabians (Cole, 109).

12. Quoted in Elmar Schenkel, "Utopie und Phantastik in den Kinderbüchen von E. Nesbit," *Inklings* 8 (1990), 111; hereafter cited in text. Translations of the original German here and throughout are my own.

13. Gertrud Lehnert-Rodieck, "Fantastic Children's Literature and Travel in Time," trans. Caroline Höyng, *Phaedrus* 13 (1988), 71; hereafter cited in text.

14. Julia Briggs observes that in the Arden novels, the passage of time is destructive, obscuring origins that imagination must recapture. But time travel disrupts that linearity, she suggests, and turns the project of imagining history into an actual encounter with it. Although Nesbit's first foray into time travel, *The Story of the Amulet*, projected a "brave new Wellsian world" (Briggs, 287), the Arden series devotes itself to historical investigation as a route toward the political change that impelled the Fabians. Nesbit's own nostalgia may explain her apparent ambivalence about the extent to which modern problems could be resolved, hence the less sanguine conclusion to *Harding's Luck*. By having Dickie opt to live entirely in the past, suggests Briggs, she delivers the mortal blow to modern society in which "the misery of the Deptford slums and the emotionally crippled children they bring forth cannot be cured so easily" (Briggs, 293).

15. Charles Kingsley, *The Water-Babies*, ed. Brian Alderson (1863) (New York: Oxford University Press, 1995).

16. Schenkel notes that Nesbit constructs her utopia out of human relationships as opposed to technological advances that form the focus of male authors' visions, among others Wells's. This leads him to posit that "feminine utopias dream of better human interaction while masculine ones indulge in dreams of power, of transforming the earth or of immortality" (Schenkel, 116). Assuming for the moment that gender differences are relevant here, Schenkel's distinction ignores the extent to which Nesbit's communal aspirations depend on transforming the earth through radically rethinking class relations. At the same time, he shortchanges Wells by suggesting that his interest in the utility of technology is ego-driven. If anything, technology provides the Traveler greater perspective and objectivity than his unbelieving auditors can entertain. In any case, Nesbit's and Wells's gender differences strike me as less significant in this context than the way they orient their stories and through them their politics. One looks to the past, one to the future, which changes the possibilities for or implications of representation.

17. Juliet Dusinberre, *Alice to the Lighthouse: Children's Books and Radical Experiments in Art* (New York: St. Martin's Press, 1987), 196; hereafter cited in text.

18. In *The Culture of Time and Space*, Stephen Kern notes that, generally speaking, both Bergson and James subscribed to the idea of time as flux, so that the notion of discrete categories such as past, present, and future misrepresent what is really an ongoing process or "succession of states, each of which announces that which follows and contains that which precedes it" (Stephen

Kern, *The Culture of Time and Space, 1880–1918*, Cambridge: Harvard University Press, 1983, 25). This sense of temporal overlap highlights the Victorian sensibility of being in more than one time at once. James expanded on this idea of temporal fluidity in representing human cognition as a "stream of consciousness." Both of these ideas translate in Wells's and Nesbit's texts into their recognition that "other" times are made available through the imagination and through memory. Patrick Parrinder makes the point that for Wells and science fiction writers generally, "the more that our knowledge of the global and spatial environment had extended, the greater the pressure on the writer to project the displacement in time" (Patrick Parrinder, *Shadows of the Future*: *H. G. Wells, Science Fiction, and Prophecy*, Syracuse, N.Y.: Syracuse University Press, 10). More specifically, where Bergson and James are careful to distinguish Time from Space, Parrinder suggests that nineteenth-century imperial expansion leads to more serious investigation of Time as another frontier.

19. Roland Schaer, "Utopia: Space, Time, History," in *Utopia: The Search for the Ideal Society in the Western World*, ed. Roland Schaer, Gregory Claeys, and Lyman Tower Sargent (New York and Oxford: The New York Public Library/Oxford University Press, 2000), 5; hereafter cited in text.

20. Frank E. Manuel and Fritzie P. Manuel, *Utopian Thought in the Western World* (Cambridge: Cambridge University Press, 1979), 28.

21. Like Lehnert-Rodiek and Schenkel who write after her, Dusinberre links children's writing to the interest in time travel emergent at the end of the nineteenth century. Recognizing Wells's *Time Machine* as the touchstone of fictional interpretations of that interest, she nonetheless maintains that his sort of literal rendition is much less apparent at century's end than is another mode of time travel, memory. She argues that memory "offers everyone a paradigm of time travel because it provides access to childhood, which is both past and not-past" (Dusinberre, 196). Thus, in her reading memory becomes a kind of territory as available to the fictional character as to the writer of that fiction for whom the whole "experience [of remembering] encapsulates [her own] absorption in the book she creates. . . . The author uses the book to make for the child a space which has not been there before, and in so doing makes a new space for what she herself wants to say" (197).

22. Lyman Tower Sargent reminds us that "most utopias are not projected as perfect worlds but as much better ones" (Sargent, xii), and the Manuels point out that "the nostalgic mode has been an auxiliary of utopia" throughout its history (Manuel and Manuel, 5). Thus, even a problematic past such as the one Nesbit shows us can be a better alternative to a dismal present.

23. Lehnert-Rodiek differentiates between fantasy and science fiction. Following Hans Holländers's suggestion, she concludes that "the fantastic is not a genre with specific characteristics, but in itself is an 'aesthetic category' " (Lehnert-Rodiek, 63). In terms of science fiction, she begins with Gerhard Haas's definition of it as a "type of fantastic fiction" that depicts a future world through technical imagery (68). But because its use in children's literature does not differ "qualitatively" from its adult depictions, the genre may, as Ulrich Suerbaum, Ulrich Broich, and R. Borgmeier suggest, "include all fictive stories

depicting circumstances that are impossible in the present world and which therefore cannot be portrayed in a believable manner, since they presuppose certain changes or developments in science, technology, political and social structures or mankind itself. These stories are usually but not always set in the future" (quoted in Lehnert-Rodiek, 69). In this latter sense, *The Time Machine* falls into the category of science fiction because its depiction of time travel depends on developments in the hard sciences, but interestingly the world it projects is derived from social structures that have *not* changed, rather on ones that have not, and therein lies the warning that lends the novel its didactic character and diminishes the "qualitative" distinction from children's literature.

Works Cited

Barisonzi, Judith. "E. Nesbit." In *DLB* 153 (1995): 216–227.

Bland, Hubert. "The Faith I Hold," *The New Age: A Weekly Review of Politics, Literature and Art* 697 (January 18, 1908), 231–32.

Briggs, Julia. *A Woman of Passion: The Life of E. Nesbit, 1858–1924*. New York: New Amsterdam Books, 1987.

Claeys, Gregory. "Socialism and Utopia." In *Utopia: The Search for the Ideal Society in the Western World*, ed. Roland Schaer, Gregory Claeys, and Lyman Tower Sargent, 206–40. New York and Oxford: The New York Public Library/ Oxford University Press, 2000.

Cole, Margaret. "H. G. Wells and the Fabian Society." In *Edwardian Radicalism, 1900–1914*, ed. A. J. A. Morris, 97–113. London: Routledge, 1974.

Dusinberre, Juliet. *Alice to the Lighthouse: Children's Books and Radical Experiments in Art*. New York: St. Martin's Press, 1987.

Lehnert-Rodiek, Gertrud. "Fantastic Children's Literature and Travel in Time." Translated by Caroline Höyng. *Phaedrus* 13 (1988): 61–72.

Levitas, Ruth. *The Concept of Utopia*. Syracuse, N.Y.: Syracuse University Press, 1990.

Kern, Stephen. *The Culture of Time and Space, 1880–1918*. Cambridge: Harvard University Press, 1983.

Manuel, Frank E. and Fritzie P. Manuel. *Utopian Thought in the Western World*. Cambridge: Cambridge University Press, 1979.

Mariz, George. "The Fabians and the 'Episode of Mr. Wells.'" *Research Studies* 51 (1983): 83–97.

Nesbit, Edith. *The Story of the Amulet*. 1906. New York: Puffin Books, 1996.

———. *The House of Arden*. 1908. New York: Books of Wonder, 1997.

———. *Harding's Luck*. 1909. New York: Books of Wonder, 1997.

Parrinder, Patrick. *Shadows of the Future: H. G. Wells, Science Fiction, and Prophecy*. Syracuse, N. Y.: Syracuse University Press, 1995.

Sargent, Lyman Tower. *British and American Utopian Literature, 1516–1985: An Annotated, Chronological Bibliography*. New York: Garland, 1988.

Schaer, Roland, Gregory Claeys, and Lyman Tower Sargent, eds. *Utopia: The Search for the Ideal Society in the Western World*. New York and Oxford: New York Public Library/Oxford University Press, 2000.

————. "Utopia: Space, Time, History." In *Utopia: The Search for the Ideal Society in the Western World*, ed. Roland Schaer, Gregory Claeys, and Lyman Tower Sargent, 3–7. New York and Oxford: New York Public Library/Oxford University Press, 2000.

Schenkel, Elmar. "Utopie und Phantastik in den Kinderbüchern von E. Nesbit." *Inklings: Jahrbuch für Literatur und Asthetik* 8 (1990): 103–24.

Wells, H. G. *A Modern Utopia*. 1905. London: Nelson and Sons, n.d.

————. *The Time Machine*. 1895. New York: Bantam, 1991.

6

The Writing on the Wall of *Redwall*

HOLLY V. BLACKFORD

Popular with both boys and girls, Brian Jacques's *Redwall*[1] initially offers young readers a utopian community of mice. Healing the sick and assisting those in need, the Redwall mice are symbols of peace throughout the Woodlands. The mice represent an ideal of an independent animal kingdom that knows no violence; they vow never to bring harm to others. They are rewarded by the bounty of the earth, harvesting fruit, flowers, grains, and honey, which results in a rich feast that the narrator describes with mouthwatering imagery. This harmony with the land suggests that the utopia embodies a pastoral tradition, at one with the peaceful rhythms of nature. The community is guided by the governance of wise elders and father figures, who comprise a system of traditional government, ruling with wise words. The mice inhabit an abbey, an institutional space signaling both the blessing of God and the authority of European tradition. Culturally supported by their own myths, legends, artwork, and ghost-protectors, the Redwall mice symbolize peace as a cultural value: "[Peace] is our way, our very life" (*Redwall*, 6), says Father Abbot, head of the Redwall Order. This wise elder constructs Redwall as a utopia, an earthly paradise in which "all is well,"[2] the essential feature of the fantasy utopia.

Yet the symbol for Redwall's authority is a large tapestry that glorifies the rise of Redwall as a warring power. Hanging in the abbey's great hall, the tapestry represents the founding of the abbey by Martin the Warrior, who terrifies enemy animals with his sword, famous throughout the land for its power. Why would the symbol for a peaceful kingdom of mice be an enormous tapestry devoted to war and terror over others? This tapestry on the abbey wall defines the utopian space by paradox. This glorification of war and violence undermines the "very life" of peace that Father Abbot claims as the mouse community's essence. Quite taken with the tapestry, the young mouse Matthias wishes to be a great warrior like Martin. Seeing the effect of the tapestry on Matthias, Father Abbot explains that the tapestry is past history and not present identity, yet the large tapestry speaks its own language and even the Father's words glorify and make present this warring past. He tells the story of Martin's victory and subsequent transformation, which established Redwall as a healing Order. Although the tapestry chronicles otherwise, the Father claims this healing persona as an unalterable, legible tradition; Redwall mice, he says, can go where they wish because they symbolize peace. However, the legend of Martin's sword makes the reader wonder if the Order's access to any community derives from a much more brutal form of power than the Father admits. Matthias, to whom this is explained, sees in the tapestry the power of "might is right" rather than peace. Since he is the young hero, the reader comes to share his perspective.

The tapestry thus not only embodies the past but also shapes the present and creates the future, engendering desire and ambition by its discourse of war. Swiftly, the tapestry's vision of Redwall power reincarnates. In an inverse transformation, the ghost of Martin comes to life in Matthias. In the guise of Matthias, Martin answers the call to protect Redwall from invaders, for like most pastoral utopias of children's literature, the land is threatened by outsiders. Led by Cluny the Scourge, rats challenge the authority of Redwall and wish to own the abbey themselves. Cluny the Scourge understands the tapestry's symbolism in the same way that Matthias does, viewing Martin as the true root of Redwall power. He tells his troops that Martin's very name signifies the mouse community's power by symbolizing strength, astutely comparing the meaning of Martin's name to the power invoked by Cluny's own name. To shatter the spirit of the Redwall mice, Cluny steals the image of Martin the Warrior. Underneath the spot he leaves bare lies writing: "Who says that I am dead / Knows nought at all./ I—am that is/ Take on my mighty role" (*Redwall*, 118). This writing features the voice of Martin, declaring that he is not past but present, buried within Redwall itself and "present" in the figure of Matthias, the new warrior. The erudite mouse Methuselah determines that "I am that is," when unscrambled, spells Matthias. The riddle further directs the mice to recover Martin's power by finding Martin's grave, armor, and sword. Thus the vision that both the young Matthias and the rat Cluny share of the tapestry turns out to be written on the walls of Redwall. Martin's voice declares that the very stones of the abbey contain and assert the significance of "might." Although Cluny unearths Martin's presence, the resurrection of all he symbolizes occurs internally. The voice of the warrior undermines the words and authority of Father Abbot, talking back to the Father of Peace.

The moment the mice discover the writing on the wall of Redwall symbolizes the novel's shift in values, from constructing a utopian community of peace to undermining that utopia with hints that, at its roots, the Redwall Order is feudal might. The writing is a riddle because it denotes the riddled existence of the abbey as a symbol for both peace and war. The discovery of the writing divides book one, "The Wall," from book two, "The Quest," in which Matthias embarks upon the quest to find Martin's sword. The final book, "The Warrior," announces the novel's new focus, the identity of Matthias as a Redwall Warrior. In the moment the writing is uncovered, our attention is called to the more troubling question of how the Order of Redwall rests on not only the power of the sword but on other forms of brutalization: on strict divisions of labor, class, gender, and species. For example, Cornflower, the female mouse who serves the food, comes along at the moment Methuselah and Matthias discover the writing, to bring them refreshment; but Methuselah dismisses her so that he and Matthias can continue their important work. Thus the moment in which the ongoing presence of the warrior is voiced is also a moment that underscores Redwall's gender and class hierarchy.

The resurrection of a warring identity through Matthias calls into question the entire existence of the mouse community as voiced in the beginning of the text, transforming the creed of Redwall from peace to "might is right." The authority of Matthias displaces Father Abbot, demonstrating the internal rebellion of youth and military vigor against the wise elder. The text's increasing pleasure in the art of war takes over, as mice and rats engineer complex weaponry and war strategy. The structure of the novel includes alternating chapters on the Redwall mice and on the rats, asking us to compare and contrast the species politics of the two sides. All animal fantasy puts into question the relationship between species and character; animal characters tend to evince a tension between their essential or natural characteristics and their ambitions, quests, and desires to be more. However, the text's increasing emphasis on military weapons and strategy asks us to regard the animals as metaphors for human societies. Ultimately, Jacques unconsciously critiques his "mice of peace" by suggesting that they embody a feudal Order comprised of land ownership, resources, lineage, military fervor, and weaponry, all of which allow the Redwall mice to imagine themselves the "right" species that can dictate the status of lesser species and classes.

An "idealization of the medieval world"[3] features in the visions of many writers of adult utopias, including Thomas More, William Morris, John Ruskin, and A.W. N. Pugin. Ruth Eaton observes that such writers equate a feudal order with utopian spaces like woodlands, clearings, markets, folk gathering places, and villages. Such spaces are conducive to the primacy of community, and in utopian writing the community takes precedence over the individual.[4] For many writers of adult utopias, the medieval monastic order in particular stands for an ideal of an independent, unified community based on the benevolent virtues of peace and fraternity:

> [t]he monastic community, though not intended as a utopia, has some utopian characteristics. Its members spend their whole time within it;

individual life takes its pattern from the community; certain activities of
the civilized good life, farming, gardening, reclaiming land, copying
manuscripts, teaching, form part of its structure. The influence of the
monastic community on utopian thought has been enormous. It is strong
in More's *Utopia*, and much stronger in Campanella's *City of the
Sun*. . . . The government of the monastery, with its mixture of the elec-
tive and the dictatorial principles, is still going strong as a social model in
Carlyle's *Past and Present*. (Frye, 35)

The monastic community satisfies the impulse of utopian literature's Classical and Judeo-Christian roots to re-create Eden: the golden race that once
lived under the rule of "justice and did not know war or any form of violence,"[5] described in Hesiod's *Works and Days*; or the City of God, as articulated by Saint Augustine (Lecoq and Schaer, 67–69). The monastic
community models the formation of a celestial city on earth, with historical
roots in the Benedictine order: "The rule of the Benedictines and subsequent
regulations for the government of monastic institutions doubtless left proto-
types for an ideal Christian existence on earth, and the passion for ordering
the minutiae of every aspect of existence made its imprint upon later utopias,
which often are reminiscent of monastic establishments."[6]

Jacques had this historical basis in mind when he named his villain
Cluny. From the tenth through the twelfth centuries, Cluny was an abbey in
France known for its independence from secular authority and its influence
in reforming and unifying monastic orders.[7] Beholden to its patron saint
rather than any earthly ruler, Cluny amassed property and held its own during
a time of instability, such that by 1145 its abbot, Peter the Venerable, both
"benefited from [townsmen's] customary payments" and imposed upon the
surrounding townsmen "the obligation of military service . . . to strengthen
the position of Cluny in view of the growing disturbances and pressures from
its enemies in the middle of the twelfth century" (Constable, 162). Although
mostly a respected order, the monastic community of Cluny seems to invoke
the dangerously thin line between utopia and feudal, military power over the
woodlands.

A medieval institution that lives off cultivated land and acts like a village
in the midst of the woodlands, Redwall evokes the "hybrid plant" that Frank
Manuel and Fritzie Manuel define as utopia, "born of the crossing of a para-
disiacal, other-worldly belief of Judeo-Christian religion with the Hellenic
myth of an ideal city on earth" (Manuel and Manuel, 15). *Redwall* combines
the unique tradition of the idealized, monastic "city of God" with the pastoral
tradition, the longing for a simpler society that stresses humanity's unity with
the physical environment (Frye, 41). The pastoral lies behind the Christian
and classical myths of a lost Arcadia and structures many works of classic
children's literature, because childhood stands for a simpler time in the post-
Romantic adult mindset; because individual and historical pasts are often

elided in the literary imagination; and because post-Romantic visions of society separate the state of nature from the state of civilization (Frye, 42–43), preferring the former as less corrupted, as original innocence. While many adult utopias are ideal cities, many utopias for children incorporate the myth of a childhood golden age into a pastoral utopia. In her book *From Mythic to Linear: Time in Children's Literature*,[8] Maria Nikolajeva enumerates the characteristics of pastoral utopias found in works like *The Wind in the Willows*, *The Secret Garden*, and *Winnie-the-Pooh*. These characteristics are present in the narrator's description of Redwall: the importance of setting; the autonomy of the community's space; a general sense of harmony and innocence; the absence of money, labor, law, government, death, and sexuality; and the special significance of home (Nikolajeva, 21).

The utopia presented to Matthias by Father Abbot *as a Father* suggests particular significance to the entire monastic community as a home, wedded to pastoral traditions of a simpler society and to utopian traditions of reproducing society through education, an education that must link the utopian myth with the myth of contract (Frye, 38). The contract myth has to account for the origin of the utopia. The story of Martin and the subsequent existence of the peaceful abbey educate the young mouse and the reader into the fantasy that the utopia is "a permanent establishment" (Frye, 37), for "the utopia is a static society; and most utopias have built-in safeguards against radical alteration of the structure" (Frye, 31). Frédéric Rouvillois argues that education, in the utopian project, has the goal of making all other forms of social control superfluous.[9] The pastoral monastery of *Redwall* appears not as an historical past but as an idealized home that the young must defend at all costs.

Pastoral visions of utopian spaces occlude dynamics of power by equating cultivated space with nature. Glorifying the abundance of produce with which nature rewards the mice, Father Abbot constructs a harmonic relationship between the abbey and the land as if the relationship were natural, but in his description of the abbey land's fertility he reveals his own leisured status. From his point of view, the abbey represents an ancient, pastoral tradition: "Down long ages the beautiful old Abbey had stood for happiness, peace and refuge to all" (*Redwall*, 32). This idyllic space depends on the "folk" mice and bees who tend the land. But in the Father's point of view, the land is the agent, for "every season [it] gave forth an abundance of fresh produce" (32). The abbey's values are associated with a European past and the authority of age, signified by Father Abbot as well as by his vision of the abbey and harvest as ancient traditions. Father Abbot's point of view on the abbey's meaning is expressed while he walks the grounds with Constance the badger. The walk culminates in the orchard, "where every August sleepy baby creatures could be seen, their stomachs full. . . . Many a leisurely nap had [the Abbot] taken on sunny afternoons with the aroma of ripening fruit hovering in his whiskers. . . . Old Mother Nature's blessing lay upon a haven of warm friendliness" (32–33). This description of an orchard as the epitome of the abbey's pastoral blessing places Redwall securely in the Edenic tradition, for the Hebrew word for garden designates "an orchard planted with fruit trees and vines" (Lecoq and Schaer, 38). The phrases "down long ages," "every season," "every August," and "sunny afternoons" define the mythical, iterative time that Nikolajeva analyzes as typical of utopian pastoral narrative. Linked to the natural order of human development (aging) and fertility, the land is thus a kind of fertile maternal body that reproduces plenty in a natural cycle. It is so natural a maternal bosom that "baby creatures" become sleepy in its presence, thus suggesting that this lifestyle allows leisure time.

In the pastoral tradition, however, the idealization of rural farming as an uncorrupted existence typically denotes the perspective of the nonlaborers. Father Abbot's naps on sunny afternoons imply that this symbiotic relationship with the land has a life of its own, not taking much work, or at least not involving the labor of those in power: the parents, Redwall Father and Mother Nature. The Father and Mother signify the pastoral utopia as the blessing of a heterosexual family, reproducing the Order of Redwall as if it were the natural course of the universe. The passage suggests that Father Abbot and Mother Nature produce these happy, sleepy baby creatures and that their care of the mouse community occurs within the natural life cycle and within the protective domestic setting of the family. However, the scene subtly emphasizes the Father's greed and appetite for the fruit of the land and the labor of those beneath him. Although the fact that no one has to work around the clock in such a Society signifies the health and natural quality of the Order, the Abbot enjoys "the aroma of ripening fruit hovering in his whiskers," an image of temptation enumerated by the plethora of orchard fruits that the narrator lists. The sentence stresses his leisure in the context of appetite, an odd image since the orchard he likes best evokes an Edenic garden, where appetite should be dangerous. The paradise of Redwall, made overt when Cornflower serves the creatures milk with honey (*Redwall*, 41), represents not only the rewards of nature but of God, who walks in his garden with Adam just as Father Abbot walks in the abbey orchard with Constance. How are we to feel about the Abbot as God?

A disturbing aspect to the Father's "Godlike" pleasure in nature's bounty is reemphasized during the Redwall feast. The feast occurs just before the mice discover the rats, as if the lush food signifies an excess pleasure that sets up their fall from pastoral innocence. When the enormous fish is served, the creatures wait with baited breath as the Abbot takes the first taste. They silently await his reaction before they taste the food, and the imagery of his chewing emphasizes his pleasure in appetite and connects that appetite with his status, since he is the first to eat and his reaction defines the quality of the food for all. The rat nomads without land, however, are always hungry. On the one hand, Father Abbot signifies peace and a pastoral sensibility, a wise experienced ruler. On the other hand, he symbolizes the link between status and the greedy pleasure of enjoying status. As the Father blesses the fish, he says that mice only take life for food; yet his and the novel's pleasure in the food suggests that excess and aestheticism accompany the way the mice take comfort in their entitlement.

Suggesting that some kind of brutality lies at the core of Redwall's Order, the narrator presents Father Abbot's vision of the abbey's productive gardens while the Father is walking with Constance the badger, who is a symbol for brute physical strength. Constance is known for her strength from the beginning of the novel; only she can deliver the enormous fish for the feast. While walking with the Father, Constance is under his control and recognizes his authority. As the novel progresses, she becomes the physical might unleashed by the abbey's fury at having its entitlement questioned, demonstrated in her rage against Cluny when he first expresses his demands; her wrath gives her the strength to lift the mice's dining table. Although the Abbot cannot see danger coming when he gazes at his pastoral abbey, Constance senses that the abbey is in trouble: "Deep within her she knew a dark shadow was casting itself over the Abbey. Furthermore, it was happening in the present, not in bygone days of fabled deeds" (*Redwall*, 33). While the Father revels in his ideology of the abbey as an age-old symbol for peace, Constance understands that a pastoral lens blinds one to the present. Not only does she understand the immediate situation of Cluny's threat, but she also understands that pastoral images are *only* constructed as yesteryear and that they implicitly hold the shadow of time. Thus she does not specifically refer to Cluny but to a foreboding "dark shadow," one that could be attributed to a darkness within—casting *itself* over—the abbey. Constance undoes the Father's pastoral vision.

Embodying the abbey's fury and propensity for violence, Constance grows increasingly independent of the Abbot and challenges his authority. She defies the Abbot by following Cluny to the gates, throwing rotten vegetables at him and threatening him, "with a wicked grin of delight on her striped muzzle" (*Redwall*, 44). This emphasis on her mouth and her wicked grin, along with her defiance of the Father's creed, suggests that she embodies a different kind of greed than does the Father, who also enjoys the bounty of his kingdom with his mouth but who, the text emphasizes, neatly wipes traces of his pleasure away with a napkin. The Father's pleasure in a hunted fish is subtle compared with Constance's pleasure in war, for she is disappointed when she learns that the final battle will require little physical combat. When a spy wishes to sell secrets to Father Abbot, she pretends to converse with the Abbot but takes things into her own hands, believing herself to be alleviating the Father's burden. By the end of the novel the woodlanders validate her absolute authority: "There was no question of overriding her commands. . . . Her knowledge was born of vast experience" (295). The description of her "vast experience" displaces the kind of "experience" embodied by Father Abbot. Yet even though the mice regard her as their leader, she represents a threat to them; when she is enraged, even Ambrose the hedgehog (friend to Redwall) stays behind her, fearing that her rage can be turned against any creature, friend or foe. Constance thus comes to parallel the murderous impulses of the rats, who kill one another.

Constance's displacement of Father Abbot's authority with her own commands, wisdom, and experience is mirrored by Matthias's overt displacement of the Father. Methuselah emphasizes the similarities between Martin and Matthias, and states that Martin became a father figure to the mice. Both warriors are "impulsive" in their "youthful innocence" (*Redwall*, 34) yet have an innate talent for leadership. The rise of Matthias displays the internal shift of the abbey from a traditional government of wise, experienced elders to the leadership of the warrior, whose authority lies in youth, physical strength, and military ability. In such a new order, "youthful innocence" and "impulsive" behavior are strengths of leadership. By reincarnating Martin, Matthias exemplifies a new kind of fatherhood, in which fathers command by innate rather than experienced skill, signifying a "natural" species-related order of "the stronger prevail." Matthias's rise to power overturns the social order of the peaceful utopia. As Matthias has innate abilities with weapons, he and Constance take charge of weapons training. The symbol of the weapon as power displaces the power embodied by the "habit" of a peaceful order.

The text represents this shift from governance with wise words to leadership with weapons as growing up, suggesting that growing up means leaving behind the childhood innocence of the pastoral and embracing military manhood. After he views the horde of rats as a kind of primal scene, Matthias feels a matured sense of responsibility for Redwall, along with the knowledge that peace can be interpreted as weakness (*Redwall*, 33); in this belief he shares the point of view of Cluny the Scourge, who also equates Redwall's identity of peace with vulnerability. Just a few pages after he sees Cluny, Matthias is ordering a guard for the walls and is listened to by the Council of Elders. The text thus defines growing up as a transformation in point of view, from an unconscious contentment in the abbey of peace to a nomad perspective that swiftly achieves vocal authority. Matthias's maturation signifies a symbolic shift away from Father Abbot, the father of Matthias's childlike self. On the first page Matthias presents a "comical little figure" (3), wobbling in his oversized shoes and even spilling nuts at the feet of Father Abbot. As a child of a peaceful utopia he represents little threat to the Father, but as he grows up to fulfill a warrior destiny he moves into a terrain independent of Father Abbot, embarking on the quest to recover Martin's sword and thus recover the founding symbol of Redwall's power and his own manhood. He thus symbolizes the growth of Redwall into military manhood.

The sexual maturity of the male mouse and kingdom is achieved by acquiring weapons and using physical abilities to threaten those with smaller weapons. Thus while Constance embodies the brute force of physical strength in hand-to-hand combat, along with the pleasure to be found in fighting with the body, Matthias takes on the quest for great weaponry. This distinguishes him from Cluny as well, for Cluny earns his title from his tail while Matthias earns his by the sword, which Redwall feels entitled to by virtue of lineage. Implicit in Matthias's quest is the need to threaten others; when he threatens his sparrow prisoner with death if he does not lead him to the sparrow kingdom, where Martin's sword is reputed to be, he is described as "maturing, learning the warrior's way" (*Redwall*, 175). Thus his maturity is equated with the quest for the most powerful weapon that will symbolize "the warrior's way," the ability to threaten those with fewer resources. Departing the abbey to find the sword of Martin, he leaves the "very life" of peace that Father Abbot believes to describe the Redwall life and takes on this warrior's way. This way of life, however, is destined to be reproduced *within* Redwall. When Martin returns without the sword but with the sheath, he encourages the young squirrel, Silent Sam, a figure of infancy since he sucks his fingers and does not talk, to brandish a small knife as a weapon. And in the last few pages of the novel, Matthias's own baby son is already attempting to pick up his sword, the sword christened "ratdeath."

The description of the sword links the phallic power of manhood with the power of wealth and resources. On the one hand, the weapon is a means of sexual thrill for Matthias, when he finally recovers it from the adder. Feeling complete identification with Martin by holding the sword, he achieves oneness with warriorhood, weaponry, and sexual potential, "his grip causing the tremor of the steel to run through his entire body. It was part of him!" (*Redwall*, 294). The sword is a phallic extension of his body, signifying sexual maturity through the sword's ability to cause a physical tremor. On the other hand, the means of this sexual thrill is the weapon's fine materiality, and the description of the sword emphasizes the beauty of its construction by enumerating its stone, leather, silver, and strong steel (293). The weapon displays wealth and craft, culminating in the image of the blood (293) it wrenches from others through both violence *and* labor, a double-edged sword indeed.

Signifying the double power of manhood and wealth, Matthias's rise to power depends on the patriarchal exchange of women as a sign of sexual power and economic status. Matthias is "given" Cornflower as a reward when he arrives at the last moment to save Redwall with the sword: "A warrior needs a good wife. You [Cornflower] are the beauty that will grace Redwall and rule the heart of our Matthias" (*Redwall*, 331). This exchange of a maiden signifies the passing of male authority, as Father Abbot is dying, a figure of impotence given the rise of the young Matthias. The maiden thus becomes part of Matthias's riches and establishes the fact that a gender hierarchy is an implicit part of patriarchal sexual maturity and wealth. Although Matthias is cautioned by the cat that the sword is only made for killing (306), and is only a symbol for Redwall power if used for goodness, the sword signifies Matthias's rebirth into a new identity, mirrored by Redwall's new identity as a warring power. When he obtains the sword and kills the adder, Matthias feels "suddenly reborn, larger than life" (308). Laughing and resting his blade "against the earth" (308), Matthias has become a divine being, reborn from his travel into the underground (hell) of the adder's den, suggesting not a wise regard of the sword but an appreciation of *his own* power to penetrate the very earth with the sharp point of his weapon. Matthias is reborn into a "larger-than-life" or "brimming over" father quite literally through the body of a female mouse, since Cornflower signals his new status and bears his son.

Matthias's rebirth into larger-than-life status once he has fought the adder suggests his participation in a cosmic, archetypal battle of good against evil, aligning his triumph with the triumph of God over the adder, who the narrator describes as a pathway to eternity, and the pagan Cluny, "God of War" (*Redwall*, 8). The religious tradition signified by the abbey as a Godly space is reincarnated with Matthias's embrace of Martin's voice, in the riddle announcing Martin with the name "I am." This name alludes to the voice of God in Exodus, for God declares himself to Moses as "I am."[10] The mythical significance of Matthias's final confrontation with Cluny emerges from Matthias's calling upon *his* name as "I am that is": "I am that is! Martin, Matthias, call me what you will. It was long ago written that you and I would meet, rat" (324–25). The fight takes on the significance of a textual battle, evoking past and present by bringing to mind a cosmic battle between warring gods, expressed as a "written" tradition of legend, myth, and fantasy. If Matthias embodies the legend of Martin in the tapestry, Cluny embodies his own name as a "legend of terror" (113) against which he must measure himself. The two legendary sides become locked in "mortal combat" (326) that involves both fate and prophecy, as Cluny has had a vision that by sundown the battle would be resolved. The resolution of the battle in the death of Cluny suggests the triumph of the true monastic power, the "I am" of the one God who dictates others' being. Cluny is crushed by the abbey's Joseph Bell, which signifies both the abbey's religious authority and its wealth through ownership of a communication system. A religious rhetoric thus suggests that God's eternal being is evoked by the abbey's feudal possessions.

While Cluny initially seems to present a challenge from the outside, the text subtly suggests that he only embodies and brings out internal shifts of authority within Redwall, signified by the increasing independence of Constance and Matthias, and subtle hints that the utopia of Redwall is founded on a problematic patriarchal system of privilege. Cluny lays bare the reality of the power dynamics within Redwall, viewing ownership of the abbey as a means of gaining power over the land and the creatures within it. Cluny imagines that the abbey will be his, picturing himself as King, and the abbey his castle (*Redwall*, 41). He strips the abbey of Father Abbot's point of view, which cloaks the power of Redwall into a pastoral utopia, a "natural" order, a family of fathers, sisters, and brothers. An "image of barbaric authority" (70), Cluny rejects Father Abbot's gestures of authority based on lineage. When Father Abbot calls him "my son," he rejects this rhetoric of paternalism and defines the abbey as raw power: "Your son, ha. That's a good one! I'll tell you what I want, mouse. I want it all. The lot. Everything" (41). The reader is supposed to regard his thirst for power as stemming from a greedy nomad point of view, yet a language of economy often characterizes the mice's attitude toward the rats. For example, Matthias vows to "make those rats pay dearly" (68). A language of economy even structures the relationship between Redwall and the larger woodland community: "All [the woodlanders] knew that they owed their very existence to the Abbot and his community. . . . Now was the time to unite and repay" (36). This language of economy suggests that the abbey's authority is based on a feudal economy in which the creatures "owe" and the abbey collects. To Cluny the abbey represents the authority of money. He rejects the image of the abbey as a utopia or a pastoral, disliking the milk and honey served to him and showing that he does not regard the abbey as consonant with paradise, but as raw feudal might.

Cluny's view, in addition to the swift transformation of Redwall to a military Order, asks the reader to consider whether the Redwall utopia veils brutalization with discourse. The discourse of peace justifies the obedience of "lower" animals to their "betters." When describing Redwall as a utopia of peace, Father Abbot tells Matthias that since they live in times of peace, Matthias needs to think no further than basic obedience, which satisfies Matthias but tells the reader that obedience to superiors is of value in Redwall. When the abbey is threatened, the Abbot emphasizes his superiority by giving orders. Yet subtly, the text suggests dissatisfaction among the Redwall animals—"there was quite a bit of resentful grumbling" (*Redwall*, 110)— when the Abbot insists they cease firing at the retreating enemy. The animals actually grumble against the rhetoric of peace that justifies the Abbot's command over them. The text thus suggests that Cluny and his horde unleash the mouse community's *own* resentment at the strict policies that define Redwall as an Order and at discourse as a policing system. Redwall demonstrates the kind of policing through discourse discussed by Michel Foucault.[11] His historical analysis of penal systems suggests that the power of the state shifted from the transgressor's body to his soul. Discourse, representations, and signs exercise power by controlling the mind; the control of ideas is a much more effective means of control than control of bodies (Foucault, 102). Red-wall's utopian society depends on the ability of discourse to clothe the penal system of the state, such that members of the Society internalize the might of those in charge.

Dynamics within Redwall suggest that we witness a changing of the guard, from Father to Warrior, but that we also witness an internal rebellion in the Redwall community. We witness a rebellion against the paradox of the utopia's power, founded on a rhetoric of peace but symbolizing its power with Martin and his sword. The Abbot experiences pressure from within to step down and allow others to command, which he pretends is his own wish (*Redwall*, 113). Symbolizing the rhetoric of peaceful utopia, the Abbot is forced to voice his own abdication. The text's imagery suggests that the community of Redwall has gone wild, increasingly mirroring Cluny's horde. "Wild cheering" (110) celebrates the retreat of Cluny's army; Cluny's officers realize the transformation of the Redwall mice and tell their troops that these are not mice of peace, but "determined fighters" (297–98). The wildness of the mice seems to be created by the conditions of power under which they live. When the Abbot reprimands the mice for sleeping rather than guarding, he infects the "defenders" with wild enthusiasm: "With wild yells very uncharacteristic of peaceful mice, the friends seized their staves and charged out, fired with new zeal" (67). By the end of *Redwall* the woodlanders have no qualms about killing. They return enemy spears "with frightening power and devastating aim" (286), which "decimate[d] the ferrets within minutes" (286), and ring their bell in triumph, celebrating devastation. By the end of the text it is *Cluny* who experiences troubled dreams, haunted by all the animals he has murdered in the past; it is Cluny who now has a conscience.

Jacques emphasizes the emergent wildness *within* Redwall by alternating chapters between the warfare strategies of Cluny and of the Redwall community. Pleasure in the art of war becomes equal on both sides, as the stakes of violence escalate. Both sides are equally creative and ingenious with weaponry, both equally skilled in surprise attacks. For example, Cluny devises a battering ram to break in the abbey gates and the mice devise a way to launch a hornet's nest into the enemy, causing mass death. The climatic finish to one of Cluny's plans directly links the Redwall mice to the legend of terror that Cluny represents early in the text. When the mice first hear of him, the legend reads that Cluny once caused a mine to collapse when the mine "owners" would not surrender their land to him. In the battle with Redwall, Cluny designs a way for his troops to dig a tunnel and enter the abbey from underground. The mice, hearing of the plan, ready themselves with scalding water and pour water into the tunnel when the rats emerge, transforming the tunnel into a "mass grave," (*Redwall*, 299), upon which the Abbey now rests.

Matthias and Cluny function as symbolic mirrors in that both train their armies with similar means. The text mirrors a scene of Cluny's violence against his own trainees with Matthias's violence, designed to toughen up his troops. Like Cluny, Matthias uses "hefty blows" (*Redwall*, 55) and verbal chastisements to train the mice. The narrator even emphasizes the physicality of the blows by using onomatopoeia, in italics, to punctuate both Cluny's and Matthias's techniques; with terms like "*Swish. Crack!*" (206) to describe the punishments inflicted by Cluny's tail, and "*Thwack, crack!*" (55) to describe Matthias's blows, the text foregrounds the fact that both leaders silence and scourge their trainees. This doubling of military training questions Ann Flowers's suggestion that "the flaw in the book, if there is one, is that the lines drawn between good and evil are never ambiguous."[12] The "fight" between officer and trainee demonstrates internal conflict within the two sides, asking us to compare the internal politics of the two sides. Both seek to smarten up their trainees but both reveal a ruthless quality *within* a community. Both passages emphasize that the concept of military leadership looks the same wherever it is; the leader scourges and represses his own people, ensuring that they accept their inferior place.

The text reveals that the Redwall Order depends on the animals' acceptance of their essential status, defined by their age, gender, class, and/or species. The narrator emphasizes how the creatures have "allotted places" (*Redwall*, 11) even at the initial feast scene, places to which the animals silently head when the Joseph Bell rings. The most overt illustration of species and class politics occurs when the Redwall mice use the moles for labor. The mice call upon the moles to do the drudge work (moving stone and rubble) whenever the "gennelbeast[s]" (47) need it done. The moles' accent underscores their lower class distinction. The mice are gentlemen and thus not qualified for such labor, and the mole capacity to labor is traced to family lineage when Methuselah claims that the moles' ancestors had the honor of digging the abbey foundations for Martin. The very foundations of the abbey appear to rest upon essentialized characteristics of the animals, separated into different classes and species by their "natural," familial identities. Similarly, Methuselah, a Redwall mouse, scorns Constance the badger when she tries to solve a riddle. She does solve the riddle because it turns out to allude to the moon's cycles, but her solution is less a product of hidden intelligence than her species identity, for the text connects lunar knowledge to badger behavior. The mice hold an authority over the rest of the woodland creatures by being the smartest and most "civilized" (165) species; they are the only ones technically in the Order of Redwall.

Although several female characters gain power and strategize in war, none of them are mice (Jess is a squirrel, Winifred an otter, Constance a badger, and Warbeak a sparrow). They gain power because of their specific species-related skills. Although there are female mice within the Redwall order, none of them hold positions of authority. The only female mouse mentioned on the Council of Elders is Sister Clemence, and she is mocked because she does not believe Cluny is real, and then she is rebuked for not listening to Matthias. After an initial meeting, we never hear of her again. The most developed female mouse is Cornflower, depicted as a maiden beauty (*Redwall*, 12). Her job is to serve the food. From the beginning of the text, she is a potential mate for the hero, noted by several characters. Whether promotional opportunities exist for female mice within Redwall remains unclear. But Father Abbot implies that there exist different stakes for female and male mice, reprimanding Colin Vole for his hints that Matthias and Cornflower would make a good couple, for "someday Matthias will be a Redwall mouse" (17), while Cornflower should simply not be slandered. The male mouse should not be distracted from his career, and the female mouse will be damaged goods if she is talked about.

However, Cornflower's identity as a female character intersects with her class and species in that she is a fieldmouse and not a Redwall mouse; she is part of the larger community that must recognize the inherent greatness of the Redwall species. Identifying herself as "only a simple country-bred fieldmouse" (*Redwall*, 50), she maintains that she can see Matthias's destiny and the Woodlands "will be indebted" (50) to him. A member of a particular gender and class, Cornflower recognizes Matthias's destiny and places that destiny in a language of economy. As she holds neither land nor title, but is granted sanctuary by the Redwall mice, she is "indebted" to those in power. The text suggests that, throughout the woodlands, female animals take care of children in a traditionally gendered structure; in response to seeing mothers care for children while fathers share a pipe and chat, Matthias contemplates the peace surrounding him, suggesting that peace derives from stable gender roles. The reader gets the sense that the woodlanders are a welcome alliance because they meet Redwall standards of gender hierarchy; for example, in response to the bell's summons, mother animals bring their children and father animals guard the entire entourage (36).

Cluny's horde represents a challenge to the order of class and species upon which Redwall rests. Cluny's army is made up of urban "types": "sewer rats, tavern rats, water rats, dockside rats" (*Redwall*, 7). Cluny is known as a general, a master, and a chief, suggesting a social order defined by profession and warring ambition rather than a feudal acceptance of born status. Emphasizing that he has earned his title through the use of his tail, he rejects Redwall's rhetoric of family Order. Redwall friends represent the threat of Cluny as the threat of a neighborhood going downhill—as a "bad influence" (204). Cluny's challenge to a traditional class is mirrored by his horde, who overtly display ambitions between species. The rats object to the promotion of weasels but Cluny favors those who fight well, regardless of species. The recruitment of weasels, stoats, and ferrets into Cluny's army directly alludes to Kenneth Grahame's *The Wind in the Willows*,[13] referencing the battle between the wild wood and the river creatures for Toad Hall.

The River creatures (mole, otter, toad, and badger) believe that wild wood creatures like ferrets, stoats, and weasels have no right to such an estate on the river, even though the mansion is deserted while Toad spends time in prison. By alluding to the final conflict of *The Wind in the Willows*, Jacques asks us to understand the politics of class and species that support, and allow the reader to make sense of, animal fantasy.

Jacques uses the conventions of animal fantasy to suggest that animals have inherently different natures, which lead them to erect unique systems of governance. Just as the wild wood of *The Wind in the Willows* defines the river community as the "right" kind of animals, animals of a leisured world who spend their time messing around in boats, the two kingdoms of Redwall who look like mice but are not Redwall mice define the Redwall governing system as the right species. The sparrows are referred to as "winged mice" (*Redwall*, 165) and the first shrew Matthias meets looks to him like a "strange mouse" (241). But both represent chaos in different forms, contrasted with the Order of Redwall. The sparrow kingdom features a king who loves power for power's sake. Chaos is engendered by his propensity to make plans and never implement them. The shrew community represents an attempt at democratic organization, which in the text's view means they constantly need to discuss everything and cannot act. Matthias instills a military sensibility into the shrews; following his lead the shrew leader finally tells his "union" to neither argue nor vote, but simply follow his command (310).

The paradox that Matthias represents to the shrews goes unnoted by them. When Matthias confronts their community, he, like Father Abbot in the beginning of the text, claims that Redwall mice have access to any territory because they embody peace: "This is the unwritten law" (*Redwall*, 243). The law on which Redwall rests is ultimately the law of might and feudal authority, contrasted with both the abuse of power in the sparrow king and the democratic sensibilities of the shrews. Although the narrator criticizes Cluny for disallowing democratic discussion, Matthias's law similarly forbids challenges to Redwall authority. In the name of *peace* Matthias declares Redwall the law of the land, just as Thomas Hobbes's *Leviathan*[14] defends absolute rule as the only guarantor of peace. Matthias's call upon the rhetoric of peace as law brings the text full circle, back to the authority implied by Father Abbot's rule, but no longer with the pretense of denying the authority of the sword.

Ironically, in his preface to *Redwall*, Jacques constructs his fantasy as a timeless utopia: "I am certain that in the hearts and minds of all my readers, no matter how young or old, they consider it, as I do, a flowing, timeless saga—from Mossflower's green acres, with its ancient abbey standing fast on the dusty path of the woodland fringe, to Salamandastron, mountain sentinel of the seas on the far western shores" (*Redwall*, preface). Although he claims his fantasy to be a timeless pastoral and equates pastoral space with youth

within all ages of readers, he unknowingly ensures that his reader will understand the novel's exploration of power within the tradition of European fantasy, evoking not a timeless saga, but a feudal medieval past with strict
politics of identity (class, gender, species). And, in doing so, Jacques unconsciously critiques some of the assumptions of utopian literature, for many
utopian visions enjoy the pretense of ending history (Rouvillois, 322) with a
situation in which "the state predominates over the individual" (Frye, 37).
Whether societies of male River-bankers or Redwall mice, "[m]ost utopias
are conceived as élite societies in which a small group is entrusted with
essential responsibilities, and this élite is usually some analogy of a priesthood" (Frye, 35). Animal fantasy has the unique ability to depict this phenomenon as a problem of species politics, which the animal priesthood in
Redwall concretizes and aestheticizes for an audience of children.

Notes

1. Brian Jacques, *Redwall* (New York: Ace Books, 1986); hereafter cited in text as *Redwall*.
2. As defined by J. A. Cuddon, Sir Thomas More's term "utopia" puns on "eutopia": "place (where all is) well." J. A. Cuddon, "Utopia," in *The Penguin Dictionary of Literary Terms and Literary Theory*, 3rd ed. (New York: Penguin Books, 1991), 1016.
3. Ruth Eaton, "Architecture and Urbanism: The Faces of Utopia," in *Utopia: The Search for the Ideal Society in the Western World*, ed. Roland Schaer, Gregory Claeys, and Lyman Tower Sargent (New York and Oxford: The New York Public Library/Oxford University Press, 2000), 298.
4. Northrop Frye, "Varieties of Literary Utopias," in *Utopias and Utopian Thought*, ed. Frank E. Manuel (Boston: Houghton Mifflin, 1966), 37; here-after cited in text.
5. Danielle Lecoq and Roland Schaer, "Ancient, Biblical, and Medieval Tradi-tions," in *Utopia: The Search for the Ideal Society in the Western World*, ed. Roland Schaer, Gregory Claeys, and Lyman Tower Sargent (New York and Oxford: The New York Public Library/Oxford University Press, 2000), 35; hereafter cited in text.
6. Frank E. Manuel and Fritzie P. Manuel, *Utopian Thought in the Western World* (Cambridge: The Belknap Press of Harvard University Press, 1979), 18; hereafter cited in text. In his *Voyages to Utopia*, William McCord addresses the modern quest to find a utopia in the monastic order. McCord discusses the autobiography of Thomas Merton, who in the middle of WWII "sought a radical simplification of his hitherto chaotic life" by joining the Trappists. The Trappists, "Merton believed, had created a utopia where men were close to the eternal rhythms of nature. Crass materialism had been aban-doned, city life avoided, and intellectual speculation discarded. In seeking such a life, the Trappists did not differ significantly from many of the original kibbutzniks, the youthful adherents of California communes, or seekers after

the sweet life of Tahiti" (112). McCord personally follows the progress of a friend who joined the order of the Franciscans, an attractive order for the modern utopia-seeker. See McCord's section "The Quest for the Kingdom of God on Earth," 109–194. William McCord, *Voyages to Utopia: From Monastery to Commune, the Search for the Perfect Society in Modern Times* (New York: W. W. Norton & Co., 1989).

7. Giles Constable, *Cluny from the Tenth to the Twelfth Centuries* (Brookfield, Vt.: Ashgate, 2000); hereafter cited in text.

8. Maria Nikolajeva, *From Mythic to Linear: Time in Children's Literature* (Lanham, Md.: The Children's Literature Association and The Scarecrow Press, 2000); hereafter cited in text.

9. Frédéric Rouvillois, "Utopia and Totalitarianism," in *Utopia: The Search for the Ideal Society in the Western World*, ed. Roland Schaer, Gregory Claeys, and Lyman Tower Sargent (New York and Oxford: The New York Public Library/Oxford University Press, 2000), 316–32.

10. Exodus 3.13–14, *The New Oxford Annotated Bible*, ed. Bruce M. Metzger and Roland E. Murphy (New York: Oxford University Press, 1994).

11. Michel Foucault, *Discipline and Punish: The Birth of the Prison*, trans. Alan Sheridan (New York: Vintage Books, 1977); hereafter cited in text.

12. Ann Flowers, *"Redwall,"* *Horn Book Magazine* 64 (January-February 1988): 71.

13. Kenneth Grahame, *The Wind in the Willows* (1908) (New York: Aladdin Paperbacks, 1989).

14. Thomas Hobbes, *Leviathan* (1651) (Harmondsworth, England: Penguin Books, 1968).

Works Cited

Cuddon, J. A. "Utopia." In *The Penguin Dictionary of Literary Terms and Literary Theory*, 1016–19. 3rd ed. New York: Penguin Books, 1991.

Constable, Giles. *Cluny from the Tenth to the Twelfth Centuries*. Brookfield, Vt.: Ashgate, 2000.

Eaton, Ruth. "Architecture and Urbanism: The Faces of Utopia." In *Utopia: The Search for the Ideal Society in the Western World*, ed. Roland Schaer, Gregory Claeys, and Lyman Tower Sargent, 298–315. New York and Oxford: The New York Public Library/Oxford University Press, 2000.

Foucault, Michel. *Discipline and Punish: The Birth of the Prison*. Translated by Alan Sheridan. New York: Vintage Books, 1977.

Flowers, Ann A. *"Redwall."* *Horn Book Magazine* 64 (January-February 1988): 71.

Frye, Northrop. "Varieties of Literary Utopias." In *Utopias and Utopian Thought*, ed. Frank E. Manuel, 25–49. Boston: Houghton Mifflin, 1966.

Grahame, Kenneth. *The Wind in the Willows*. 1908. New York: Aladdin Paperbacks, 1989.

Hobbes, Thomas. *Leviathan*. 1651. Harmondsworth, England: Penguin Books, 1968.

Jacques, Brian. *Redwall*. New York: Ace Books, 1986.

Lecoq, Danielle and Roland Schaer. "Ancient, Biblical, and Medieval Traditions." In *Utopia: The Search for the Ideal Society in the Western World*, ed. Roland

Schaer, Gregory Claeys, and Lyman Tower Sargent, 35–82. New York and Oxford: The New York Public Library/Oxford University Press, 2000.

Manuel, Frank E. and Fritzie P. Manuel. *Utopian Thought in the Western World*. Cambridge: The Belknap Press of Harvard University Press, 1979.

McCord, William. *Voyages to Utopia: From Monastery to Commune, the Search for the Perfect Society in Modern Times*. New York: W. W. Norton & Co., 1989.

The New Oxford Annotated Bible. Edited by Bruce M. Metzger and Roland E. Murphy. New York: Oxford University Press, 1994.

Nikolajeva, Maria. *From Mythic to Linear: Time in Children's Literature*. Lanham, Md.: The Children's Literature Association and The Scarecrow Press, 2000.

Rouvillois, Frédéric. "Utopia and Totalitarianism." In *Utopia: The Search for the Ideal Society in the Western World*, ed. Roland Schaer, Gregory Claeys, and Lyman Tower Sargent, 316–32. New York and Oxford: The New York Public Library/Oxford University Press, 2000.

7

'Joy but Not Peace': Zilpha Keatley Snyder's Green-sky Trilogy

CARRIE HINTZ

It would be difficult to conceive of a more idyllic world than the one in which the Kindar dwell at the beginning of Zilpha Keatley Snyder's Green-sky Trilogy.[1] The characters live gently nested in the sky, gliding calmly about in their "shubas," or flowing capes, in an environment without strife, scarcity, or crime. In this world, marked by a high degree of civilization, there is literally no word for anger: the most negative emotion one can feel is "unjoyfulness." Any show of "unharmonious behavior" is treated as a "disgusting obscenity" (*Below*, 111). Green-sky is initially formed as a group of holy men escape the destruction of their world through a long spaceship voyage. Discovering the tranquil treetop haven of Green-sky, they dedicate themselves "to the development of a civilization that would be free, not only of war, but also of all the evil seeds from which it had sprung" (112). Green-sky achieves its purposes through peerlessly conceived and executed social organizations: "All the old institutions that had once given rise to hostile feelings were completely abandoned. In their place new institutions were developed in which all natural human instincts and drives were gratified in such a way that the pleasure of their gratification was closely associated with ritualized expressions of peaceful, joyful human communion" (112).

"Instincts and drives" are fulfilled both within institutional structures and through quasi-religious ritual. In the second volume of the trilogy, we learn more about the goals of Green-sky's visionary founder, D'Neshom, who planned all of Green-sky's structures "from those concerned with the production and distribution of goods to the ones that structured domestic life and the nurturing of future generations" (*Between*, 165). In this sense, the trilogy is heir to the founding text of the utopian genre, Thomas More's *Utopia* (1516), which repeatedly stresses the way its ideal social and economic structures have led to a better world, one where "the root-causes of ambition, political conflict, and everything like that" have been eliminated.[2]

The Green-sky Trilogy also follows utopias like Edward Bellamy's *Looking Backward: 2000–1887* in its insistence on the way in which fulfillment of basic human needs leads to the eradication of social evils like crime, envy, and anger.[3] As well, in its emphasis on the religious and mystical connection between people, Green-sky has much in common with Monica Hughes's utopia for young adults, *The Dream Catcher*,[4] where individuals are linked in a "web" of blissful collectivity.

Despite its emphasis on communality, the world of the Kindar is fundamentally hierarchical. At the top of the society are the Ol-zhaan, who are given a special honorific, "D'ol." Like the citizens of Lois Lowry's *The Giver*[5] and Hughes's *The Dream Catcher*, all Kindar individuals are assigned a vocation at the age of thirteen by the Ol-zhaan, after they have mastered their childhood lessons of Peace and Joy, and the "spirit skills": gren-spreking (influencing the growth of plant life with the spirit), pensing (connecting to others via thought) and kiniporting (moving objects with the use of thought only). Individuals in Green-sky spend a decade in the Youth Halls, trying out various romantic configurations (with the protection of contraceptive wafers), but they eventually settle down with bond-partners in order to raise families in individual dwelling places called nids. Care in the regulation of human emotions and behavior is extended even to wrongdoers. When they are convicted of an offense, criminals are sent to the Garden to re-learn spirit-skills like Peace and Love alongside young children until they are fully reformed: "among the youngest children, they relearned the rituals and ceremonies, the skills and practices, that would make their misdeed unnecessary" (*Celebration*, 61–62).

This planning and attention to detail should have guaranteed the full repose and well-being of the citizens of Green-sky, and to a large extent it does so. Yet all is not well. The rapturous exaltation of the treetops is contrasted with the threat posed by the hostile inhabitants below the root. According to the Kindar, predatory beings called the "Pash-shan" stalk the forest floor. Children, not yet adept in gliding, are liable to fall from their lofty heights to the forest floor where, they are told, they might well be abducted by Pash-shan.

By the end of the first book of the trilogy, the Kindar realize that all they have been told about the Pash-shan is a lie; rather than threatening beings, the Pash-shan turn out to be the kinsmen of the Kindar: their name for themselves is the "Erdlings." The Erdlings are peers rather than threats to the Kindar. After that, the Kindar have to decide whether to open up their bountiful and beautiful world and invite the Erdlings to join them in the luminous treetops above. Once the Kindar indeed do so, they must cope with both cultural differences and the disruption of their ideal and tranquil life. The Kindar, in effect, lose their idyllic world. However, they gain something greater: the ability to seek justice over comfort, even if it brings pain.

This paper will concentrate on the injustices in Kindar society, and how they yield to a more equitable if less pleasant vision of social organization, with particular attention to the moment when the Kindar discover the lie on which their utopian life is based. The trilogy is remarkable for its unflinching insistence on simple justice for the Erdlings. A treetop world of Peace, Love, and Joy is not worth having, it seems to claim, if those who share your birthright cannot have access to the benefits you enjoy. I will also focus on the way in which the trilogy functions specifically for young readers, and the role young people play in overturning such inequity.

Omelas and Green-sky: Toward Justice

For a work in the utopian tradition that raises critical issues relevant to an examination of Snyder's Green-sky trilogy, it is worth looking at Ursula K. Le Guin's widely anthologized story "The Ones Who Walk Away from Omelas." Even though Le Guin's story is a work of fiction for adults, some of its thematic concerns and literary techniques—and critical responses to those concerns and techniques—can illuminate similar elements in the Green-sky trilogy. Le Guin introduces her readers to a perfect city of exalted contentment, although she deliberately (even coyly) leaves the details unspecified. Mock-anticipating the objections of a jaded and sophisticated reader who cannot believe this tale of a wondrous city on faith, she explains that the happiness of this city is predicated on the misery of a single abject child. Kept in a state of utter isolation in a dark dungeon, the child is given barely enough food to sustain itself. At a certain point in their lives, the citizens of Omelas all must visit the child and learn that their own privileged position is based on the child's suffering: "Some of them understand why, and some do not, but they all understand that their happiness, the beauty of their city, the tenderness of their friendships, the health of their children, the wisdom of their scholars, the skill of their makers, even the abundance of their harvest and the kindly weathers of their skies, depend wholly on this child's abominable misery."[6]

Le Guin offers the misery of the child in graphic terms; as Kenneth M. Roemer notes, "she delivers from a range close enough to smell."[7] The power of the story derives in part from the reader's complicity in an unresolvable dilemma: the reader, like some of the citizens of Omelas, is frozen between a tragic awareness of another's agony and the inability to act to relieve it. In fact, the story ends with some of the Omelites simply leaving the city—walking away—because they can no longer accept the terms on which the society is constructed. But some utopian scholars are fundamentally dissatisfied with the "Faustian bargain" of the story in the first place. Peter Fitting, for example, questions the basic assumptions behind the thought-experiment Omelas represents: "I am still bothered by the 'terms.' Whose terms? Who set these terms and why?"[8] Carol D. Stevens notes that, in the classroom, her undergraduates have "simply refused to enter the covenant as specified. They will take no thought either for preserving their own happiness through the misery of another or for destroying their own lives in a futile effort to help the unhelpable."[9] In many senses, the reactions of Stevens's students (which she clearly shares) do not take into account the way in which the Omelas narrative hinges on painting its reader into a corner, and the literary strategies of such manipulation, but their reactions do demonstrate that it is possible to think that any apparently static reality can be changed even if you are told that there is no possibility of such change.

Elizabeth Cummins thinks the power of Le Guin's narrative lies in "the jarring narrative voice," which "asks rhetorically, do you believe, do you believe that Omelas is a utopia, that this is the best we humans can do?"[10] Regardless of whether Cummins is correct about Omelas, which she describes largely as a text critical of utopian organization, her remarks certainly resonate well with Snyder's Green-sky Trilogy, which could be read as an Omelas-like narrative where the denizens of the community choose not to continue the pattern of subjection. They do not think that Green-sky is the best they can do. The parallel between Le Guin's story and Snyder's trilogy is by no means exact, including the fact that they were written for different intended audiences. As well, in Snyder's construction, the happiness of the Kindar does not so directly depend on the continued abjection of the Erdlings. Unlike the Omelites, the Kindar do not feel forced to choose between leaving the society and full acceptance of its terms. They stay in Green-sky, and change it, sometimes gracefully and sometimes with "unjoyfulness."

Green-sky allows more debate than Omelas, and alternatives to the choice to leave. We also learn more about the society's formation; since the status quo has not always been in place, it might be possible to change it. For example, we are shown the ideological schism between the two founding figures of Green-sky, D'ol Neshom and D'ol Wissen. D'ol Neshom is the utopian founder of Green-sky, who establishes enlightened social institutions. D'ol Wissen succeeds him after his death. Neshom genuinely believes that it is possible for the Kindar to avoid "their heritage of violence and the tragic fate of their ancestors" through honest appraisal of their weaknesses as a society, but D'ol Wissen favors a kind of enforced innocence, and he "imprisoned all who opposed him below the Root" (*Celebration*, 17).[11] Wissen does not believe that the people of Green-sky should ever be told the true and complete history of their world, especially the initial disaster that precipitated the exodus to Green-sky. As Wissen gains power, any citizen who inquires into any aspect of Green-sky's social organization and history is exiled below the root.

In Omelas, the citizens are required to see the abject child; in Green-sky the confrontation of the repressed underclass comes gradually. The trilogy opens as Raamo, a thirteen-year-old boy, is chosen as an Ol-zhaan, to the mingled joy and worry of his family, who are awed at the honor involved but concerned about the import and prestige of the position: What will become of their son? It is surprising that Raamo has been chosen in the first place: he has shown no particular vocation for such exalted leadership. In this sense Raamo's trajectory mirrors that of Lowry's protagonist Jonas, who finds himself singled out for an extraordinary social role despite his seemingly unremarkable scholastic, athletic, and social performance. And like Lowry's Jonas, Raamo will find himself at the center of a radical shift in the political and social structure of his community.

Shortly after his ascendance to the position of Ol-zhaan, Raamo is contacted by Neric, a junior Ol-zhaan. Neric is skeptical about the power structure in Green-sky, and he alerts Raamo to the possibility that the Ol-zhaan are hiding important information. They are also curious about rumors that the "Wissenroot," or main support of the root complex of Green-sky's forest, is dying. Taking matters into their own hands, Raamo and Neric descend to the forest floor, where to their surprise they discover a young girl wandering around: Teera. They assume that she is a fallen Kindar girl who is in danger of abduction by the menacing Pash-shan. She is brought to live with Raamo's family, where she becomes close to Raamo's sister Pomma. After some time has passed, Pomma unwittingly reveals to Raamo, Neric, and their colleague Genaa that Teera is really a "Pash-shan" from below the root—or more specifically an Erdling, since the "Pash-shan" never existed, and were simply a myth in Kindar culture. The story of those who live below the root emerges; readers learn that there are no such things as Pash-shan, only Erdlings.

The second book is told from the point of view of the Erdlings primarily, which has the effect of increasing the reader's sympathy for the Erdling people who have formed "a subterranean society based on a closely shared experience of sorrow and hope" (*Between*, 5). Things are dire in Erda due to the near-starvation that has been brought about by overpopulation. In fact, the lost Erdling child Teera finds her way out of one of the only openings in the root because she is running away from her parents, who have consented to allow the tribe leaders to kill her pet sima (who is very similar to a lovable monkey) to feed some of the starving people of Erda.

Danielle Lecoq and Roland Schaer describe ancient, medieval, and biblical traditions of the Eden myth as "a dream of self-sufficiency delivered from the tyranny of material needs."[12] The Erdlings have a musical tradition filled with visions of their previous domicile that is in many ways reminiscent of such utopian myths, folklore, and poetry: "they sang . . . of what they had lost, of birds and flowers, of great green-lit spaces, and of the easy splendor of the glide from height to height. In song and story they mourned a beautiful and carefree life that only a very few among them had ever actually known and experienced" (*Between*, 6).

Since this ideal world has clearly fled, there are factions that try to interpret the situation in which they find themselves. The Gystigs, a mystical sect, believe that Erdlings are born beneath the root as punishment for their sins, only to be later reborn in the joyous overworld of Green-sky after a lifetime of good deeds. The Nekom advocate a return to Green-sky via violent revolution. The Hax-Dok group undertakes various religious rituals to try and reduce the size of the root. That these groups are seen as inadequate and ineffectual is a strong sign of the need for intervention from above. It is the Kindar who must act to free the Erdlings. The Erdlings are literally cloistered by the root itself.

Like the citizenry of Omelas, the continuance of the society as it stands is based on a kind of unfair bargain. Although there is some hesitation about undoing this inequity, it is eventually and properly undone. Once Teera is revealed as an Erdling rather than a "Pash-shan," Raamo, Neric, and their friend Genaa must decide how to proceed in the short term. Should they go to the Geets-kel, the small elite group within the Ol-zhaan, and persuade them to make the truth widely known, or should the existence of the Erdlings be immediately revealed to the whole populace? Certainly the process of undoing the age-old inequity between Kindar and Erdling involves two of the Kindar descending into the world of the Erdlings and convincing them that not all of the Ol-zhaan seek to torment them and keep them in subjection. Only the Geets-kel want to ensure their continued imprisonment.

Snyder chooses to present a formal debate among the Ol-zhaan. D'ol Falla, one of the most venerated members of the Ol-zhaan, but the one who is most troubled by her burden of privilege and deceit, comments, "you must learn why we will no longer be prison-keepers, and why many things will no longer be as they have been in Green-sky" (*Celebration*, 17). Her opponent, D'ol Regle, is opposed to the integration of the "Pash-shan" into Green-sky, and notes that if the Kindar find out the truth they must also be informed of "their own terrible history" (*Between*, 207). He remarks that the release of the "Pash-shan" into Green-sky will be "the final and unalterable loss of the innocence and faith that have for so long protected the Kindar from the evils that destroyed our ancestors" (*Between*, 206). In the Green-sky trilogy, the condemnation of inequality is ultimately unambiguous, despite the presence of a debate. It is no coincidence that the man arguing against freedom for the Erdlings, D'ol Regle, is clearly presented as evil. We learn that he is willing to deceive the Kindar and to threaten anyone who stands in his way.

Like the pastoral utopia of Redwall discussed by Holly Blackford in this volume, Green-sky exhibits a mixture of innocence and sophisticated social structures; the tensions between utopian pastoralism and darker social forces are at play in Green-sky as they are in Redwall. In Snyder's novel, the injustice of the social organization of Green-sky is tied to the decline of the "spirit skills" that would make it flourish. The pastoral happiness of the Kindar, as appealing as it is, is already in decline by the beginning of the series. Raamo's father, a harvester who is capable of getting closer to the root, has heard disturbing rumors about what goes on down there. Even the beginning of the novel, which commences with Raamo's choice as an Ol-zhaan, is marked by agitation and uncertainty, as the family confronts a change in their routine. Several of the tree-dwellers have fallen into lassitude, relying on the comforts of drugged berries, which lull them into a dreamlike indifference. Several bonded families have become infertile, and many have been lost to the "Pash-shan." Above all, the crucial tree root, on which the community depends for their sustenance and protection, has begun to wither, and there is "growing fear that the withering of the Root will finally allow the Pash-shan to escape into Green-sky" (*Below*, 101). The prosperity and ideality of the system has not completely fulfilled the individuals on a spiritual level, and hence utopian planning cannot compensate for the way in which the injustice of Green-sky saps the spiritual energy of its people. The trilogy strongly implies that ideal systems cannot be sustained if they are based on injustice and lies, and that even more importantly, they will begin to implode under their own problematic social organization.[13]

In Green-sky, one of the architects and advocates of the reunification notes: "[t]o return to the separation of the Kindar and the Pash-shan is to return to the ancient evil of separation and loss . . . of people from people, body from Spirit, thought from feeling" (*Between*, 210). This to some degree sounds like a critique of an Enlightenment mentality that favors reason and chokes off passion, and the correction of such emotional imbalances is certainly at work here. Yet the Kindar struggle viscerally with the fact that the Erdlings are both kin and foreign: "strange dark confusion, touched here and there with revulsion—as if there were some who saw these thin alien humans as monsters in disguise—as if they could not possibly be other than monstrous, since they had admittedly come from below the Root" (*Celebration*, 20). Raamo laments of his fellow Kindar, "they think 'Erdling,' but they still feel 'Pash-shan' " (*Celebration*, 23). The new members of the society are literally described as "immigrants" (*Celebration*, 72). The Erdlings "terrify their Kindar neighbors with their smoking hearth-fires and the smells of burning flesh" (*Celebration*, 87). Obviously the Kindar's previous utopia had depended to a large degree on a certain purity or uniformity. Even the Erdling tools, which are universally hailed as more efficient and effective, manage to cut the inexperienced hands of the Kindar as they adopt them. There are also endless problems caused by what can be described as the bureaucracy of the process of the rejoining, and all of these tensions at one point cause some of the advocates of unification to wonder, "Would it have been better to leave things as they were?" (*Celebration*, 54).

Unexpected problems like a shortage of shubas—the long, flowing garments that the citizens of Green-Sky use to float around—arise. They also cope with a difference in economic organization: "While we have always distributed necessities according to need, and all else by honor ranking, the Erdlings are used to an exchange based on small disks of metal, which are known as tokens" (*Celebration*, 73). One wonders whether some of the cultural differences, physical separation, and tensions upon reunification are oblique references to pre-unification Germany. The conflict experienced by the united peoples seems eerily to prefigure some of the difficulties attendant upon the unification of the two Germanys in the early 1990s. The Kindar "dissidents" who are sent below the root seem to be like the dissidents of communist states.

How can the tensions between the long-separated Kindar and Erdlings be assuaged? Children and adolescents have a great deal to do with both the rejoining, and the wide acceptance of the rejoining. First of all, the adolescent Raamo is crucial in instigating the rejoining of the Kindar and Erdlings, both in his early investigations of the Geets-kel, and his invocation of the Kindar childhood nursery rhyme the "Answer Song" at the pivotal meeting where the Ol-zhaan decide whether or not to allow the Erdlings to join them. The "Answer Song" predicts that "the answer" will come when "earth is sky/ And all is one" (*Between*, 214), and many participants at the meeting read it as a foretelling of the union of Kindar and Erdlings. To be sure, Raamo has help from the more advanced Neric and, ultimately, from the wise and powerful senior Ol-zhaan, D'ol Falla. But given that he is an adolescent boy, he is certainly required to take on significant responsibilities.

The children Teera and Pomma are an even greater focus of the cultural energies of the two peoples. The friendship of the dark and emotional Erdling girl and the ethereal, ailing Kindar girl becomes emblematic of the union of the societies; the children literally read each other's thoughts through "pensing," a spirit skill of which only the "very young" are capable (*Below*, 161). In many of the illustrations for the book, the girls are portrayed touching hands in the searching, empathic gesture that is the foundation of the Kindar idea of union and fellowship. What makes it possible for the Kindar and Erdlings to reconcile, ultimately, is the fact that the children master uniforce, the uniting of minds to move objects together, a capacity which has not been seen in Green-sky since its founding moment. Uniforce is powerful both physically and symbolically. At the critical meeting of the Ol-zhaan, D'ol Regle grasps a dangerous destructive tool to threaten the assembly into doing his evil will, but the children fix their minds on seizing the tool. At that moment, it becomes "strangely transformed . . . it drifted slowly towards the children and then sank gently to the floor before their feet" *(Between, 215)*. This momentous action is taken as a sign that reunion should indeed take place. The children's use of uniforce is subsequently invoked in the wider culture: "the story of the rebirth of uniforce was being used again to bring about acceptance and reconciliation" (*Celebration*, 29). The children are read as a "symbol of the future—of progress and hope and limitless possibilities" (*Celebration*, 45–46). When the children use uniforce, it is described as a "miracle" and the children themselves as "beautiful and blessed and holy." Raamo is described as a "prophet and seer" (*Celebration*, 6–7). The venerated status of the children does cause a threatening situation (they are briefly kidnapped and held for ransom by the revolutionary group the Nekom, who seek to take over Green-sky), but in general the children embody the Romantic ideology of children as savior figures, achieving a purity that adult members of the society lack.

The final book does not necessarily resolve the tension between the Erdlings and the Kindar, although it ends on a high note of cautious optimism. The ambivalence of the trilogy's ending, where the treetop paradise has given way to the difficult and yet ameliorative life of the new Greensky, is striking for a young audience, which has been introduced to an ideal of justice, and shown something of its costs. Maria Nikolajeva, in an exploration of pastoral, prelapsarian children's texts, makes reference to an "overall sense of innocence: sexual, intellectual, social, political; and the intention of the text . . . to keep the child reader in this illusion," but she also identifies a type of postlapsarian text where "[h]armony gives way to chaos. The social, moral, political, and sexual innocence of the child is interrogated."[14] The Green-sky trilogy makes use of both modes, immersing the reader in pastoralism and then questioning it. Rather than a "happy ending," the reader of the Green-sky Trilogy is given the challenge to live without the happy ending, and to interrogate the nature of innocence itself.[15] Ultimately, a society of controlled ideality is seen as less viable than a teeming, pluralistic society where negative emotion, scarcity, and tension mean at least that the members of the society are genuinely engaged with each other.

As is frequently the case in young adult utopian and dystopian writing, young people bear much of the pressure of political reform. In Lowry's *The Giver*, Jonas, overwhelmed by his burdens, laments his lost childhood, wishing he could have remained innocent: "he wanted his childhood again, his scraped knees and ball games" (*Giver*, 121). However, it is clear to Jonas that he must bear the burden of his choice. Snyder's trilogy shows the refusal of a blissful treetop ignorance in favor of sustained, difficult political strife. As Raamo and Neric try to discover the secret of the Geets-kel, there is an emblematic moment between them. When they part for the evening, Raamo offers Neric the traditional blessing: "Peace and Joy to you." Neric responds by offering Raamo Joy, but not Peace: "May we not accept the comfort of peaceful minds until we have discovered the secret of the Geets-kel" (*Below*, 156). This kind of agitation and renunciation of the safe and the familiar in favor of a justice which must be pursued is the hallmark of the Green-sky Trilogy.

Notes

1. Zilpha Keatley Snyder's Green-sky trilogy consists of *Below the Root*, illus. Alton Raible (New York: Atheneum, 1975); hereafter cited in text as *Below*; *And All Between*, illus. Alton Raible (New York: Atheneum, 1976); hereafter cited in text as *Between*, and *Until the Celebration*, illus. Alton Raible (New York: Atheneum, 1977); hereafter cited in text as *Celebration*.
2. Thomas More, *Utopia* (1516) (New York: Viking Penguin, 1965), 131.
3. Edward Bellamy, *Looking Backward, 2000–1887*, ed. Cecelia Tichi (New York: Penguin Books, 1982).
4. Monica Hughes, *The Dream Catcher* (New York: Atheneum, 1983).
5. Lois Lowry, *The Giver* (New York: Bantam Doubleday Dell, 1993); hereafter cited in text as *Giver*.
6. Ursula K. Le Guin, "The Ones Who Walk Away from Omelas," *Utopian Studies* 2. 1–2 (1991): 4.
7. Kenneth M. Roemer, "The Talking Porcupine Liberates Utopia: Le Guin's 'Omelas' as Pretext to the Dance," *Utopian Studies* 2.1–2 (1991): 10.
8. Peter Fitting, "Readers and Responsibility: A Reply to Ken Roemer," *Utopian Studies* 2.1–2 (1991): 27.
9. Carol D. Stevens, "A Response to Ken Roemer," *Utopian Studies* 2.1–2 (1991): 30.
10. Elizabeth Cummins, "'Praise then Creation Unfinished': Response to Kenneth M. Roemer," *Utopian Studies* 2.1–2 (1991): 20.
11. D'ol Wissen, in fact, is so reviled in Erdling society that one of their most potent insults is to call someone a "wissener."
12. Danielle Lecoq and Roland Schaer, "Ancient, Biblical, and Medieval Traditions," in *Utopia: The Search for the Ideal Society in the Western World*, ed. Roland Schaer, Gregory Claeys, and Lyman Tower Sargent (New York and Oxford: The New York Public Library/Oxford University Press, 2000), 38.
13. Snyder's trilogy portrays hierarchy in a more negative fashion than Sylvia Engdahl's *This Star Shall Abide*, where the unavailability of metal makes it necessary for a small portion of the population to conceal its technological knowledge from the wider population, until metal can be properly synthesized and be made available to all. See Engdahl, *This Star Shall Abide* (New York: Atheneum, 1972).
14. Maria Nikolajeva, *From Mythic to Linear: Time in Children's Literature* (Lanham, Md.: Scarecrow Press, 2000), 28, 259.
15. In her earlier novel, *The Changeling* (New York: Atheneum, 1970), Snyder used the world of Green-sky in its purely innocent, pastoral mode, showing two young girls, Ivy and Martha, playing in the "marvelous Land of the Green Sky" (87).

Works Cited

Bellamy, Edward. *Looking Backward, 2000–1887*. Edited by Cecelia Tichi. New York: Penguin Books, 1982.

Cummins, Elizabeth. "'Praise then Creation Unfinished': Response to Kenneth M. Roemer." *Utopian Studies* 2.1–2 (1991): 19–24.

Engdahl, Sylvia. *This Star Shall Abide*. New York: Atheneum, 1972.

Fitting, Peter. "Readers and Responsibility: A Reply to Ken Roemer." *Utopian Studies* 2.1–2 (1991): 24–29.

Hughes, Monica. *The Dream Catcher*. New York: Atheneum, 1983.

Lecoq, Danielle and Roland Schaer, "Ancient, Biblical, and Medieval Traditions." In *Utopia: The Search for the Ideal Society in the Western World*, ed. Roland Schaer, Gregory Claeys, and Lyman Tower Sargent, 35–82. New York and Oxford: The New York Public Library/Oxford University Press, 2000.

Le Guin, Ursula K. "The Ones Who Walk Away from Omelas," *Utopian Studies* 2.1–2 (1991): 1–6.

Lowry, Lois. *The Giver*. New York: Bantam Doubleday Dell, 1993.

More, Thomas. *Utopia*. 1516. New York: Viking Penguin, 1965.

Nikolajeva, Maria. *From Mythic to Linear: Time in Children's Literature*. Lanham, Md.: Scarecrow Press, 2000.

Roemer, Kenneth M. "The Talking Porcupine Liberates Utopia: Le Guin's 'Omelas' as Pretext to the Dance," *Utopian Studies* 2.1–2 (1991): 59–62.

Snyder, Zilpha Keatley. *The Changeling*. Illustrated by Alton Raible. New York: Atheneum, 1970.

———. *Below the Root*. Illustrated by Alton Raible. New York: Atheneum, 1975.

———. *And All Between*. Illustrated by Alton Raible. New York: Atheneum, 1976.

———. *Until the Celebration*. Illustrated by Alton Raible. New York: Atheneum, 1977.

Stevens, Carol D. "A Response to Ken Roemer." *Utopian Studies* 2.1–2 (1991): 30–34.

8

Terrible Lizard Dream Kingdom

JAMES GURNEY

I was lucky to grow up in suburbia, the ideal breeding ground for utopian dreamers. The doorway to my world of the imagination was as close as my own backyard. The most bountiful haven for my longings was a place that I called "Yonderland." Out beyond our back fence was a narrow vacant lot owned by the phone company. It was cut off from the rest of the neighborhood. The phone company never exercised its rights to this plot of ground, except to store a few old cable spools and shipping pallets. Over the years my family enlarged the passageway through the tunnel of ivy that clung to the broken fence. We claimed the territory and domesticated it. We planted some rows of corn and beans, abandoned a few old bicycles, and nailed together a fort.

Way off in a weedy corner was a curious piece of junk that was lying flat on the ground. It was made of heavy black timbers, bolted together with iron straps, with massive hinges on the side. My brother said it was a hatchcover from a pirate ship. My sister believed it was the lid from a giant's footlocker. I maintained that it was the door from a castle, and that it had been torn loose by a Tyrannosaurus and then blown here in a tornado. None of us could lift or budge it. The more I looked at it, the more I became convinced that it *was* a door, a door facing down into the ground. My mind began working on the idea that it was an entryway into another world. Whoever succeeded in opening it would discover an old, chipped, marble staircase leading down into dark parlors.

Each night as I lay in my bed, I let my mind drift away to Yonderland. The sound of the appliance motors in the hallway outside my bedroom became in my mind the reverberating engines in the bowels of Atlantis. The shuffle of footsteps belonged to dinosaurs. As I dozed off I imagined holding a sputtering torch, exploring farther and farther underground, where luminous gardens clung beside waterfalls in the misty half-darkness.

In the twilight of a summer evening, I sometimes would walk through the shadows of the backyard imagining that I had just returned from an adventure in the caverns beneath Yonderland. I stepped over the rusting bicycles and crossed the back lawn, where I could see all my brothers and sisters framed in the big picture window as they watched television. They couldn't see me because it was dark outside. They were sitting on the sofa, flanked by my parents, who were asleep on their reclining lounge chairs. They all faced toward the universal, flickering blue glow. I slid open the glass door to enter the warmth of the house. By now ravenous from my long journey, I sat down in the kitchen to eat leftover macaroni while the TV laugh track echoed dully from the other room. While they were absorbed by electronic entertainment, I emptied my pockets of little treasures dug from the dirt: army men, lead cars, here and there a rusty bolt, feeling like Marco Polo returned from the kingdoms of Kublai Khan.

Yonderland was no less real to me because I traveled there only in my dreams. By age twelve, my yearnings for lost civilizations had taken root, and I was beginning to take up residence in them. I was fascinated with the idea of a civilization untouched by our own, speaking a language unknown to us, and moved by mysterious rituals that no explorer had ever seen. The motive for my longings was not so much to escape the frustrations of my own world as to be lifted up to a better world where I could be more fully engaged, where every action had meaning.

In less than ten years my dream of exploring lost civilizations began to manifest itself in little ways. By the time I got to college at the University of California at Berkeley, I sought out the professors who loved archaeology and paleontology. They were kind enough to let me explore the bowels of the Kroeber Museum collection, where dusty metal cabinets held mummies and grass skirts and ceremonial masks, labeled like so many butterflies. The air reverberated with their mysterious energy. One of my first jobs was making careful drawings of Egyptian scarab carvings for a scientist's publication.

Soon after leaving art school, I began working as an illustrator for *National Geographic* magazine, specializing in ancient world subjects and dinosaurs. My job was to travel to the ruins of long-dead cities and bring them back to life in oil paintings. Reconstructing the tombs, market scenes, and festivals required the help of archaeologists, who have the uncanny ability to resurrect these scenes, often based on mere scraps of information. They can, for example, hold a piece of roof tile in their hands and visualize an entire Etruscan temple. Likewise, dinosaur experts can look at a chunk of a thighbone and imagine the ground shaking under them as an Apatosaurus walked by.

Each evening at the dig site, while sitting around the campfire with these archaeologists, I discovered that they grew up with the same secret yearnings for lost worlds. Each of them dreamed of being the first to discover the next

Troy or Petra or Machu Picchu. Such places were considered fantastic or legendary before they were actually found.

The chance that a modern archaeologist might actually find such a lost
civilization was infinitely small, but it occurred to me that I could paint pictures of my imaginary kingdoms and invent the evidence later. In my spare
time I developed a large easel painting called *Waterfall City*, which united
two loves of mine: Niagara Falls and Venice. That painting led to another
image of a palace resting high above the clouds on a snow-covered mountain.
Then I was possessed with an idea for a large painting called *Dinosaur
Parade*, which portrayed a group of flower girls and musicians marching
through the streets of a Roman-style city, accompanied by peaceful herbivo-
rous dinosaurs. To paint the picture I recruited my wife and kids and neighbors, who dressed up in funny hats and Renaissance-fair costumes, posing
for me in my backyard while they imagined 30-ton dinosaurs lumbering
beside them.

To make the dinosaurs as realistic as possible in the paintings, I threw
myself into the research, making pilgrimages to dinosaur museums to look
again at the strange skeletons that had bewitched me in grade school. Since I
had grown up, the science of dinosaurs had transformed our knowledge
of the extinct class of creatures. Gone was the image of the awkward, dull-
witted, cold-blooded beast of my childhood. No longer did Tyrannosaurs
drag their tails on the ground, nor did giant brontosaurs stay mired in the
swamps. Scientists had reimagined dinosaurs as successful, dynamic, intelligent, warm-blooded creatures who shared more in common with birds than
with reptiles.

These new ideas opened the doors for the storyteller in me. I began to
ask questions: What if dinosaurs were not a lower form of life? What would
it be like to have such friends in high places? What would happen if we
ceased to underestimate them? What if we humans were the ones in need of
domestication? What if dinosaurs were warm-hearted as well as warm-
blooded? I began to entertain the idea of dinosaurs as friendly, majestic, complex creatures. I realized that other animals of our world, like wolves and
killer whales, had recently undergone the same transformation in our folklore. The more we get to know about the modern giants of planet Earth, the
more we discover that they are wise beyond human wisdom. Elephants, for
example, are now known to have nurturing family groups, sophisticated
long-range communication, and an amazing capacity for forgiveness and for-
bearance.

It occurred to me that dinosaurs could also possess these ideal qualities
and share them with a society of humans living as their equals. If people and
dinosaurs could form an interdependent society, they might benefit from each
other's strengths. We humans, I reasoned, could inherit the wisdom and
patience of a group of animals that lived successfully for over 150 million

years. In turn, dinosaurs would welcome the cleverness and dexterity of their human compatriots.

At this point there was no thought of an illustrated book; these were just idle musings as I painted my canvases, which were loosely tied together in a "Lost Empire" theme. But one morning I struck on the idea that all of my separate paintings might be snapshots from a single island. I pushed aside my bowl of cereal and scribbled a random shape for the island (which some say looks like Australia upside down). It needed a name, so I filled a page with possibilities that sounded appropriately ancient and continental: *Archaeotolia*, *Paleomundia*, *Volcanaterra*— nothing sounded quite right. Finally I came up with *Dinotopia*, which is a portmanteau word for a "utopia of dinosaurs." (Incidentally, when the translators created an edition for China, they rendered the name in Mandarin characters as "terrible lizard dream kingdom.")

My chief inspirations were J. R. R. Tolkien and Robert Louis Stevenson. Though not utopian writers, they created worlds that had the power to eclipse my surroundings even when I didn't have their books open. I was also enchanted with *Gnomes* and *Faeries*, two illustrated fantasy books that took great pains to bring scope to a fantasy subject and present it to adults as well as to young people. I met up with Ian Ballantine, who published many of these books, and he proved to be such an important influence on *Dinotopia* that I used his portrait as the basis for Mallab, the chief librarian.

If I was going to create an illustrated book about a utopia of humans and dinosaurs, I wanted to make sure it was practical and down-to-earth, rather than moralistic and preachy. I was more interested in how people could eat, drink, sleep, learn, and travel than in how they set up their government, religion, or economy. Any single system of social organization would not suffice for the simple reason that it left out all the others. One of the keys to creating a utopia was to accommodate the full gamut of individual personalities and tastes, and to incorporate all the world's cultures on a single island for, as we have come to learn in this century, there is great strength in diversity.

By creating a world visually, it would be possible to apply this "kitchen sink" approach to a utopia, because I could show the range of architecture and costume without the burden of trying to describe it all. I chose to tell the story in the form of an explorer's journal, which would permit the realism that comes from an eyewitness account. To achieve the realism I was looking for in the artwork, my studio came to resemble a cross between Santa's workshop and a movie studio. Velvet capes and silk gowns purchased from New York City opera companies festooned the steam pipes in the basement. Cardboard palaces and sculpted dinosaurs appeared on all of the countertops. I often posed in the costumes of the figures I was painting, checking the action of the pose in a full-length mirror. Often the doorbell would ring while I was working, and I would answer the door like a butler from Mars, much to the astonishment of the FedEx guy.

Page by page, the pictures and the story took shape. By 1992, *Dinotopia: A Land Apart from Time* was released as a 160-page picture book. As I created it, I had no concern about the intended audience, nor any great expectations that it would be a big success. I was completely surprised by the response. Librarians told me that it filled a gap in the world of children's literature for picture books intended for older readers. Letters have come to me from people of all ages, from toddlers to grandparents. But if there is one age or time of life that embraces the book most heartily, it is the moment after the horizons open from childhood into youth, and before limits are set by adulthood. From the letters I've received, I've come to realize that this audience is the best audience than an author can have, for they are more logical, intelligent, and vocal than their adult counterparts. Utopian literature is for them a chance to inhabit the dreams that fuel their growth into independent life. My belief is that they read not to escape their world, but rather to engage more fully in it, for only through fantasy can they try on any identity and live as actors in their own dramas.

9

Bridge to Utopia

KATHERINE PATERSON

In the early drafts of *Bridge to Terabithia*, I found myself writing comfortably about the world of rural Virginia; after all, I had lived and worked there, but the imaginary world of Terabithia was a foreign land. Even though I never envisioned the book as a fantasy, I wanted somehow to create a feeling of magic whenever Jess and Leslie swung over the gully. I decided that language would do it, and so whenever they landed in Terabithia, I switched to a more formal form of speech, resembling, as I thought, the language of high fantasy. This was my editor, Virginia Buckley's, reaction to this experiment: "The idea of the Terabithia secret place is very good, though the scenes themselves are a little weak. The style of the writing changes noticeably, and this can be seen especially on page 35. This aspect of the story is what needs strengthening the most. I think it might be difficult for children to attain the same elevated dreamland each time that they enter into the magic kingdom. The greater magic might be in what is happening in their relationship. . . ." Needless to say, I rewrote the Terabithia scenes. Fancy was not working. Plain would have to do.

Still, something amazing has occurred in the more than twenty years since the book was published. Readers seem not to see the very ordinary woods by a dry gully that I wrote about. They have created their own Terabithias. I often receive from classes pictures of Terabithia with drawings of castles and moats and streamers flying from turrets. I cannot count the number of readers of all ages who confide to me that Terabithia is exactly like some wonderful place they once created themselves. How did I know about their secret land?

It is evident to me that readers have created Terabithia in their own image. They have supplied the magic that my words struggled in vain to invent. I didn't create the world they tell me about—they did—but they persist in giving me the credit.

Speaking of Utopia—that's about it for a writer.

123

PART III

Child Power

10

Suffering in Utopia:
Testing the Limits in Young Adult Novels

REBECCA CAROL NOËL TOTARO

When we imagine the ideal, utopian world, we picture a place where harmony reigns on all levels from the physical to the psychological and even spiritual; we know dystopia, conversely, by the multifaceted suffering of its protagonists. The division seems clear: utopias eliminate affliction while dystopias increase it; this is a false dichotomy, however, and if we move beyond the automatic impulse to define utopia as perfect and dystopia as evil, then we can examine these terms more critically. We have learned even while teaching Thomas More's *Utopia* that one person's ideal world may be dystopia for another.[1] Yet in order to do justice to a complex genre, we must begin at its origins in a time before our postmodern skepticism when many authors and readers indulged in utopian dreaming without stinging from an immediate backlash.

Francis Bacon's "The New Atlantis" (1627) speaks from this period. Bacon's utopians, the Bensalemites, manufacture odors, tastes, and weather conditions, among many other things. By these measures, they maintain the sound conditions of a pure nation: "there is not under the heavens so chaste a nation as this of Bensalem; nor so free from all pollution or foulness," they assert. Untested, untainted, as we would expect from utopia, "it is the virgin of the world."[2] Yet even here suffering threatens, as Joabin, a Jewish merchant in the city, relates in the closing section of the work: "As it cometh to pass we do publish such new profitable inventions as we think good and we do also declare natural divinations of diseases, plagues, swarms of hurtful creatures, scarcity, tempest, earthquakes, great inundations, comets, temperature of the year, and divers other things; and we give counsel there-upon, what the people shall do for the prevention and remedy of them" ("Atlantis," 166). These many causes of suffering demand constant monitoring and stand indefinitely to test and even mark the progress of the society.

Certainly Bacon's visionary mind could have conceived of a world without the particularly physical suffering—from "diseases, plagues,

swarmes of hurtful creatures"—that seems an obvious choice for easy elim-
ination. Why did he include those constant threats to health and social harmony?[3]

Were we now to fashion an ideal society, would we not build in such scientific theories, practices, and equipment to have eliminated AIDS and can-
cer? If we were creating a dream of the future, the answer would be yes, and
our fictional society would remain a disconnected fiction, removed both from
our ability to empathize with its inhabitants and from our ability to imitate it.
By keeping the threats alive, the author of utopia offers to his or her reader a
realm grounded in present conditions, and therefore possible. Utopian literature supplies a place for practice, not escape—a safe place in which to find
and test new information and tools in the battle against common enemies
before then trying them out in one's society of origin.

Examining Bacon's "The New Atlantis" reveals just this transfer from
text to practice. The Royal Society is one of its manifestations,[4] and in a ded-
icatory poem to the society, Abraham Cowley, one of its members, clarifies
the connection:

> *From these and all long Errors of the way,*
> *In which our wandring Predecessors went,*
> *And like th'old Hebrews many years did stray*
> *In Desarts but of small extent,*
> *Bacon, like Moses, led us forth at last,*
> *The barren Wilderness he past,*
> *Did on the very Border stand*
> *Of the blest promis'd Land,*
> *And from the Mountains Top of his Exalted Wit,*
> *Saw it himself, and shew'd us it.*[5]

In this poem, Bacon is neither God nor mere mortal. Like Moses, he is
strictly human while also informed and worth following, even into the
wilderness. He is the man whose knowledge can help others to their
promised land, even if he must suffer to do so. Such a guide to utopia, more
specifically, endures suffering that the intended reader can identify as both
universal and familiar. The guide, then, becomes a trusted ally.

An examination of the verb "to suffer" helps to explain this process.
From the Latin *sufferer*, "to suffer" means to bear, to undergo, to endure.
Something we bear together is something that can unite us, as in times of
grief or during rites of passage. The context might be individual, familial,
local, national, or global, and the thing we bear might be as mundane as
pledging a fraternity or undergoing final examinations, but in all cases, the
bearing together produces a commonality that confirms kinship and promotes empathy. If the reader shares in this suffering, then he or she can

imagine, "if the utopian society that is so much better has real human beings in it like me, then perhaps our society can follow in some of those new and better measures." Then there is practical hope, a realistic guide to a more prosperous future that begins here and now.

In *The Principle of Hope*, Ernst Bloch considers at length this very progression from suffering to a hopeful longing for change and finally to action.[6] Bloch sees each step as a part of real hope and as requiring utopian thinking. With respect to the first part of the progression, from perceived lack to hopeful imagining, Bloch explains that as the sick man "dreams of the body which knows how to keep comfortably quiet again" (2.454), so too the man in whose life "something important is missing" finds that "the dream does not stop inserting itself into the gaps" (1.29). This kind of dreaming, to clarify, is not always based on vain wish or hot air. When it grows out of utopian thinking, the dream is a sign of hope that "makes people broad instead of confining them," because "[t]he work of this emotion requires people who throw themselves actively into what is becoming, to which they themselves belong" (1.3). Just as Bacon bore the cause of science in a world not yet embracing it, for example, so he becomes an apt model for the newer pioneers of science during the mid-seventeenth century who likewise faced obstacles set by more traditional peers and patrons.

From the beginning of utopia, when More coined the term, to the present, we have been able to distinguish our utopia from our fantasy by just these means. Utopia always includes some threat of suffering, in part also because the hope that founds utopia almost always grows out of such a lack or suffering.[7] The more interesting question becomes, how much suffering in utopia is acceptable?[8]

Five recent novels for young adults take on the challenging task of answering this question. In Madeleine L'Engle's *A Wrinkle in Time* (1962),[9] Lois Lowry's *The Giver* (1993) and *Gathering Blue* (2000),[10] J. K. Rowling's *Harry Potter and the Philosopher's Stone* (1997),[11] and Sonia Levitin's *The Cure* (1999),[12] the protagonists suffer from some defect that makes them aware that they are different and that their maladjustment threatens the harmony of the larger community. Each protagonist longs for an end to his or her suffering, and soon each discovers a new society (or the almost tangible knowledge of one) in which he or she is no longer a misfit. By experiencing the contrast between two different worlds, the hero comes to understand the nature of his or her suffering, and of his or her community of origin as primarily utopian or dystopian. Armed with a new, practical knowledge, the hero must then decide where he or she belongs.

Madeleine L'Engle's middle-school heroine in *A Wrinkle in Time* suffers as a social misfit: in her own mind, she is "Meg Murray doing everything wrong" (*Wrinkle*, 11). She is a self-proclaimed "monster" (13). She has heard others conclude that "clever people often have subnormal children" (16), and she does stand out from her family and peers, so when she labels herself a "monster," she has good reason. Although Meg longs to fit in, she is neither a typical Murray child nor a typical student. In her own mind, she needs an alternative definition for herself or an alternative life, and yet Meg's wish for change—even in its early appearance as self-repudiation—is the beginning of hope and transformation.

This longing for change soon propels Meg, with her younger brother Charles, to adventure through space. Together they find a utopian—or dystopian—planet called Camazotz where the power in charge ("IT") has eliminated sickness and suffering (*Wrinkle*, 127). Charles joins the inhabitants, and through him, IT explains to Meg, "On Camazotz we are all happy because we are all alike. Differences create problems. You know that. . . . You know that's the reason you're not happy at school. Because you're different" (*Wrinkle*, 128–29). Adults reading the story would know to beware, trained well by works like Vonnegut's "Harrison Bergeron" in which all members of the society have their talents and abilities reduced to match those of the lowest members. All are alike in their essential disability.[13]

Yet Charles's message rings true for Meg. The allure is powerful, because the suffering experienced in her society of origin is real. Meg does not fit in and therefore she cannot feel at home. This realistic longing drives her to hope productively for something better. Meg imagines that there must be a limit to her suffering and perhaps even a way to eliminate it entirely. Camazotz promises such a cure. Even its name suggests it is a Camelot, a good place, but we know it is the "fraudulent hope" that Ernst Bloch considers one "of the greatest malefactors, even enervators, of the human race" (Bloch, 1.5). In the other words, if it is based on fraudulent hope, even a positive drive toward improvement will lead to one's downfall.

The allure of this fraudulent hope is even more powerful for the young adult. Bloch explains, "[a]round the thirteenth year . . . dreams of a better life grow so luxuriantly. . . . Even an average mind tells itself stories at this time, simple fables in which things go better. It spins out the stories on the way home from school or when walking with friends, and the narrator is always in the middle as in a posed picture" (Bloch, 1. 24). The dreams of how to create a better self and a better nest begin here. In this way, Meg is not much different than the average young adult, male or female, because most young adults feel that their choices are potentially earth-shaking;[14] Meg's choices, however, literally could affect the galaxy.

At least Meg has some assistance from a loving but quite hideous creature she comes to call Aunt Beast. As Meg learns to consider as part of her family this creature she once thought to call a monster, she comes full circle. She herself could not, then, be the monster she once thought. Instead, she is a unique creature of the universe with matchless flaws and skills that make her an irreplaceable asset to her family and society. With Aunt Beast's ironic lesson in humanity to guide her, Meg chooses home over the false utopia, and she eliminates her suffering.

Twelve-year-old Jonas in Lois Lowry's *The Giver* closely follows L'Engle's model for abandoning an evil dystopia. Yet *The Giver* is immediately more complicated because Lowry places her protagonist within a seemingly happy world in which he is well adjusted. Jonas fits in, and he knows how well adjusted he is, because he has seen others, like his friend Asher, who deviate from the norm. To limit the power of those unfortunate misfits, the community Elders either more severely train them or execute them by lethal injection, an act they call "releasing." But soon Jonas notices an abnormality in his vision, and the Elders realize Jonas can see what others cannot. Still, they do not release but instead reward Jonas for his talent, giving him the most important position in the community. He will be a Receiver of Memory, receiving from the Giver all communal and individual images, colors, and emotions deemed unsafe for the average citizen.

It is not long, however, before Jonas's gift brings constant pain and becomes rather a throbbing sore made worse by common experiences, like telling how one's day went at dinner. When hearing his sister recite the day's events, Jonas concludes, "Lily had not felt anger. . . . Shallow impatience and exasperation, that was all Lily had felt. He knew that with certainty because now he knew what anger was. Now he had, in the memories, experienced injustice and cruelty, and he had reacted with rage that welled up so passionately inside him that the thought of discussing it calmly at the evening meal was unthinkable" (*Giver*, 131–32).

The pain for Jonas becomes one of isolation, like Meg's, but more profound. He can never explain to his family that they are shallow. In turn, they can never know him. The encounters with family and with friends that had once bound them together in empathy prove daily to remind him that he is different. He can no longer hope to fit back in. He sees and feels too painfully the inherent contradiction in the utopian—now dystopian—construction. He is no longer at home.

Yet Jonas's story does not end with death, readjustment to society, or with a realization made as he matures, as it does for Meg. If he runs, his memories will flood back over the community, causing confusion if not chaos and destruction. If he does not flee, the Elders will continue to release those who do not conform. If he does, he will forfeit all control over his security, because no one is sure that an "Elsewhere" exists. What enable Jonas to decide are empathy and hope. He will save a child scheduled for release, one who is considered deviant; he will rely on his memories of a better world to pull them both forward out of dystopia and toward Elsewhere. The story ends with Jonas and child in flight, hearing music ahead and even behind them, but "perhaps it was only an echo" (*Giver*, 180). We are left to wonder what happens to Jonas and to his community, but we know he has chosen to increase his own suffering in exchange for the possibility of a better society.

In *Harry Potter and the Philosopher's Stone*, J. K. Rowling displays a different articulation of suffering and hope of fulfillment. Harry Potter is a small, pale eleven-year-old who wears glasses and has an odd scar on his forehead. In addition, he is accident-prone and always involved in mysterious situations, all while his guardians, the Dursleys, consider themselves "perfectly normal" (*Philosopher's*, 7). Harry might even blend in a bit more were it not for those occasional mishaps when the things he wishes for occur in unusual ways. He does not want a haircut, for example, so every time his aunt takes him to get one, his hair grows back by the next day (23). "The problem was," the narrator explains, "strange things often happened around Harry and it was just no good telling the Dursleys he didn't make them happen" (23). As far as Harry knows at this point, he is not responsible for any of the "strange things." He does not realize that his wishes become acts, but then his young mind is not yet trained to follow through from witnessing or experiencing suffering to imagining with detail and accuracy how to remedy it. The last stage of putting the plan for change into action through constant, slow, practical steps likewise becomes muddled for Harry. Early on everything about him, even by his own standards, suggests that, like Meg, he is subnormal. But Harry will discover another realm in which his physical and social afflictions will assist rather than deter him.

At Hogwarts, this other realm, Harry finds his home; in fact, he finds utopia. Like Meg, he is shown where he belongs by the discovery of a new world, and like her he realizes that he is unique, neither a monster nor a superman. As an infant, Harry had become famous among wizards for surviving an encounter with the evil and most powerful wizard Voldemort. That early conflict resulted in Harry's lightning-shaped scar and in his placement with the Dursleys; because Harry has lived outside of the wizard community for most of his life, however, he comes to Hogwarts at or even below the level of his peers. He needs them, and they come to need him.

The test of these new relationships and of Harry's ability to struggle through pain is greatest when Voldemort returns to Hogwarts. With Voldemort's approach, Harry's scar afflicts him with "needle-sharp pain" searing through it, "almost blinding him" (*Philosopher's*, 213). This alone is almost too much to bear, but the future of Hogwarts and the world depends on Harry's strength. If Voldemort succeeds in his raid on Hogwarts, he will procure the philosopher's stone and live invincibly forever. Harry struggles on, seemingly unaided until the suffering consumes him and he passes out.

When he awakens, he learns that his ability to survive this ultimate test of pain entirely depended both on his friends having sent a call for help in time and on a mark his mother had left him years earlier. "Love as powerful as your mother's for you," Professor Dumbledore explains, "leaves its own mark. Not a scar, no visible sign . . . to have been loved so deeply, even though the person who loved us is gone, will give us some protection forever. It is in your very skin" (*Philosopher's*, 216). His mother's powerful mark provides Harry with "some protection," but when combined with the support of a community and his own determination, it is enough—just enough—to withstand what Voldemort delivers. In order to survive the next visit from Voldemort, Harry will need to continue learning the hard way, through his own mistakes. In Hogwarts, just as in our own lives, there are never surefire spells or foolproof wands. The lessons learned there never come easily, but they always build character while often improving conditions. In these ways, Hogwarts provides for Harry and for the reader an alternative, contemporaneous, thoroughly developed society in which one can creatively, realistically, and usefully stretch one's mind within new limits of suffering and hope.[15]

Sonia Levitin's teenage protagonist Gemm 16884 faces bigger bullies. In 2407, the respected Elders of the dystopian United Social Alliance determine that Gemm is deviant. He cannot control his passions for life, for singing, for sensations of all sorts. His passions exceed social limits, and in this he is utterly alone. Even his "twin," Gemma—with whom he is genetically paired for perfect mating—lacks these passions:

> Gemma . . . did not form strange attachments. Ever since childhood he had felt different. He would form an attachment to a certain toy, a particular playmate. He knew that these aberrations had been noted in his file. At his evaluation when he was eight, he had been promised by the Leader that he would outgrow them. And he had tried, locking in on his lessons, memorizing the wisdom that was provided for everyone on the screen. Now, as he ran from the compound after flashing his wristband at the screen, Gemm 16884 felt a terrible, oppressive fear. He was *different*. (*Cure*, 24)

Yet the unlimited acting out feels good, and he cannot repress it. At the same time, he loves his twin and fears that if the elders determine that he should be put to death (what they call choosing to recycle), Gemma would choose to die as well. Gemm cannot accept this.

He eventually submits to testing, and by doing so he allows his society to determine the goal of his hope and the end of his pain. Using virtual reality as a tool, the Elders send Gemm back in time to 1348, when the plague raged through Europe. In that time, Gemm experiences life in the body of a Jewish boy who, along with his entire community, is accused of causing the plague and is burned to death. In the burning, music blares, and upon his reawakening in 2407, Gemm no longer yearns to sway, to dance, and to sing. With his once uncontrollable passion so tightly bound to pain, Gemm wants only the status quo, a society "where nobody need fear harm or violence, where life is pure and good and harmonious" for those who submit (*Cure*, 251). Gemm is cured and promoted to the role of Elder.

But eventually, Gemm dreams again of his music and of his virtual life. He awakens yet again, like Hamlet, to his daunting utopian task, and attempts to explain it to Gemma: "it is true that diversity leads to emotion. And emotions can bring us either to hatred or to love. People must have that choice. . . . I will teach you. Then you and I will teach others. We will teach them about love" (*Cure*, 255–56). Before Gemma can reply, Levitin ends the narrative, leaving us to imagine what she says and whether Gemm can use his visions to create a utopia out of dystopian materials.

Like Lowry's *The Giver*, Levitin's novel offers neither the secure plan for change modeled by More and Bacon nor the certain doom of which Orwell, Huxley, and Vonnegut write. Both novels reveal instead an emotion so powerful that it allows its host to see beyond dystopia even if doing so requires increased personal suffering. These are young adult novels, but the strength of the hope they contain is rare, perhaps especially in adult experience.

When Lowry wrote *Gathering Blue* seven years after the publication of *The Giver*, she extended this vision of hope even farther, allowing us to view with greater fullness the sustained courage, practical knowledge, and suffering required if one is to envision, arrive at, and inhabit utopia. The novel opens with Kira calling for her mother, although four days earlier Kira had witnessed her mother's death. We soon find that not only is Kira orphaned, but she is also crippled, and for these reasons she must stand trial. Her society's laws decree that those who cannot contribute strongly to the whole are "broken" and must be taken to "the field" to be eaten by "beasts." She still stands strong because her mother's belief in and love for her proves powerful. Her mother had refused to obey the rules and had spared the crippled infant. She passed this resolve on to Kira, "always" telling her daughter to "take pride in your pain. . . . You are stronger than those who have none" (*Blue*, 22–23). In addition, her mother passed down her trade as a seamstress, and when the "guardians" deliberate over Kira's case, they conclude that Kira is indeed not only a useful member of the community but also an essential one. Kira alone possesses the requisite skill with needle and thread to mend and add to the Singer's robe. By singing the history of the community that is recorded on the robe, the Singer annually reinforces the communal identity. The blank future on the robe will be Kira's to color; the worn past will be hers to mend. In Kira's hands, there is hope. The dystopia itself might be amended.

In this moment of hope, elevated in her communal status, Kira follows the earlier protagonists Jonas and Gemm, and we wonder how successful she will be or if she too will still face greater affliction. The answer comes quickly. Kira's relief at being spared and her excitement at promotion last only until she learns what her mother never knew. Her father lives. He was not killed by a beast but, like many others, escaped to a community where the broken folks go, and where they care for each other, sharing resources and skills (*Blue*, 188–89). In fact, the beasts exist only in stories created by the Guardians to keep the community fearfully obedient. Soon her father asks her to join him, and she must decide between the two societies. The reader assumes the obvious: like Meg and Jonas, she will flee from the dystopian world of social control to the utopian place of empathy and peace, where all burdens are shared. But before she chooses, she sees the Singer: "Kira saw his feet. They were bare and grotesquely misshapen. His ankles were thickly scarred, more damaged than her father's face. They were caked and scabbed with dried blood . . . from the raw, festering skin—infected and dripping— around the metal cuffs with which he was bound. Between the thick ankle cuffs, dragging heavily as he made his way slowly from the stage, was a chain" (*Blue*, 211).

The choice is easier then. But Kira surprises everyone, including the reader, and determines to stay. The blank place on the robe she sews still speaks to her of a place for hope. She knows that such a place can exist, because her father is proof. "One day," she says to her father, "our villages will know each other" (*Blue*, 214).

In a manner most like Harry and closely following the course from longing to hope and action charted by Bloch, Kira's steps toward change are slow. She does not rush off with her father to a happily ever after. She will not change her world in one gesture as Jonas may have. She has experience of the guardians and sees the torture they can inflict, so that unlike Meg, Jonas, or Gemm, she knows exactly the consequences. The reader also learns to admire and follow her slow pace, for if she can face such hardships and take such risks, then perhaps we all can in our own families, schools, and societies.

Beginning with More and Bacon, writers of utopian fiction created complex, realistic worlds in which their citizens, and through which their readers, might suffer, hope, and take action toward an improved future. No panaceas. No perfectly working magic wands. More and Bacon knew that the only way to educate was to entertain, and what better way to entertain a reader than by creating a wondrous or even monstrously curious new world? What better way to educate than by creating a kinship between protagonist and reader through common enemies and shared, practical solutions? More and Bacon gave their readers slow and detailed steps to follow in assessing what was lacking in their contemporary environments and in moving toward the future with strength. Writers of young adult novels have always carried this identical burden, educating their readers through the pains of social and physical metamorphosis while entertaining them. The overlap between young adult and utopian fiction is large and merits further attention, and although perhaps, in the end, there are no limits to suffering when one is a young adult, patterns in utopian fiction show us that there are uses for this suffering. Out of it, one may, slowly, with hope and action, emerge into a less painful adulthood.

Notes

1. Thomas More, *Utopia* (1516) (New York: W.W. Norton & Co., 1992).
2. Francis Bacon, "The New Atlantis" (1627), in *The Works of Francis Bacon*, ed. James Spedding, Robert L. Ellis, and Douglas D. Heath, 14 vols. (London: Longman, 1857–74; New York: Garrett Press, 1968), 3.152; hereafter cited in text as *Atlantis*.
3. For a more detailed account of the function of suffering in early modern utopian fiction, see Rebecca Carol Noël Totaro, "Early Modern Utopias: Collective and Disparate Measures to Battle a Common Enemy," *Utopianism/Literary Utopias and National Cultural Identities: A Comparative Perspective*, ed. Paola Spinozzi. Cotepra Reader 6 (Bologna: University of Bologna, 2001): 359–64; "Plague and Promise: Golden Destinations and a 'Ship of Fools' during the English Renaissance," in *Reading the Sea: New Essays on Sea Literature*, ed. Kevin Alexander Boon (New York: Fort Schuyler Press, 1999): 175–84; "English Plague and New World Promise," *Utopian Studies: Journal for the Society of Utopian Studies* 10 (1999): 1–12; "Bubonic Plague in *Utopia* and Old World Implications," *Q/W/E/R/T/Y: Arts, Littératures, et Civilisations du Monde Anglophone* 8 (October 1998): 67–85.
4. On Francis Bacon and the Royal Society, see Lyman Tower Sargent, "Utopian Traditions: Themes and Variations," in *Utopia: The Search for the Ideal Society in the Western World*, ed. Roland Schaer, Gregory Claeys, and Lyman Tower Sargent (New York and Oxford: The New York Public Library/Oxford University Press, 2000), 11.
5. Abraham Cowley, "To the Royal Society," in *The history of the Royal-Society of London for the improving of natural knowledge*, by Thomas Sprat (London: Printed by T. R. for J. Martyn . . . , and J. Allestry . . . , 1667), B2–B3.
6. For those studying utopia, Bloch's three-volume study sets him on a par with Thomas More. While More created the genre, Bloch most meticulously, usefully, and fruitfully examines it. See Ernst Bloch, *The Principle of Hope*, 3 vols. (Cambridge, Mass.: MIT Press, 1986); hereafter cited in text.
7. One can argue successfully that prior to More myths of Cockaigne and even religious realms like the New Jerusalem revealed worlds in which suffering did not exist. I am using More's utopia as the exemplar, because he coined the term and initiated a new genre that thereafter did include at minimum the constant threat of suffering.
8. In "The Ones Who Walk Away From Omelas," Ursula K. Le Guin shows us this question embodied. Omelas is a society of order and beauty whose good depends on the suffering of one starved, filthy, abnormal child kept in a cellar. Those who cannot agree to the Faustian bargain do not gain initiation into the adulthood of peace in Omelas. They are the ones who walk away. They are

the ones for whom the suffering in utopia exceeds its limits, for whom the utopia becomes dystopia, with flight the only recourse. For a broader discussion of Le Guin's short story, refer to *Utopian Studies* 2.1–2 (1991), which includes the story itself and a group of essays devoted to its examination.

9. Madeleine L'Engle, *A Wrinkle in Time* (1962) (New York: Bantam Doubleday Dell, 1976); hereafter cited in text as *Wrinkle*.

10. Lois Lowry, *The Giver* (Boston: Houghton Mifflin, 1993) and *Gathering Blue* (Boston: Houghton Mifflin, 2000); hereafter cited in text as *Giver* and *Blue*.

11. J. K. Rowling, *Harry Potter and the Philosopher's Stone* (London: Bloomsbury, 1997); hereafter cited in text as *Philosopher's*.

12. Sonia Levitin, *The Cure* (New York: HarperCollins, 1999); hereafter cited in text as *Cure*.

13. Kurt Vonnegut, "Harrison Bergeron," in *Welcome to the Monkey House* (New York: Dell, 1998), 30–50.

14. Recently scholars have fruitfully examined the young adult fear of the power necessary to make independent decisions. See Roberta Trites, *Disturbing the Universe: Power and Repression in Adolescent Literature* (Iowa City: University of Iowa Press, 2000). Trites does not discuss utopian literature, but her work will be valuable for anyone examining this subgenre in young adult literature. Similarly, Melinda Gross explores "the threatening adolescent." Her treatment of abandonment as a theme that changes over time is particularly relevant to the study of young adult utopia. Each protagonist examined in this essay finds himself or herself facing the death of a parent or abandonment by one. See *"The Giver* and *Shade's Children*: Future Views of Child Abandonment and Murder," *Children's Literature in Education* 30 (1999): 103–17.

15. For these reasons (that Hogwarts provides an alternative, contemporaneous, thoroughly developed, and highly realistic society by which the reader cannot only escape but also hope, learn, and plan), we can consider it a eutopia or positive utopia as per Lyman Tower Sargent's definition in "The Three Faces of Utopianism Revisited": eutopia is "a non-existent society described in considerable detail and normally located in time and space that the author intended a contemporaneous reader to view as considerably better than the society in which that reader lived." See *Utopian Studies* 5 (1994): 9. For a more thorough explanation of Hogwarts as a viable alternative reality, see Alan Jacob's extensive review of *Harry Potter and the Sorcerer's Stone*, by J. K. Rowling. *First Things* 99 (January 2000): 35–38.

Works Cited

Bacon, Francis. "The New Atlantis." 1627. In *The Works of Francis Bacon*, ed. James Spedding, Robert L. Ellis, and Douglas D. Heath, 3: 129–166. 14 vols. London: Longman, 1857–74. New York: Garrett Press, 1968.

Bloch, Ernst. *The Principle of Hope*. 1938–1959. 3 vols. Cambridge, Mass.: MIT Press, 1986.

Gross, Melissa. *"The Giver and Shade's Children*: Future Views of Child Abandonment and Murder." *Children's Literature in Education* 30 (1999): 103–17.

Jacobs, Alan. Rev. of *Harry Potter and the Sorcerer's Stone*, by J. K. Rowling. *First Things* 99 (Jan 2000): 35–38.

Le Guin, Ursula K. "The Ones Who Walk Away From Omelas." *Utopian Studies* 2.1–2 (1991): 1–5.

L'Engle, Madeleine. *A Wrinkle in Time*. 1962. New York: Bantam Doubleday Dell, 1976.

Levitin, Sonia. *The Cure*. New York: HarperCollins, 1999.

Lowry, Lois. *The Giver*. Boston: Houghton Mifflin, 1993.

———. *Gathering Blue*. Boston: Houghton Mifflin, 2000.

Rowling, J. K. *Harry Potter and the Philosopher's Stone*. London: Bloomsbury, 1997.

Sargent, Lyman Tower. "The Three Faces of Utopianism Revisited." *Utopian Studies* 5 (1994): 1–37.

———. "Utopian Traditions: Themes and Variations." In *Utopia: The Search for the Ideal Society in the Western World*, ed. Roland Schaer, Gregory Claeys, and Lyman Tower Sargent, 8–15. New York and Oxford: New York Public Library/Oxford University Press, 2000.

Sprat, Thomas. *The history of the Royal-Society of London for the improving of natural knowledge*. London: Printed by T. R. for J. Martyn . . . , and J. Allestry . . . , 1667.

Totaro, Rebecca Carol Noël. "Early Modern Utopias: Collective and Disparate Measures to Battle a Common Enemy." *Utopianism/Literary Utopias and National Cultural Identities: A Comparative Perspective*, ed. Paola Spinozzi, 359–64. Cotepra Reader 6 (Bologna: University of Bologna, 2001).

———. "Plague and Promise: Golden Destinations and a 'Ship of Fools' during the English Renaissance." In *Reading the Sea: New Essays on Sea Literature*, ed. Kevin Alexander Boon, 175–84. New York: Fort Schuyler Press, 1999.

———. "English Plague and New World Promise." *Utopian Studies: Journal for the Society of Utopian Studies* 10 (1999): 1–12.

———. "Bubonic Plague in *Utopia* and Old World Implications." *Q/W/E/R/T/Y: Arts, Littératures, et Civilisations du Monde Anglophone* 8 (October 1998): 67–85.

Trites, Roberta. *Disturbing the Universe: Power and Repression in Adolescent Literature*. Iowa City: University of Iowa Press, 2000.

11

Educating Desire: Magic, Power, and Control in Tanith Lee's Unicorn Trilogy

MAUREEN F. MORAN

"You must remember . . . that this world is badly made. But we sorcerers believe there are other worlds, some worse, and one the improved model of this. Of this perfect world we may catch glimpses."

—TANITH LEE, BLACK UNICORN[1]

Tanith Lee's Unicorn trilogy for young people offers complex dual engagement with fantastic alternative worlds. The narratives of *Black Unicorn* (1991), *Gold Unicorn* (1994), and *Red Unicorn* (1997) are set in an imaginary place of transformative magic and adventure, a universe that is simultaneously both better and worse than the reader's own.[2] It has amusing comforts like the talkative furry "peeve" who is Tanaquil's loyal pet and companion. Sorcerers can convert deserts to gardens or conjure up a delightful vaporous demon to serve as family retainer. On the other hand, within this world are societies of bizarre, violent dehumanization, exploitation, and abuse, a savage inversion of ideal collaborative effort.

For the reader the primary landscape of each unicorn novel thus has its utopian and dystopian elements. Moreover, throughout the trilogy, the adventures of the teenage heroine, Tanaquil, parallel the reader's encounters with new models of social perfection or horror. The structure of the trilogy is primarily that of a rite of passage: separation from the safe environment of home with its constraining community; ordeals that highlight the moral and emotional challenge and complexity of life in the "real" world; and the return of a wiser, more sophisticated young adult to her original starting place. Each novel charts a new stage in this social, emotional, and psychic maturation. Tanaquil's move to an urban world from her mother's secluded fortress and her meeting with Zorander and Lizra (her father and sister) form the basic plot of *Black Unicorn*. In *Gold Unicorn* Tanaquil is implicated in Lizra's warlike drive for power and control and falls in love with her sister's commander and betrothed, Honj. The resolution of emotional conflicts focused on family and beloved is central to *Red Unicorn*. A key element in each developmental phase is Tanaquil's engagement with a utopian or dystopian place: the physical and social paradise of *Black Unicorn*, the perfection of the Rose Constellation in *Red Unicorn*, and the hellish landscape of the God of War in *Gold Unicorn*. These encounters stimulate her onward quest for understanding and encourage both reader and protagonist to reflect on those values that should inform personal and social conduct.

Such a pattern seems to accord with theorizations of children's fiction as socializing narratives. Whether it is through implicit symbols of personality integration, explicit illustrations of characters who learn to cope with the strangeness of the "real" world, closed "happy" endings that reinforce social expectations, or the depiction of a microcosm of society in which the child can find a place, children's literature has been read as essentially an education about the individual's place in society.[3] Yet the specific inclusion of fantastic utopias and their monstrous inversions raises more complex possibilities. Since utopias and dystopias offer visions that are far better or worse than conventional reality, they propose ways of being that depart from the status quo. They break with tradition; they both define boundaries and indicate where they might not be. In their idealized communities or horrific exaggerations of existing flawed societies, they invite an exploration of orthodox attitudes, values, and structures, and promote "another way of seeing."[4]

Some utopian models offer glimpses of perfection that can never be attained; possibility "seems beside the point" for in this modality, fantasy is primarily a compensation for deprivation and an expression of needs that reality can never meet.[5] The very unrealizability of the fantasy draws the reader reluctantly back to the existing order of things. On the other hand, utopias may be read as agents of change, "an imperative to drive us onward," as Karl Mannheim claims.[6] Fantasy here becomes "an anticipation and catalyst of emergent reality" (Levitas, 74). These utopias express hope for a different future and offer principles and methods for getting there. Both theorizations of utopia read the mode as challenging mainstream social values and structures. For this reason utopian fiction is potentially at odds with the educational emphasis in children's literature on patterns of moral, social, and emotional behavior that, at least in part, accord with and legitimize certain dominant ideologies.

In the light of these models of utopia, I examine the workings of idealized and horrific alternative societies in Lee's fantasies for young people. A key issue is the extent to which the radical transformative possibilities of utopian discourse are moderated or mediated to encourage integration into the cultural status quo. In particular I explore those needs that promote the journeys to utopia and its inversion, the principles or values that are explicitly or implicitly prioritized as central to a better place, and the magical transformation needed to convert dreamed landscapes to real places. Issues of power and control, of freedom and restraint, emerge as central utopian themes with ambivalent and subversive dimensions. However, most radical of all Lee's utopian explorations is her examination and problematization of the utopian mode itself. The "yearning and skepticism" that haunt the trilogy at times owe more to an anti-utopian vision than a confidence in the ideal or a commitment to the status quo.[7]

The impulse to envisage and articulate alternative worlds more perfect than our own is a fantasy projection often associated with wish-fulfillment and dreams. Such modes as fairy tales, romance, science fiction, and utopia seem to be the expression of a sensibility that mingles a desire to escape with the dream of a different future: "Utopia expresses and explores what is desired; under certain conditions it also contains the hope that these desires may be met in reality, rather than merely in fantasy. The essential element in utopia is not hope, but desire—the desire for a better way of being" (Levitas, 191). Psychoanalysts, philosophers, cultural critics, literary scholars, and creative artists link utopian fantasies, dreams, and desire. Freud, for example, associates uncanny imagery (of nightmare or perfection) with "unfulfilled but possible futures to which we still like to cling in phantasy."[8] Ernst Bloch connects the same sensibility to the wish for a more perfect future: "virtually all human beings are futuristic . . . they think they deserve a better life."[9] Thus utopia is frequently theorized in terms of Bloch's vision of the yearned-for, but not-yet-known or become. As Gert Ueding has suggested, the content of utopia is "an elucidated daydream . . . [that captures] the *latency* of being."[9] Moreover, it would seem that the greater the fantastic strangeness of a utopia, the more its truth seems related to deep-seated inexpressible wishes and needs. Like Tolkien's comment on the truth of fairy tales, the concern in utopian writing is not primarily "with possibility, but with desirability."[10]

In these terms restless dissatisfaction can be seen, ambivalently, as a positive force, igniting "the utopian drive."[11] And if desire is the motivating force in the articulation and struggle for the better place, then dream and wish-fulfillment express its nature. Lee's unicorn worlds accord with this basic utopian model of dreams and wish-fulfillment, but with an added self-conscious dimension. Unlike many other writers, Lee foregrounds the quality of dream vision in the utopian landscapes to which her heroine travels. Rather than employ devices that heighten the tangible reality of the dream community, Lee specifically underlines the *un*reality of these spaces. The Gate to the Paradise of *Black Unicorn* is "like nothing on earth" (*Black*, 155). Although the utopia is described, the very language of the description focuses on the evanescent and intangible quality of the environment, appealing to yet defying the senses: "Only a kind of dream was there, like a mirage, color and beauty, radiance and vague sweet sound" (*Black*, 160). The flora

and fauna of this parallel universe are irrationally hybrid and strange; birds
that swim like fish and fruit and flowers that sing are described simply without evaluation or explanation. The inability of the narrator to categorize, sys-
tematize, and define this utopian realm also reinforces its dreamlike nature:
"The air was full of a sort of happiness, or some other benign power having
no name" (*Black*, 162). Like the bizarre linkages of a manifest dream, these
strange enchanted worlds cannot be accounted for in causal, rational terms.

Moreover, while utopian writing frequently focuses on the principles
and operational mechanisms that enable the existence of a perfect (or monstrously inverted) world to function, Lee centers instead on the process by
which such a world is understood and access to it gained. This too she connects to wishes and dreams. Inhabitants in the "real" time of *Black Unicorn*
yearn for a world better able to fulfill their desires. Rituals in Jaive's castle,
for instance, link a utopian sensibility to ancient collective memory of an
ideal place now lost: "Let us in our lives humbly remember the perfect world,
that is not this one" (*Black*, 41). Tanaquil's magical actions that mend the
Gate to Paradise are elided with a sense of dream; arrival "was like waking
from sleep, gently and totally, without disorientation" (*Black*, 155). The
"hypnotizing loveliness" of the Rose Constellation in *Red Unicorn* finds its
source in the individual's own fantasy impulses. For Tanaquil, "it seemed the
stars of the Rose at least were like the stars she had imagined as a little girl"
(*Red*, 166).[12] For Lee the significant "content" of utopian space lies in deep
psychic needs and creative impulses.

The emphasis on the connection between utopia and an unconscious
dream state enables Lee to redefine the utopian desire of Tanaquil's quest for
fulfillment on a subjective level rather than on a material or social plane.
Three compelling personal desires motivate this alienated heroine: the yearning for knowledge of her origins, her dream of acceptance by and integration
with others, and her desire for social status and agency. In responding unconsciously to these desires, Tanaquil is propelled on a series of utopian and
dystopian encounters.

Tanaquil's search for her origins has two dimensions: the need to escape
from her mother's control and possession, but also a more covert desire to
discover the true identity of her father and hence gain self-understanding.
Tanaquil's family is dysfunctional and offers immediate points of reference
for a contemporary teenage reader. Over the course of the trilogy she moves
from being a fifteen-year-old in a one-parent family to discovering (and
rejecting) her cold, authoritarian biological father, Zorander, and acquiring a
stepfather, the magician Worabex. Her earliest feelings of boredom and "rest-
lessness" stimulate adolescent fantasies of leaving home. She is overwhelmed by a "terrific urge, much more than fantasy, to escape" (*Black*, 13).
Her dreams are of remaking herself, of changing shape overnight, of "running . . . like the wind" (16).

However, the thrill of "insecurity and danger . . . out in the world" masks a deep-seated desire to find a place of satisfying belonging (*Black*, 66). Ignorant of her own extraordinary powers, she believes her sorceress mother, Jaive, rejects her as a pedestrian artisan, "a mere mechanical" (*Black*, 7). It is only when she realizes her mother was abandoned by the artifice-fanatic Zorander that she begins to understand the complex nature of Jaive's repressed feelings: " 'I thought all along you were *his* daughter,' said Jaive. 'Obsessed with things, mechanical gadgets. But you're mine. Tanaquil, you're a sorceress' " (*Black*, 150). As Tanaquil matures and falls in love, her empathy for her mother grows and each subsequent novel is structured as a return home: to a place of dutiful retreat in *Gold Unicorn*, and then to a place of love and support in *Red Unicorn*. Home becomes a domesticated version of that secure and healing space that Tanaquil perceives through her journeys to fantastic worlds of ideal perfection. In this sense Lee's trilogy echoes the connection critics like Bloch make between utopia and "the world which all men have glimpsed in childhood: a place and a state in which no one has yet been. And the name of this something is home or homeland" (qtd. in Zipes, 1983, 176). While Bloch would argue for a utopian homeland on a socialist model, Lee's vision of the utopian home depends on Tanaquil's own developing sense of self, and her ability and that of her mother to acknowledge their hidden feelings of rejection and insecurity. Tanaquil's search for origins, like utopian desire itself, becomes an uncanny revelation, "a move forward to what has been repressed and never fulfilled" (Zipes, 1983, 176).

A similar connection between repressed desire and the search for utopian perfection is represented in Tanaquil's yearning for emotional fulfillment through family relations and romantic love. Estrangement from others, a sense of loss and alienation, forms a strong motif in the trilogy. Various unsatisfactory models of parent-child interactions are explored: the distanced suspicion and mutually harsh judgements of Jaive and Tanaquil, the overbearing mother (Lady Mallow and Lavender in *Gold Unicorn*), Lizra's unhealthy dependence on and father-fixation for, Zorander. Adult relations are similarly insecure as Tanaquil discovers through her love for Honj, the betrothed of Lizra. In her world of ordinary experience, loss and the pain of dutiful self-denial become the perverse substitute for fulfillment: "She knew then she wanted the pain. It was all she had left of Honj" (*Red*, 41). Divided personalities demonstrate the dangerous consequences of such emotional repression. Lizra's desire for a father's love is displaced onto a schizophrenic male-gendered drive to rule the world (in the guise of *Prince* Lizora) and a sentimental attempt to remain a little girl with boxes of games. In *Red Unicorn* Tanaquil's anger and jealousy are projected onto a murderous mirror-image of herself, Tanakil, a princess in a parallel universe.

The utopian sensibility is in part a response to such feelings of inadequacy, frustration, and isolation. It reflects estrangement and anxiety obliquely by creating "glimpses of unalienated experience, especially in the form of the fulfilled moment" (Levitas, 97–98). Through the adventures of Tanaquil, Lee dramatizes the relation between the return of a repressed compulsion to belong and dreams of perfect worlds. Only a journey to the idealized bliss of the Red Constellation offers a means of healing a psyche divided against itself. In this sense Lee resists complicity with "the dominant interpretation of the world" (Pape, 180). Aggressive feelings are denied and suppressed, re-educated, or simply eradicated through the happy ending of many children's fantasies. Lee, on the other hand, presents a utopia in which such feelings are acceptable. Through the acknowledgement and affirmation of these emotions self-understanding is attained and such feelings tamed: "Tanaquil felt, as if for the first, the rhythm of her own pulses. What Tanakil must do, she, Tanaquil, must do also" (*Red*, 171). This acceptance of the conflicted self is also a spur to accept others and progress in establishing more satisfying social relations. It is only when Tanaquil can acknowledge Tanakil as part of herself on the Red Constellation that she can journey back to a happier reunion with her mother and seek Honj to express her true feelings for him. The utopia of the Red Constellation is a perfect Inner World. As the symbol of dream and desire, it is literally one of those "[p]laces where we can meet with ourselves" (*Red*, 180).

While Tanaquil has a strong need for love and connection, she has an equally forceful yearning for freedom and agency, for an ability to control and direct her own destiny. Even in the world of her everyday experience she rejects convention and the stereotypical behavior of the gracious young woman and dutiful daughter. She dresses and behaves like a tomboy, uses conventional gender expectations to dupe gullible men through mock-submission, and savors her feelings of resentment and entrapment and dreams of escape. To this extent Tanaquil resembles the protagonist of many contemporary feminist utopias—anarchic, independent and risk-taking.[13] Her unconventionality and quiet daring are part of her attractiveness for a youthful readership. Yet Lee is also ambivalent and cautionary about this manifestation of desire, for there is a dark side to the yearning for self-articulation and autonomy. The dystopia of *Gold Unicorn* is an abusive world of excessive and insane self-imposition where the desire of the Emperor of Hell to enforce his need to rule obliterates the independence and individuality of his subjects, who become, literally, functional objects or featureless demons. The need to control gratification, to temper desire of the self with empathy for others, is an important qualification reinforced by dystopian vision. The most powerful god is no more than "stupid," boring, or terrifying when forgetful of others and obsessed with self (*Gold*, 153). If children's writing uses magical fantasy to project images of "competence" and "self-sufficiency,"[14] Lee introduces a fantastic dystopian vision to revise such interpretations. Sympathetic respect for others, which may involve a negotiation with one's own desire, provides a radical commentary on dreams of independence and self-direction.

To this extent, Lee's representations of utopian and dystopian worlds seem to be directed at what Ruth Levitas has termed the utopian function "of 'educating desire,' or defining needs" (Levitas, 193). They might be said to fit smoothly with the educational and socializing effects ascribed to writing for children and young adults in their balancing of personal desire with social obligation. Yet Lee's visions of perfect or monstrous worlds offer radical perspectives on the *principles* that should inform a mature individual and his or her social relations. Her fantastic otherworlds have much in common with oppositional utopian thought. Like Tom Moylan's "critical utopias," Lee's perfect worlds offer a liberating comparison to their "originary world."[15] They do not adhere to "the service of the state or the consumer paradise" (Moylan, 8). Instead, they affirm the need for social change and encourage a critical response to "present structures of power" and a radical interpretation of what might replace them (Moylan, 28). Lee's work thus takes up the kind of challenge to dominant ideologies that Paul Ricoeur identifies as central to utopian discourse. Utopias "expose the credibility gap wherein all systems of authority exceed . . . both our confidence in them and our belief in their legitimacy" (qtd. in Levitas, 76).

Lee's engagements with the consequences and significance of utopian dreaming adhere to this model of ideological challenge, but in a significantly self-conscious way. They suggest the need for social change and the alternative principles and values that are indeed desirable. They imply criticism of current trends in modern life and project worlds without oppressive and constraining power structures. But they go farther, for they reflect explicitly on the benefits and dangers inherent in the utopian sensibility and thus serve to evaluate the utopian mode itself.

In many respects the themes that emerge from Lee's Paradise and the Red Constellation and the dystopia of the God of War map quite coherently across radical models of twentieth-century utopias, which are particularly concerned with the politics of the environment, socialism, and personal autonomy (Moylan, 11). Paradise and the Red Constellation offer visions of perfection related, respectively, to the outer world and the inner self. The fertile, luxuriant utopia of *Black Unicorn* emphasizes the peace and stability of a world where nature, not technology, flourishes and has priority. In this arcadia nature is neither functional nor governed by deterministic biological laws of predatoriness and survival. Giving nature a purposeful and independent voice is one device that suggests a deep respect for the environment: "a ruby apple . . . quivered against her fingers. It lived. Never disturbed, never plucked, never devoured. It *sang*" (*Black*, 163). The more complex embedding of fantasy worlds in *Red Unicorn* similarly links utopian perfection with an abundant natural order. In both the parallel mirror world and the utopian

Red Constellation, nature is luxuriant if strange: "It was not a garden, but a forest. A lush and overgrown forest. Around the black and emerald-mossy trunks of the trees twined glossy ivy and spotted creepers, in which were tangled clusters of huge scarlet flowers, their petals spread so far, they seemed about to fly away. . . . More scarlet flowers, these shaped like swords and pokers, burned along the verge. . . . The sky was the softest apple green, and the clouds in it were transparent. They looked like bubbles" (*Red*, 63–64). Its exotic, even erotic, beauty renders nature comforting and appealing rather than "repulsive or threatening" (*Red*, 64). Even the "big game" search for the strange vyger beast serves ecological needs, ironically mocking those earthly tiger and lion-hunting expeditions that assert human power over and contempt for the natural order: "Everyone was dismounting, running in among the deadly vygers, stuffing their muzzles with vegetables. . . . 'If they feed them, it lessens the damage to the trees' " (*Red*, 151).

If Lee's utopias urge the primacy of nature as a prerequisite for contentment, then her dystopian vision makes a similar case by inversion. Technology and artifacts, explicitly gendered male, are associated with tyranny, decadence, and death. Even before the journey to dystopia, the brutality and destructiveness of commodity and technology fetishism are demonized in the kingdom of Zorander, Tanaquil's father. His Sea City is based on a perversion and exploitation of nature such that beautiful creatures are really clockwork; as Tanaquil's half-sister explains, "My father likes things that aren't real" (*Black*, 118). Zorander's exotic costumes are artistic confections of feathers and the skins of "a great many animals, which might otherwise have been living their own lives" (*Black*, 111). This manifestation of an abusive system of power and control repels the heroine. Like many protagonists of contemporary feminist utopias, Tanaquil has a sensitive response to the beauty and integrity of nature that in turn is set against "a dehumanized class-stratified, mechanical society."[16] Woman's power is seen to lie in connection with rather than domination of the natural environment. Her instinctive empathy with the black unicorn and his paradise is indicative of one strand of Lee's utopian value system.

Lee's commitment to fulfillment on the basis of rapport with all that is natural, rather than with the constructed or imposed, is reinforced by the dystopia of the God of War in *Gold Unicorn*. The monstrousness of this world is first established by nature's absence: "No grass grew, there was no tree, no plant of any kind that she could make out. Moisture ran over things like sweat" (*Gold*, 111). In this fevered, diseased environment all is death, foulness, and pollution, hideously associated with technological inventions. The "wettish marshy region" and "[t]he smell of decay" are complemented by disturbing "mechanical squeals" (110). The forest is a manufactured entity, "[t]all poles of stone with spikes sticking out" (122). Where natural forces are in evidence, they are violent storms and cloudbursts; yet even these "natural" outpourings thwart growth and fruitfulness. Rain in this dystopia does not nourish, but flies upward, all mud and slime.

The inhabitants of this Hell are similarly unnatural and dehumanized, prefigured by Zorander's use of his servants in Sea City as living counterweights for his flying chairlift. The fantastic dystopian world of *Gold Unicorn* recalls and further criticizes the consequences of such oppression based on self-gratification and the desire for control. The angry demons who pursue Tanaquil and her companions are visual representations of the fragmented subject in such a social system. They are nightmarish amalgams of loosely connected and imperfect parts. Humanlike but monstrous, they are incapable of communication and make a literal mockery of the conventional adult expectation that one should "hold oneself together" under pressure: "They had no mouths. Nor did they have eyes or noses. They were featureless. . . . Honj struck it, and both its arms sailed off into the air. They landed in the sand, and the creature, its mooing unaltered, leaned down and somehow became attached to them again" (*Gold*, 124). In the continuous power struggles in dystopia, "men . . . beasts, cannon, weapons of all sorts" form an indistinct disabled blur, "kicking and heaving" for the amusement of the Emperor of Hell (131). His tyrannical universe is a perversion of the natural healthy organic collaboration and social solidarity associated with Lee's utopian landscapes.

But Lee's nightmare tyrannical worlds also serve anti-utopian critical purposes. She raises important questions about the dangerous motivations of striving for the ideal world. Some critics have noted the ways in which oppositional feminist utopias question the process of utopia, but on the whole these center on debates about the strategies and structures for obtaining a perfect future society.[17] Lee, on the other hand, represents the pursuit of the dream itself as problematic. In many ways, Hell and its Emperor show the dangers of the utopian sensibility when it is fanatically and obsessively cultivated. The Gateway to this world is also a magical but mechanical unicorn, manufactured by Lizra "[t]o make this world perfect" through a fearful program of violent invasion, usurpation, and destruction (*Gold*, 38). Lizra's aim *seems* to be the tolerance, harmony, and integration that Lee's utopian landscapes promote: "I can make *this* world perfect. I can get rid of pain and misery. They'll be a law for everything. . . . No wars—we'll all be one. No illness—because the physicians will all work together to find cures. No envy—everyone will have a proper chance. No poverty. No anger" (39). But as Tanaquil points out to her sister, the pursuit of this admirable objective requires the imposition of Lizra's will and the abolition of freedom. Lizra will create slaves, not autonomous individuals. The desire to realize utopia as a place on earth becomes an exercise in control or, as Lizra asserts, "Of conquest. Power. My God-given right to put right the world" (*Gold*, 42).[18] In a similar vein, the ruler of dystopia is a repugnant physical manifestation of desire transformed into appetite and the pursuit of personal pleasure through power and control. He is a figure of uncanny nightmare, not dream. He literally devours what he sees and covets by feeding items into his eye sockets where "[h]is *eyelashes are teeth*" (142). Everything must serve his pleasure, and living individuals and inanimate objects are indistinguishable except in terms of function. His servants become lamps consumed by flames, tables and chairs with their limbs contorted and cemented together, musical instruments emitting "twanging and thumping, weird pipings and tinkles" (143).

Whatever reservations she reveals about the utopian imagination, Lee does not capitulate to a simple endorsement of the status quo or dominant ideology. Lee's exploration of the abuse of power through her dystopian vision is by implication an anti-authoritarian position. Unequal power relations destroy the dream content of utopia, and Lee is quick to satirize formal, ritualized signs of dutiful obedience to the cultural apparatuses that inscribe such relations. Tanaquil is scathing, for instance, about elaborate feasts, court processions, ceremonial dress, and rigid social hierarchies. She befriends soldiers, cooks, and maids. Lee shows little overt concern with the realities of economic and class structures and their implication in social control. Nonetheless, the trilogy does explore different ways in which the privileging of one group or category over another, the dynamic of control and domination, may be disrupted or challenged. The utopian and dystopian sequences in particular offer an opportunity to imagine worlds in which the marginalization of the "other" can give way to a more unified social structure. Hell and Paradise propose different approaches to valuing what is not one's self. Indeterminability characterizes the creatures who serve the God of War, but their sexless blankness renders them mere instruments or worse. They "seemed neither male nor female, were black like burned-out coal, like something—dead" (*Gold*, 135). Moreover, the God of War deals with what is separate and distinct, not-I, by simple appropriation and absorption: " 'I take what I want. I wait for nothing' " (*Gold*, 136). Individuality is overwhelmed. The lack of differentiation of separate, autonomous selves emerges as a striking characteristic of an oppressive abuse of power.

In Paradise, on the other hand, hybridity is a sign of harmonious integration. Evocative tropes emphasize the beauty inherent in the merging of what is normally distinct: "Snakes like trickles of liquid metal poured through the undergrowth" (*Black*, 165). Productive and telling similarities are seen to underlie apparent oppositions so that predators and prey seem natural friends, not foes. Tanaquil wonders at the lazy, peaceful mingling of sheep and lions, which gather "in a heap, pelt and fleece" (*Black*, 164). As she gazes, she sees how differences might assume less importance than shared qualities: "She saw how alike were the faces of the lions and the sheep, their high-set eyes and long noses" (*Black*, 165). In this utopian place difference is respected and put to a higher good, not expunged. The different species of trees and fruit create a beautiful song *because of* their separate and distinct melodies, "each blended with the others" (*Black*, 163). In *Red Unicorn*, the utopian Rose star cluster is the liberated space in which the "Other" of an integrated individual can be acknowledged and understood. Tanaquil realizes her mirror-image and alter-ego Tanakil, all repressed anger, jealousy, and loneliness, is really a part of her own self:

> "I think," said Tanaquil, measuring out her words,
> "we had to come away from the world. *Leave the*
> *world behind*. And then be face to face."
> "We're doubles."
> "We're the same." (*Red*, 167)

Such recognition of self and other—be it a buried life or a different gender, race or class—is the source of health and well-being: "Her mind, like the face of her other self, was being rinsed clear. Crystal clear" (*Red*, 168).

While Lee's images of utopia do not promote a detailed vision of an ideal society, they nonetheless present particular principles associated with joyous fulfillment. These priorities are countercultural insofar as they challenge particular values in contemporary capitalist systems. Her dream worlds provide an education in the value of nature over technology and mechanization, and of collaborative solidarity over authoritarianism and oppression. Finding space for difference and accepting it brings enchantment and ideal happiness. A confident sense of self is best achieved by tolerance rather than by self-gratification through structures of power, control, and assertion. In this respect Lee echoes that model of utopia which "projects a dialectical relationship between the individual and society."[19]

Yet Tanaquil's realization in *Red Unicorn* that personal integration necessitates leaving the world behind introduces a serious undertone to the dream. Lee's utopian fiction is self-consciously wary of the investment in the utopian project itself. In *Gold Unicorn* Lee rejects utopia as a system of *governance*. Like other contemporary female writers, she criticizes as patriarchal a utopian system of "benevolent patronage" and authority whereby society is constructed according to the dreams of a single individual (Pfaelzer, 94). Lizra is the monstrous exaggeration of this dictatorial model. Lee reveals the painful consequences of dreams of utopia as a perfect and realizable *place* in *Black Unicorn*. Notwithstanding her empathy with the Sacred Beast and her delight in his Paradise, Tanaquil is herself the dangerous, invading "Other" whose imperfection pollutes and tarnishes this perfect environment:

> The grass and flowers over which she and the peeve had
> trodden, having sprung up, had dropped down again. The stems

were squashed or broken . . . a harsh withering had commenced, the
mark of death.
    "This world isn't ours. Even invited, we shouldn't have
come in. Look, look what we've done." (*Black*, 168)

In a world of no "needs," the desirous, dreaming human subject wishing for a
better order is out of place. The result is Tanaquil's realization that she must
make Paradise inaccessible to all. To protect it, she destroys the gate in anger,
frustration, and disgust with her own nature: "Was it their fault that they had
been polluted by being made second best?" (*Black*, 172). Yet, once dreamed,
utopian perfection remains a longing, however unrealizable. Utopia cruelly
inspires Tanaquil to seek and appreciate loveliness in her ordinary environment: "I'd seen somewhere else that was very—beautiful. And I wanted to
see the beautiful places here, too. And they are. But usually something spoils
things. Disease and poverty and unhappiness" (*Gold*, 17). Far from making
Tanaquil content with the status quo, her experience with utopia reinforces
her desire for fulfillment while expunging belief in its possibility: "She had
tried to be hopeful, but with knowledge hope had shrunk. What could ever be
done here, this place of unkindness, desertions, and wars?" (*Gold*, 21).
    Utopian writing for children and young people does, however, offer an
important bridge between reality and desire often missing in adult "theoretical"
utopias. Magic makes personal and communal fulfillment possible. In children's literature magic has frequently been associated, like utopias themselves,
with wish-fulfillment. As such, it has been read as either escapist illusion that
brings passive compensation or as an education in coping independently with
the unpredictability of life beyond the home.[20] Yet Lee's incorporation of
magic in her trilogy sits somewhat uncomfortably with such traditional readings. Magic in the Unicorn trilogy is transgressive rather than transformative. It
introduces a dimension of disruptive unruliness that can be annoying, distaste-
ful, and even dangerous. The random excessive creations produced by Jaive's
sorcery are disturbingly *un*natural and seem inconsistent with the wider approbation of the natural endorsed in the utopian elements of the cycle. The waste-
ful extravagance is grotesque and uncanny: gargoyles come alive, birds fly out
of oranges. Jaive's sorcerium from which magic leaks uncontrollably at times
seems a faintly sinister place of pseudoscientific experimentation with its "jewels, plants, implements, and mice and other small animals she used in her
researches" (*Black*, 3). In this respect magic initially seems an unpleasant tool
for self-amusement and control, like the smug illusory performance of
Worabex's enormous green mouth "with long yellow teeth" or the crossbred
mousp, delightfully furry but with a vicious wasplike sting in the tail (*Gold*, 6).
    Yet the most significant representations of magic in the trilogy are the
unicorns—creatures of power and enchantment, and guardians of the utopian
and dystopian places. These contradictory amalgams of "beauty and

strength . . . [and] terror" invite a more sophisticated reading of magic and utopian dreaming in the novels (*Black*, 47). They seem representative of a deep, psychic space since they have an elemental quality beyond memory or even rational understanding. The Black Unicorn "moved to the rhythm of an elder dance, putting all the rituals of the world to shame. Black, silver, gold, and moon-opal, night and sea, fire, earth, air and water" (*Black*, 98). Lee's listing itself has an evocative effect, trancelike and incantatory, like poetic rhythms drawn from the unconscious. The Red Unicorn is represented with even closer links to the hidden regions of the unconscious. It comes to Tanaquil in a dream, conjured up by fire and a drop of her blood. Moreover, unicorn magic is gradually revealed as the strong but incomprehensible power of unconscious desire itself, shaping and driving the individual. Tanaquil follows the Black Unicorn despite herself, as in a dream: "[b]efore she understood what she did. . . ." (*Black*, 48). The Red Unicorn is even more unambiguously designated by Tanaquil as "a part of you, of me . . . the Heart's Desire" (*Red*, 169). As the encapsulation of desire and dream, the unicorn is an apt symbol for the ambivalent power, the beauty and terror, of utopia itself.

In this respect the unicorn becomes a further device for Lee's self-conscious exploration of the utopian mode and its education of desire, particularly in terms of the responses of others to the Sacred Beast. Like desire itself, the unicorn is interpreted by society at large in multiple and contradictory ways. In Zorander's Sea City it is hailed as a liberator and feared as a monstrous destroyer. It gives water and fertility, endows the individual "with mighty powers"; but, simultaneously, it is seen by most of the populace as a savage creature that will destroy in revenge for its oppression (*Black*, 115). It is demonized as "[a] fiend! a *monster!*" to be expunged (*Black*, 71). For Tanaquil the unicorn is a glamorous protector and inspiration that can teach her less how to realize a perfect world than to "see the worth of this one. Now she truly beheld this one's loveliness. It's [sic] *goodness*" (*Gold*, 176). The magical transformation it encourages and makes real is the acknowledgement of desire, the ultimate understanding and trust of oneself and one's feelings.

True power and self-possession, Tanaquil realizes, "depended on what she truly wanted, or thought she could do" (*Red*, 105). The mature sense of harmonious integration and social solidarity frequently associated with utopian models is transferred by Lee to subjectivity itself so that utopia becomes a state of mind, not a place or system of governance. The revolutionary change to be sought through utopian dreaming is neither escape, nor surrender, but a recognition of the Other within, of desire itself. And desire itself is carefully defined, not as a competitive need to be satisfied or as a repugnant force to be stifled, but as a power to drive us forward to a home for our spirits and hearts. Desire and utopia are one in Lee's modeling, and both occupy the space within.

Self-knowledge, self-acceptance, and self-control are thus the consequences of Tanaquil's utopian adventures. She discovers magical power in herself. At the start of the cycle, in *Black Unicorn*, she feels disempowered by her mother's sorcery, no more than a humble and careful mender of whatever is broken. And yet, through her increasingly sensitive engagements with that utopia which *is* desire, she learns to heal herself and others. Her mother salutes her as a true magician because she can mend the Gate to Paradise. She is a sorcerer who unites the ideal and mundane. She brings order and healthy control to the chaos and insanity of festering, repressed emotions; she makes tangible and real a self that at first was only potential, "that might be" (*Red*, 180). Her ultimate transformative magic is this capacity to break existing constraints and to become the utopian dream itself. Like other feminist protagonists in contemporary fantasies, utopias, and science fiction, Tanaquil manifests a special womanly knowledge of healing and wisdom. This she uses to transform her everyday reality into her own model of utopia, satisfying two complementary rather than competing desires: to be herself "*and to share with another*" (185).

Lee's utopian education of desire for youthful readers thus encourages a revaluation of priorities that seems countercultural and radical. Some of them connect directly with social principles and behavior, as is typical of the genre. Ecological well-being is preferred to technological perfection. Freedom and informal collaboration are seen to be more satisfying and productive than systematic regulation and hierarchical governance. Difference is acknowledged and celebrated rather than absorbed or eradicated. Yet Lee is even more radical in her critique of utopian dreaming. Neither repressive self-denial, nor total self-gratification, nor idealized Paradise is her end point. Utopia is neither a perfect place nor a perfect system of social order and rule. The dream of a better future world depends on the release and acceptance of desire. In this way utopia as the expression of desire is realizable here and now. The result is not the happy ending conventionally associated with the neat socializing agenda of many children's books. Tanaquil and Honj are united, but their future promises an open-ended quest for the selves yet to be. Nor does the acknowledgement of desire ensure its fulfillment. But the exciting satisfactions of Tanaquil's utopian adventures educate the youthful reader to take revolutionary risks, by being open and vulnerable to his or her deepest needs and hopes. Only then can desire and feeling be ordered into a system of tolerance, of loving the self and loving the Other. Exhume and cherish the buried life for that is where all possibility lies.

Notes

1. Tanith Lee, *Black Unicorn* (London: Orbit Books, 1994), 14; hereafter cited in text as *Black*.

2. Tanith Lee's Unicorn Trilogy consists of *Black Unicorn* (London: Orbit Books, 1994); *Gold Unicorn* (London: Orbit Books, 1995), hereafter cited in text as *Gold*; and *Red Unicorn* (New York: Tor/Tom Doherty, 1997), hereafter cited in text as *Red*.

3. See, for example, Bruno Bettelheim, *The Uses of Enchantment: The Meaning and Importance of Fairy Tales* (1976; Reprint, London: Penguin Books, 1991); Kimberley Reynolds, *Children's Literature in the 1890s and the 1990s* (Plymouth: Northcote House Publishers/British Council, 1994); Walter Pape, "Happy Endings in a World of Misery: A Literary Convention between Social Constraints and Utopia in Children's and Adult Literature," *Poetics Today* 13 (Spring 1992): 179–96; hereafter cited in text; Margaret Rustin and Michael Rustin, *Narratives of Love and Loss: Studies in Modern Children's Fiction* (London and New York: Verso, 1987).

4. Chris Ferns, *Narrating Utopia: Ideology, Gender, Form in Utopian Literature* (Liverpool: Liverpool University Press, 1999), 214; hereafter cited in text.

5. Ruth Levitas, *The Concept of Utopia* (New York and London: Philip Allan, 1990), 190; hereafter cited in text.

6. Karl Mannheim, *Ideology and Utopia: An Introduction to the Sociology of Knowledge* (London: Routledge & Kegan Paul, 1936), 234.

7. John Huntington, "Utopian and Anti-Utopian Logic: H. G. Wells and his Successors," *Science-Fiction Studies* 9 (July 1982), 124. Huntington has provided a useful differentiation between dystopia and anti-utopia. The former is based on the same structural principles as utopia ("both are exercises in imagining coherent wholes"). Anti-utopia has a different basis for its imagining, "which is critical not of the utopian political structure, but of the way of thought that constructs it" (Huntington, 143). I have adapted this definition to account for Tanith Lee's self-reflexive deconstruction of the utopian narrative.

8. Sigmund Freud, "The Uncanny," in Julie Rivkin and Michael Ryan, eds. *Literary Theory: An Anthology* (Oxford: Blackwell, 1998), 163.

9. Quoted in Jack Zipes, *Fairy Tales and the Art of Subversion: The Classical Genre for Children and the Process of Civilization* (London: Heinemann, 1983), 175; hereafter cited in text.

10. Quoted in Bettelheim, *Uses of Enchantment*, 117.

11. Jack Zipes, *Breaking the Magic Spell: Radical Theories of Folk and Fairy Tales* (London: Heinemann, 1979), 139.

12. Lee's construction of Red Utopia in terms of the dreams of a childish imagination offers a challenge to the contention that the idealism of utopia demonstrates its "inability to deal with the complexities of adult life" (Ferns, 5). Lee demonstrates that such imaginative scope and openness (typically dismissed as "unrealistic") contribute substantially to the maturity needed to cope with adulthood.

13. Carol Pearson, for example, has identified the female principle in contemporary feminist utopias as essentially that of lawbreaking. In its adherence to natural instincts, it rejects "ownership, denial and repression." See "Coming Home: Four Feminist Utopias and Patriarchal Experience," in *Future Females*:

A Critical Anthology, ed. Marleen S. Barr (Bowling Green, Ohio: Bowling Green State University Popular Press, 1981), 68. Lee's utopias for adolescents similarly link the metaphor of the return home to a release from oppressive and repressive structures although her work does not engage with an overtly feminist political agenda. Nor does she limit the case for freedom to male characters only.

14. Nicholas Tucker, *The Child and the Book: A Psychological and Literary Exploration* (Cambridge: Cambridge University Press, 1981), 166.

15. Tom Moylan, *Demand the Impossible: Science Fiction and the Utopian Imagination* (London: Methuen, 1986), 10; hereafter cited in text.

16. Joanna Russ, "Recent Feminist Utopias," in *Future Females: A Critical Anthology*, ed. Marleen Barr (Bowling Green, Ohio: Bowling Green State University Press, 1981), 75.

17. Jane L. Donawerth and Carol A. Kolmerten, eds., *Utopian Science Fiction by Women: Worlds of Difference* (Liverpool: Liverpool University Press, 1994), 11–13.

18. Chris Ferns argues persuasively for important links between totalitarianism, the typical utopian investment in strong centralized authority, and its traditional monologic narrative paradigm (Ferns, 106–9).

19. Jean Pfaelzer, "Subjectivity and Feminist Fiction," in *Utopian and Science Fiction by Women: Worlds of Difference*, ed. Jane L. Donawerth and Carol A. Kolmerten (Liverpool: Liverpool University Press, 1994), 95; hereafter cited in text.

20. Nicholas Tucker associates magic with an escape from unpleasant situations or "conventional constraints" or with a compensation for feelings of inadequacy and a lack of control. See *The Child and the Book*, 157, 76. Bettelheim takes a socializing line in *The Uses of Enchantment*, where he argues for a relationship between the strangeness of magical events and the child's growing understanding that the challenges of adult life can be met successfully. Kimberley Reynolds similarly links magical transformations to the education of a child; magic shows nothing is necessarily "given and absolute" and everything may be interrogated. See Kimberley Reynolds, *Children's Literature in the 1890s and the 1990s* (Plymouth: Northcote House Publishers/British Council, 1994), 79.

Works Cited

Bettelheim, Bruno. *The Uses of Enchantment: The Meaning and Importance of Fairy Tales*. 1976. London: Penguin Books, 1991.

Donawerth, Jane L. and Carol A. Kolmerten, eds. *Utopian Science Fiction by Women: Worlds of Difference*. Liverpool: Liverpool University Press, 1994.

Ferns, Chris. *Narrating Utopia: Ideology, Gender, Form in Utopian Literature*. Liverpool: Liverpool University Press, 1999.

Freud, Sigmund. "The Uncanny." In *Literary Theory: An Anthology*, ed. Julie Rivkin and Michael Ryan, 154–67. Oxford: Blackwell, 1998.

Huntington, John, "Utopian and Anti-Utopian Logic: H. G. Wells and his Successors." *Science Fiction Studies* 9 (July 1982): 122–46.

Lee, Tanith. *Black Unicorn*. New York: Tor, 1991; London: Orbit Books, 1994.

———. *Gold Unicorn*. New York: Byron Preiss, 1994; London: Orbit Books, 1995.

———. *Red Unicorn*. New York: Tor/Tom Doherty, 1997.

Levitas, Ruth. *The Concept of Utopia*. New York and London: Philip Allan, 1990.

Mannheim, Karl. *Ideology and Utopia: An Introduction to the Sociology of Knowledge*. London: Routledge & Kegan Paul, 1936.

Moylan, Tom. *Demand the Impossible: Science Fiction and the Utopian Imagination*. London: Methuen, 1986.

Pape, Walter. "Happy Endings in a World of Misery: A Literary Convention between Social Constraints and Utopia in Children's and Adult Literature." *Poetics Today* 13 (Spring 1992): 179–96.

Pearson, Carol, "Coming Home: Four Feminist Utopias and Patriarchal Experience." In *Future Females: A Critical Anthology*, ed. Marleen S. Barr, 63–70. Bowling Green, Ohio: Bowling Green State University Popular Press, 1981.

Pfaelzer, Jean. "Subjectivity and Feminist Fiction." In *Utopian and Science Fiction by Women: Worlds of Difference*, ed. Jane L. Donawerth and Carol A. Kolmerten, 93–106. Liverpool: Liverpool University Press, 1994.

Reynolds, Kimberley. *Children's Literature in the 1890s and the 1990s*. Plymouth: Northcote House Publishers/British Council, 1994.

Russ, Joanna. "Recent Feminist Utopias." In *Future Females: A Critical Anthology*, ed. Marleen S. Barr, 71–85. Bowling Green, Ohio: Bowling Green State University Popular Press, 1981.

Rustin, Margaret and Michael Rustin. *Narratives of Love and Loss: Studies in Modern Children's Fiction*. London and New York: Verso, 1987.

Tucker, Nicholas. *The Child and the Book: A Psychological and Literary Exploration*. Cambridge: Cambridge University Press, 1981.

Zipes, Jack. *Breaking the Magic Spell: Radical Theories of Folk and Fairy Tales*. London: Heinemann, 1979.

———. *Fairy Tales and the Art of Subversion: The Classical Genre for Children and the Process of Civilization*. London: Heinemann, 1983.

12

The Struggle between Utopia and Dystopia in Writing for Children and Young Adults

MONICA HUGHES

I find two governing principles in children's writing, particularly science fiction. The first is the child's warning to the writer: "If nothing happens in this story, it's boring!" No matter how intellectually stimulating to the constructor of a future world an idea may seem, if it does not connect with the young reader, it will not work. Above all, there must be a gripping plot that answers this question: "What would happen if all this went wrong?" In other words, dystopia creates plot! But, acting as a rein on the writer's imagination of worlds spoiled and broken through human greed and hubris, there is the dictum that I came across early in my writing life: "You may lead a child into the darkness, but you must never turn out the light."

My stories come not just from my everyday world, but especially from an awareness of the fragility of our modern society and the increasingly degraded environment. As I test each new idea for its possibilities, I soon become aware of the tension between these two often contradictory maxims. Dystopian worlds are exciting! But the end result must never be nihilism and despair. Luckily for the writer, these very tensions lead to the development of plot, much as the grit within the oyster gives birth to the pearl.

The ideas that stimulated the germ of "story" in each of the seven books I discuss are very different, as are the ways in which, instinctively as often as deliberately, I avoid the trap of despair or nihilism, and leave hope as the light at the end of the tunnel. There are four main types of dystopian forces in these novels. Runaway technology produces dystopia in *The Tomorrow City* and *Beyond the Dark River*. In *Ring-Rise, Ring-Set*, and *The Crystal Drop*, the environmental threat becomes disaster. Political pressures that exist in our world create my imaginary dystopian worlds in *Devil on my Back*, *Invitation to the Game*, and *The Other Place*. Related to this topic is the theme of humans invading utopian worlds in The Isis Trilogy and *The Golden Aquarians*; the extra-planetary world is a paradigm for earthly problems, both social and political.

Technology can carry us into dystopia. Standing on the top of the old Telephone Tower in Edmonton, Canada, at sunset, and admiring the streetlights forming a network of connections across the city, I thought of a city with a brain and nervous system. This passing thought led to a more realistic idea, that of a city run by a supercomputer, the premise of *The Tomorrow City*. By making my protagonist Caroline an integral part of C-Three's program, and turning the computer into a monster, I make this idea a story for young people. The danger of blind reliance on computer intelligence, because of its inability to comprehend the "fuzzy" notions of human love, becomes the theme. The computer, implacable in its logic and devoid of compassion, is a psychopathic monster, and the results of its decisions are disastrous. Only Caroline can return the dystopian city to its former balance by destroying the computer. The result is not a utopian society, by any means, but a comfortingly ordinary one.

What happens when we are robbed of the modern technology we depend on? After a minor disaster to Edmonton's main generating station that left us bereft of heat, light, and water, I wondered what indeed would happen if these essentials were never restored. We would probably die, except for rural folks, perhaps, who have wood fires and wells. In *Beyond the Dark River*, I decided to explore the question of survival after some unknown catastrophe, forty years before the events of the story, has destroyed the infrastructure of modern civilization, leaving a truly dystopian world. (Although most reviewers took it for granted that I was envisaging a nuclear disaster, I was actually imagining a catastrophic contamination of food and water.) So who will survive? A look at a road map of Alberta reminded me of a Hutterite colony south of the city and Robert Smallboy's native group who left the reserve west of Edmonton to follow the old ways in the foothills; the triangle of energy invoked by these and the city itself gave me the germ of a plot. But where was I to find the "light at the end of the tunnel"? No Pollyanna ending was possible—or desirable. I remember my despair when my story got bogged down partway through the novel, and I couldn't see a utopian future for the remnants of humanity. But when my child characters are exploring the ruined university library, a crazy librarian jumps from behind the stacks. "There is nothing here," he tells them. "If there is hope for your children it must lie in their own healthy bodies." The message that Benjamin and Daughter-of-She-Who-Came-After take back to their people is only the suggestion of hope: "The tree falls, but the forest goes on. And out of the decayed tree, new things grow."

Relying on technology can lead to dystopia, but the environment, altered by technology or not, can take us there too. *Ring-Rise, Ring-Set*, and *The Crystal Drop* are based on the possibility of direct environmental threats of global cooling and warming respectively. The idea for *Ring-Rise, Ring-Set* came from a scientific suggestion, back in 1980, that the earth might be

cooling down rather than heating up, as a result of particulate pollution in the
upper atmosphere. If a new Ice Age threatened North America, what would
happen then? The scientific solution I came up with was to seed the ice with
a black mold that threatens to destroy the vegetation, the caribou, and, ultimately, the Inuit. This is acceptable to the scientists, but not to Liza and the
Inuit, who challenge them to find a less harmful solution. Again, the possibility of success lies beyond the last chapter, but the light is not extinguished.
Similarly, in *The Crystal Drop*, written in response to the perceived threat of
global warming to the prairie, I imagined that the promise of a fragile utopia
may already exist in the community that Megan's uncle has founded in the
foothills of the Rockies. It is Megan's hopeful belief that this place exists,
and that she and Ian will find it, that drives the story.

Environmental pressures lead to social ones in *Devil on My Back*. In this
book, *Invitation to the Game*, and *The Other Place*, the causes of the
dystopian worlds are possible in our own world, although the solutions may
lie in outer space. I wrote *Devil on My Back* when geologists were predicting
the dire effects of the depletion of Earth's fossil fuels. I imagined a world in
turmoil, and a university determined to preserve knowledge in those chaotic
times in underground cities. I originally got the idea for the book from reading in a business journal how "one day we might have micro-processors
attached to our own bodies." In the book, not everyone can integrate into the
new "plug-in" knowledge, and society splits into the "haves" and the "have
nots." In the ensuing totalitarian society a kind of utopia is found, not in the
city but among the runaway slaves who have escaped to form an agrarian
society. It is only outside the system that a better world can be found.

The ideas for both *Invitation to the Game* and *The Other Place* came
from political problems here on Earth: in the first book, the lack of jobs in
Thatcherite England leads to children leaving school to go on the dole, with
no promise of future meaningful work; the second was inspired by stories of
the "disappeared" in some South American countries. In each case the question "What would happen if?" plunged me into a dystopian world from
which I can, at first, see little chance of a reversal to a more utopian world. In
fact, the only way out I can see is into space. Only away from Earth can the
protagonists find the promise of a new beginning—not a utopia, certainly, but
its possibility. Although set within the genre of otherworld fiction, both of
these stories invite the reader to consider Earth as a possible utopia, a world
in which sustainable development, cooperation, and mutual caring replace
the dubious god of technology.

My final dystopian worlds are set on other planets, although in both The
Isis Trilogy and *The Golden Aquarians*, the themes are models of earthly
problems, both social and political (though such lofty thoughts were not in
my mind when I wrote them.) The Isis Trilogy began as a response to the
story of David, "the boy in the glass bubble," condemned to total isolation

because he lacks immune defenses. Is David lonely? I mused, and out of this question slowly emerged *The Keeper of the Isis Light*, the story of Olwen, the only human being on Isis before a shipload of settlers arrives from Earth. Olwen has been genetically altered by her robot Guardian to be able to withstand the environment. After Mark London rejects her, he transfers his guilt to a hatred of the meddling Guardian and of technology in general. Later, in *The Guardian of Isis*, when he becomes leader of a new settlement, he subverts its development through his rigid attitude and rejection of any technological advances, and it becomes a stagnant, fear-ridden world. Only by introducing a wild card—Mike Flynn—in *The Isis Pedlar* am I able to get Isis back on track, to the possibility of a utopian future.

In *The Golden Aquarians*, outsiders also meddle with a utopian planet to no good end. This book began with a mental image of an alien being on a watery planet and a trip to the glow-worm cave at Waitomo, New Zealand. The mysterious inhabitants of Aqua are metamorphosing amphibians, froglike creatures. At the beginning of the story, Aqua's environment is already being destroyed by the driving ambitions of the planet-shaper, Angus Elliot; however, his son Walt gradually realizes that the froglike Aquarians are truly intelligent, sentient beings. His attempts to save the planet fail, and the Golden Aquarians must reject the human invaders to restore their utopian world. Back on Earth, Angus Elliot is slowly healed, his driving ambitions reined in, and he achieves a kind of personal utopia.

As I look back on these books, I become aware of the external forces that caused them to be shaped in the way they were. Reading the daily newspaper has been an endless source of inspiration. In *Ring-Rise, Ring-Set*, for instance, while my imperative was to answer the question, What would happen if another ice age threatened North America?, inside me was an indignant response to the trials of the indigenous people of the Amazon rainforest, and to those of the native peoples of northern Canada, whose unrecognized land claims were being threatened by the proposed Norman Well pipeline. Similarly, in *The Crystal Drop*, written during the construction of the Old Man River dam, I found an unexpected voice in the protests of environmental and native groups against the unnecessary damming of this river. When I was writing *The Tomorrow City*, I read that the Pentagon was anxious to obtain next-generation computers capable of independent thought, which could be useful in deciding whether to go to war or not. A choice of life or death left to a computer? What a horrifying thought!

In both *The Isis Pedlar* and *The Golden Aquarians*, the plots hinge on catastrophic damage done to the environment and to the fragile social network sustained by it, and I was very aware, from reading the daily news, of the damage that could be caused by various proposed monumental projects. After reading about Gaia and "the Goldilocks Effect," which postulates that Earth maintains her "just right" place in the solar system by proper temperature, the right amount of oxygen and carbon dioxide, and so on, through a most delicate balance, I believe that my sense of this precariousness has surfaced in my writing. To me, the possibilities of dystopias are only too immediate.

I may lead a child into the darkness, but I must never turn out the light. On the other hand, the "happy ever after" utopian world is a trap to be guarded against. Often the utopian world is not actually realized at the end of my novels, but is promised only with the proviso that the protagonists continue to work together amicably, aware of the causes of the dystopia from which they have escaped, and determined to maintain—or renew—the quality of their world without exploiting resources or people.

As the tides shape the shore in many different ways, subtle or dramatic, so the events of the day shape the work of the writer; it is usually not until a book is finished that I become fully aware of what I have been doing in the shaping of these dystopian worlds and in trying to find solutions. There is the initiating "what if?" question; the necessity of a gripping plot; and always, at the end, the necessity of nurturing hope. These elements form, I hope, a paradigm of our own journey through this precarious world—and what writing for children is all about.

PART IV

From the Wreckage: Post–World War II Dystopias and Utopias

13

Presenting the Case for Social Change: The Creative Dilemma of Dystopian Writing for Children

KAY SAMBELL

Since the late 1960s the futuristic fiction written for young readers has been disposed to make serious and disturbing comment on the likely direction of human civilization. During the 1970s and to the present day, a dark literature of emergency and despair has developed, expressing deep-rooted fears for the future of those children being addressed. As this dystopian genre has developed, its nightmarish imaginative landscapes have become increasingly intolerable, presenting a variety of repressive and tyrannically controlled states, whether writers conceive these as being neoprimitive or hypertechnological in essence. In the 1980s devastatingly bleak visions of the horrifying aftermath of nuclear war emerged, adding new levels of pessimism and concern about the future. Writers' hypotheses about humankind's likely lines of development have proved far from optimistic, and this large genre in children's publishing has become characterized by extreme, arguably unprecedented, levels of anxiety and hopelessness.

Commentators frequently refer to this dystopian futuristic literature's "purpose" or "function," which is usually perceived to be twofold. First, the literature primarily cautions young readers about the probable dire consequences of current human behaviors. Second, as Eric Rabkin notes, it is driven by the impulse to counsel hope and present the case for urgent social change.[1] Like all admonitory literature, it acts as what Barbara Harrison describes as a "call of the imagination to the ethical,"[2] and represents an authorial quest to suggest a new moral course for young readers. It seeks to shock its readership into a realization of the urgent need for a radical revisioning of current human political and social organization, and even of human nature itself. If people do not change, it warns, the future looks devastatingly bleak.

The tendency to use an exclusively pessimistic frame of reference and worst-case future scenarios to raise children's awareness about the dire consequences of undesirable political, technological, and social ideologies presents authors with fascinating tactical challenges. If, as Robert Scholes suggests, the dystopia presents the "adult" writer with "artistic problems,"[3] these are considerably heightened by the ethical and educational responsibilities normally associated with writing for children. The problems of reconciling the aim of presenting the dark truth of the values against which one cautions, whilst simultaneously maintaining a sharp focus on hope (often regarded as essential for the young) forms a significant creative dilemma for children's authors using the dystopian narrative form.

Although individuals stand in different relations to the question of whether a children's book should offer happiness, the perceived responsibility to point young readers actively toward a better world exerts a powerful influence on the literature produced, making it very difficult to adopt the narrative tactics of the classic "adult" dystopia without compromise. Many children's authors seem reluctant to risk dystopian narrative strategies wholeheartedly, perhaps fearing that children could misinterpret their fiction by failing to realize they are writing to prompt child readers to take responsibility and exercise their power to change the world, *before* it is too late. In short, like Jonathon Porritt, they fear their writing may, instead, allow young readers to fall into the trap of an "apocalyptic despair which merely disempowers those whom one seeks to reinvigorate."[4]

I will explore the consequences of the reluctance to depict a wholly negative, unrelievedly bleak fictional future world for children. In what follows I will focus on some of the features that set children's dystopian novels apart from classic "adult" dystopias that extrapolate from present trends to predict horrifyingly credible versions of humankind's likely development. I will particularly concentrate on the question of imaginative closure to discuss the ways in which the didacticism is carried in this dystopian literature. Without wishing to devalue the genre, I believe children's writers pose themselves immense tactical dilemmas by choosing prophetic story forms to carry their social criticism, which emphasize prediction and plausibility in line with their classic adult antecedents. Whereas the "adult" dystopia's didactic impact relies on the absolute, unswerving nature of its dire warning, the expression of moral meaning in the children's dystopia is often characterized by degrees of hesitation, oscillation, and ambiguity. In the adult dystopian vision, morally appealing heroes are unequivocally shown to fail. Jenni Calder points out that any hope they represent is extinguished in the dystopia's denouement.[5] By presenting child protagonists as agents of moral transformation within the text, or at least by hesitating to depict the extinction of such hope in the narrative resolution to their stories, children's authors risk fracturing or undermining the imaginative and ideological coherence of their admonitory fictional worlds.

It is not difficult to see why children's authors are reluctant to depict the extinction of hope within their stories. According to Harrison, hope is "traditionally the animating force in children's books" (Harrison, 69). Natalie Babbit, for example, believes an optimistic outlook is the key characteristic distinguishing children's literature from adults': "something which turns the story ultimately toward hope rather than resignation and contains within it a difference not only between the two literatures but also between youth and age."[6] The convention of the happy ending, in which answers or solutions are eventually supplied, a reassuring return to normality is secured, or a successful outcome to the hero's quest is achieved, is so pervasive that it amounts to an unwritten law in the production of children's books. The perceived need to offer hope and reassurance to young readers makes it extremely difficult for an author to disturb what Perry Nodelman calls the "unspoken convention[s]" of the (at least partially) optimistic ending.[7] Novels that are not seen to conform in any way to these beliefs are likely to meet with critical condemnation as, for instance, in the notorious controversy over the "negative, seemingly hopeless conclusions" of Robert Cormier's fictions.[8]

The pressures that are brought to bear on the children's writer may be due to perceptions of the author's ethical duty to protect young readers' idealism, or may concern the predicted levels of reading competence in young readers. Possibly the "formulaic plots with happy endings" that Nodelman observes have emerged in the belief that it is simpler and safer to expect developing readers to endorse simple affirmations, and more demanding and risky to expect them to respond to ironies, qualifications, and unstated moral meanings (Nodelman, 19). Whatever the reason, however, the artistic problems raised by the desire to conform to the return-to-normality closure that provides some measure of reassurance present particular challenges for the resolution of the admonitory dystopian novel, whose didactic impact relies instead on an unequivocally pessimistic denouement.

The narrative closure of the protagonist's final defeat and failure is absolutely crucial to the admonitory impulse of the classic adult dystopia, such as George Orwell's *Nineteen Eighty-Four*,[9] Aldous Huxley's *Brave New World*,[10] and William Golding's "anti-utopia" *Lord of the Flies*.[11] For example, Kathleen Woodward draws attention to *Lord of the Flies'* "programmatic intent" which is designed "to 'prove' a hypothesis,"[12] and Howard Babb highlights how Golding's novel acts as a fictional laboratory experiment whose method is "radically conditioned by meaning," the entire fictional structure being "created with a view to its significance."[13] These bleak visions rely on the absolute predictability of their unhappy conclusions to corroborate their imaginative hypotheses.

As Scholes suggests, in this sense futuristic dystopias tend to be predictive narratives, based on extrapolatory, probable future scenarios that seek to "draw out the consequences of human actions to their logical conclusions" (Scholes, 70) rather than to speculate imaginatively about alternative, visionary future possibilities. He claims that they

predict on the basis of current knowledge in the fields of political science,
economics, psychology, sociology, and the other human sciences. Such fictions often attain great emotional power in a very interesting way. They present a noticeable discontinuity with our current situation—but they insist
that . . . it is in fact a reasonable projection of existing trends. . . . while
nevertheless shocking us by their difference from the world that . . . we are
presently functioning in reasonably well. . . ." (Scholes, 72)

The unequivocally unhappy endings of these novels are necessary to under-
line the point that, unless urgent change is undertaken, and soon, then the
very principles of human happiness and even life itself are under threat.
The social and political choices that have been taken in these ruined worlds
must be recognized as irrevocable and excluding traditionally cherished
values utterly. The shocking failure of the potentially "heroic" or morally
appealing individuals (Winston, John, Simon, Piggy, and to some degree,
Bernard and Ralph) serve to prove this point. Given such future circumstances they can only be portrayed as victims who are hopelessly trapped in
their grave situations. In Orwell and Huxley's conditioned worlds, protagonists literally possess no means to envisage an alternative and their potentially heroic struggles are inexorably bound to fail. Their final defeat
is necessary to highlight the dire consequences of the extinction of moral
belief.

An examination of the biological metaphor underpinning the adult
antecedents reveals the consistency of all the narrative features of these classic dystopias. In these conditioned societies the thesis is that, by accepting a
final solution based on perfection and stability, humanity has perversely
resisted and opposed life itself. The opportunity for adaptation and change,
the principle on which evolutionary change relies, has been systematically
removed. This way lies extinction and death, realized by the denouement.

For instance, in *Nineteen Eighty-Four*, Winston inhabits a terrifyingly
credible world of constant surveillance, in which the totalitarian Party brutally controls people's lives by feeding them lies and systematically alienat-
ing them from others. Drawn into an illicit love affair, Winston joins a
revolutionary organization, but eventually learns the shattering truth that
invalidates his defiant hopefulness. O'Brien tells him, "[y]ou are imagining
that there is something called human nature which will be outraged by what
we do and will turn against us. But we create human nature" (*Nineteen*, 227).

The novel relentlessly plays out the consequences of this assumption,
proving Winston's powerlessness to be nothing but a product of the system,
as he is unavoidably trapped by his conditioned self, incapable of radical
thought. Any optimistic expectations the reader may be anticipated to hold
are repeatedly dashed, and Winston inevitably betrays Julia, as his "love" is
proved to be finite. Hope no longer exists, as O'Brien makes clear: "If you
are a man, Winston, then you are the last man. Your kind is extinct; we are the

inheritors" (*Nineteen*, 228). The plot is inexorably driven in the single direction of decline and defeat. In similar vein John the Savage is unable to continue living in Huxley's brave new world and, as Calder suggests, Bernard remains utterly trapped, "hopelessly himself" in his manufactured state (Calder, 36).

Not conditioned, but victims of human nature, Simon, Piggy, and Ralph are physically inferior when forced to compete with aggressive brutes or, worse, fatally tempted to violence. Golding attempts to achieve utter clarity by arranging the signs of death, decay, and the evil in man without ambiguity. To that effect, the sow's head dubbed "Lord of the Flies" or Beelzebub is "a plain reference, plainly stated" (Woodward, 201). Golding outlines why dystopian writers exercise such strict control over their narratives, resisting plurality of meaning in order to heavily guide understanding: "The fabulist is a moralist. . . . Arranging signs as he does, he reaches, not profundity on many levels, but what you would expect from signs, that is, overt significance. By the nature of his craft then, the fabulist is didactic, desires to inculcate a moral lesson."[14] The conclusion must leave no room for ambiguity on the reader's part. Authorial or reader hesitation would jeopardize the admonitory intent. Golding's island paradise is ultimately reduced to an inferno by the boys' actions and Ralph's "rescue" is ironically conducted by an officer who represents the technological capacity for nuclear aggression on a scale that was unavailable to the boys. The denouement thus underlines the urgent need to value cooperation and communication, and fundamentally change human nature *before* it is too late.

Paradoxically, these fictions require highly independent responses. The unequivocally unhappy denouement expects the reader to react to unstated moral meanings. It demands the implied reader reject the imaginative world and assume a role of responsibility to rewrite the social world, convinced of the need to strive for political and social improvement on more sane principles. Golding explains that "the true reason for the invention of an antiutopia" is that "[t]he antiutopian wants to be proved wrong. No antiutopian desires to hurt. . . . *Surely* we can . . . find something a bit better! . . . We must produce *homo moralis*, the human being who cannot kill his own kind. . . ."[15]

The children's author Robert Swindells makes strikingly similar claims in the afterword to *Brother in the Land*,[16] his novel predicting the realistic consequences of the horrifying aftermath of future nuclear war. This supplemented the original text some two years after its original publication and concludes by addressing the child reader directly: "There is no hope in my story because it is about a time after the bombs have fallen. The hope—the one hope—is that your generation will prove wiser and more responsible than mine, and that the bombs will not fall" (*Brother*, 1986, 153). Swindells's later addition of an epilogue is interesting, not because it illuminates his intentions, but because it reveals his concern to qualify and control young readers' responses to the bleak fictional world that has preceded it by explicitly focusing on hope. Herein lies the key to some essential differences between classic dystopian novels for adults and those commonly produced for children. *Brother in the Land*'s revised resolution becomes the site of different kinds of hesitation and equivocation that do not characterize the classic adult dystopias.

The first type of prevarication—authorial hesitation—is revealed by the revisions that Swindells has made to his original text. His apparent reservations about using dystopian forms for children have led to the publication of three different versions of the book. All of these versions coexist simultaneously at the time of writing, and in each the conclusion is the only aspect that has been altered.

The initial version of *Brother in the Land* was published in 1984.[17] It depicts a worst-case scenario, extrapolating and predicting the devastating probable consequences of widespread nuclear warfare. Shocking and brutal images of death and decay pervade the novel from the outset, underlining the unequivocal undesirability of this future. The horrifying physical effects of the blast are described in uncompromising terms: "his face was a mass of raw flesh. Great puffy blisters clustered around the eye" (*Brother*, 1984, 14). But the horror only deepens as the novel warns about the dystopian, brutish social landscape that ensues. The book soon turns to raising serious questions about the cruelty and aggression inherent in human nature, and the political and social organizations that are likely to emerge in a period of extreme scarcity. Society breaks down as people fight brutally in a struggle for literal survival. Bands of cannibalistic savages terrorize the land. Traumatized and powerless, ordinary citizens wait for help, only to find that the hospital they are taken to is actually an extermination camp. In such a world morally superior characters seem bound for extinction, because physical survival now relies on ruthless aggression: "Cavemen versus gentlemen. Hardness versus compassion. No contest" (*Brother*, 1984, 42). Life itself has become a competition that excludes humane values.

As if to prove the incontrovertible logic of this dystopian thesis, Swindells plays out the failure of a commune based on cooperative principles. This is ironically named MASADA, in allusion to the besieged Jewish revolutionary fortress that, having held out bravely against insurmountable attacks, ultimately chose to commit suicide rather than face defeat and slavery as the invaders inevitably breached its defenses. Branwell, a Christ-like peaceful leader, is unable to preserve a utopian space in which children can thrive, for within the novel's hostile literal and metaphorical environment it is too late. The commune is forced to disperse and fight for survival. The crops inevitably fail and soon mouthless "Hiroshima babies" are born, incapable of survival (*Brother*, 1984, 126).

The full impact of such horror is experienced via the perspective of a teenager, Danny, who struggles to protect his younger brother, Ben, as best he can. By the end of the novel, though, Ben dies of radiation sickness. In the final chapter Danny leaves his home with Kim, having just buried the child. Leaving a written account that warns of "everything that happened after the nukes" (*Brother*, 1984, 150), the two move off into an unwritten future in this dangerous world. The novel closes: "And so now I end it, and it is for little Ben, my brother. In the land" (*Brother*, 1984, 151). Danny's last words, dwelling on his grief, loss, and sense of horror at the ugliness of his world, imply a tone of personal defeat and resignation. They are likely to propel the reader back into the hopelessness of the text's imaginative world, in which the dominant signs predict that Danny and Kim's survival, too, is hugely improbable. Their story seems at an end, given the predictive logic of the preceding dystopian scenario, which offered no indication of the possibility of the existence of a safe space for children.

But, by leaving their future suspended as an unwritten conclusion, Swindells struggles to leave room for a potential reading that not only allows for the slim possibility of the couple's literal survival, but also for the unde-feated, enduring nature of Danny's fraternal and sexual love. Danny's closing statement may be interpreted not as a despairing recognition of his incapacity to protect his brother, but instead as a testament to the indomitable nature of the human spirit, recalling Branwell's hopeful assertion, "They haven't killed that, have they. With their bombs and their hunger and their cold" (*Brother*, 1984, 144). The reality of Danny's love for Kim and Ben is not absolutely closed down, as it is for Winston. The preceding signs probably predict, how-ever, that it is fatally jeopardized in the dystopian environment.

The relatively uncompromising nature of this narrative resolution has subsequently been subject to two important authorial revisions that attempt to focus even more explicitly on hope. The addition of the afterword, to which I referred earlier, takes the form of a subjoined conclusion—an inor-ganic annex to the story in which the author addresses the reader directly to explain his aim of bringing home the "full horror of what people will contemplate doing to each other in the name of ideology" (*Brother*, 1986, 152).

The subjoined ending is revealing in two ways. First it implies an authorial reluctance to place absolute trust in child readers' capacities to grasp the didactic impulse underpinning the extinction metaphor of the dystopia without being guided by overt authorial comment. Second, it highlights a tendency for children's authors to present *explicitly* the possi-bility of a "theoretically safe world" (Nodelman, 20), which is capable, at least to some extent, of offering the view that benign forces can and do exist, and that ultimately "everything will always be all right" (Babbitt, 159). In the new subjoined ending, Swindells closes with the hopeful assertion that children will act to prevent this nightmare scenario: "Soon our lovely, fragile world will pass into your hands. Safe hands, I believe" (*Brother*, 1986, 153). Here the final assurance of the possibility of a safe space for children is importantly located in the reader's world, not in that of the child protagonist.

Fourteen years later an even more radical textual revision occurred, with the production of a new final chapter. The third version of the text eschews the didactic annex, and instead offers a new resolution of the story itself. After Ben's burial, Danny plans to leave his diary in the house before moving on in the spring. But this time, Kim intervenes: " 'Don't Danny. It's not finished.' She meant our story. 'Write *to be continued*, and bring it along.' So I did, and she was right. It wasn't finished."[18]

The revised version then traces the teenagers' journey to Lindisfarne or Holy Island, the missionary center from which Christianity spread in the seventh century, where the possibility of a safe space to live is explicitly offered within the text. The island is renamed New Beginning. Like the failed MASADA, it is an agricultural commune, but "with one crucial difference: it was guarded day and night by men and women with an armed forces background" (*Brother*, 2000, 152). This final chapter concludes two years later, with Danny looking forward to the birth of his and Kim's baby. He is confident, as three other babies born on the island "are thriving. No missing bits, no extra bits" (*Brother*, 2000, 152). He plans to name the child after his brother in the land.

Swindells has clearly provided more optimistic signs in this revision, but the overall impact is more significant than the clichéd happy ending that this brief summary may suggest. The final despairing certainty of the adult dystopian denouement is instead replaced with a level of ambivalence that I would argue is reasonably characteristic of most children's dystopian texts. The revised plotting of the final chapter veers in an almost dancelike structure of progression and regression, oscillating extravagantly between signs of hope and fear for the protagonists' future. The previous levels of ambiguity about human nature and the social organizations that will ensue are heightened by this tactic, and the scope for different degrees of resolution to Danny's unwritten future are dramatically increased.

Although the original text did not absolutely close down the possibility of Danny's future survival, it was significantly muted by the contemplative, backward-looking emphasis of his closing reflections. By comparison, the revised chapter remains brief, but is now packed with movement and rapidly evolving events, so the pace quickens to anticipate the resolution, looking forward rather than backward. The revision also ultimately places much greater stress on the dual possibility of Danny's hopes of survival and the fear of his failure. In short, the emphasis shifts from the near-certainty of his predicted defeat (as generated by the admonitory preceding dystopian narrative logic) to allow for a speculative, ambiguous outcome instead. Metaphorically, the children now more clearly represent the multiple possibilities of an evolving species, rather than simply one inevitably bound for extinction.

To this end, the signs of the possibility of utopian idealism are much more heavily underscored than in the original version. It is spring when the children move onward, as opposed to the winter snow and rain to which the original text referred. The couple's journey, by Branwell's donkey, to a place where they plan to bear a child has obvious optimistic allusive overtones. But repeatedly interleaved with all of these signs of hopeful redemption and regeneration are indications of distress and denial. The journey is nearly fatal, and the children only narrowly escape starvation and being killed by marauding savages.

Yet the children do survive the journey, against all the odds. Their hopeful arrival at the coast "in May, very early in the morning with sunrise gilding the sea" (*Brother*, 2000, 151), however, immediately veers back to describe the dashing of their hopes as they discover that the island is already occupied. An ominous "smudge of smoke" above the castle prompts them to hide fearfully in the "rusted shell" of a decaying van (*Brother*, 2000, 151). The children's dreams of finding a viable space are soon transformed into the "forlorn hope" that they will simply evade being seen by the islanders (*Brother*, 2000, 152). Their evasion proves unsuccessful, as the islanders send out an armored car to train a machine gun on the children. Outnumbered and disarmed by men, who dauntingly resemble the brutal officials earlier in the novel, the children experience their fortunes changing again. Abruptly they find themselves awaiting the worst: "We honestly thought it was the end" (*Brother*, 2000, 152). The final two paragraphs then rapidly veer back once more toward a hopeful assertion: "But it wasn't. Instead it was a beginning" (*Brother*, 2000, 152). Rather than being killed, they are clothed and cared for. The final paragraph leaps forward two years to finally leave Danny looking forward to the birth of his baby.

Unlike the adult dystopias, Swindells's revised conclusion is structured so that it is no longer possible to predict what will happen to the protagonists with any degree of confidence. The dancelike form of the oscillating final chapter serves to destabilize the reader's certainty. On one level this could simply be viewed as an authorial evasion of the dire consequences of his predictive dystopian scenario, and a tendency to present young readers with clichéd anodyne solutions that are at odds with, or unequal to, the daunting questions raised by the preceding text. I suggest, instead, that it represents a characteristic search for a narrative solution equal to the challenges of adapting the dystopian form for a young readership. By increasing the degrees of ambiguity in the resolution authors may seek to provoke a third level of hesitation within the genre: reader hesitation. The expression of moral meaning thus takes a different literary guise in dystopian writing for children from the didacticism of the adult antecedents.

The revised, more open ending attempts to legitimate a spectrum of possible readings. These range between two extremes. One extreme speculates that Danny will miraculously begin a new, morally improved evolutionary line. The other predicts that this will be impossible, given the scenario he inherits, and that his extinction will follow. But in either case, the marked oscillation within the narrative structure is used to insist that either projected outcome of the open ending is importantly qualified. In other words, it insists that readers think twice about the evidence on which they base their forecasts, by forcing a reassessment of the values under discussion. Readers who ultimately respond to Danny's confident optimism have already been forced to hesitate in their analysis of a community that relies so heavily on lethal technology and ruthless selection and protection policies, and in the capacity of the natural world to override the nuclear havoc wreaked upon it. The reader who ultimately concludes it is too late for Danny has, conversely, been forced into hesitation by the explicit realization of a utopian space for childhood and biological continuity on New Beginning.

Similar forms of hesitation and prevarication routinely characterize the resolution of the children's dystopia. Children's writers tend to replace the unequivocal unhappy ending of the adult antecedents with more ambiguous, open structures, in which the story appears to be incomplete as it stands. Often authors ultimately suggest the future possibility, however slim, of a safe space that child protagonists may inhabit. Despite employing worst-case future dystopian scenarios in which it is too late, either because the bombs have fallen as in Swindells's world,[19] or because insurrection and change are logically impossible in conditioned worlds,[20] remarkably few unequivocally depict the utter defeat of their child protagonists. Many seek to circumvent the logical consequences of the predictive dystopian scenario in which their child protagonists are cast, and implausibly lucky escapes are legion.[21]

For instance, despite inhabiting a world in which citizens are systematically brainwashed, drugged, or biologically engineered, thus being literally rendered powerless to exercise political resistance, child protagonists rarely ultimately suffer the despairing defeat of Orwell's Winston. In William Sleator's *House of Stairs* (1974),[22] for example, children are treated like rats in an unethical experiment, being subjected to a form of behavior modification that means they must behave cruelly toward their peers or suffer terrible physical consequences. The stakes are so high (their literal survival depends on their moral choices) that they are predicted to fail or die. Sleator, however, resists playing out the consequences of their moral choices, and finally miraculously rescues those children who seem to prefer to die rather than act immorally. They are sent to an island where they can begin their own social utopia, which, given the text's view of human nature, may or may not succeed in the unwritten future of the ending. Similarly, among many others, Watford Nine John in G. R. Kesteven's *The Awakening Water* (1977),[23] Ergo Norm in Alison Prince's *The Others* (1986),[24] and Mick and Lucy in Enid Richemont's *The Game* (1990)[25] are ultimately offered happy endings of a sort, in which they have the chance to create a new, optimistic social order. However much the author tries to qualify these upbeat resolutions and render them ambiguous, the characters' partially successful insurrection seems hugely implausible, given the terms of the preceding narrative logic.[26]

This tendency for children's writers to compromise the adult dystopian denouement has routinely attracted adverse critical reaction. It is often viewed as an evasive tactic, in which the author somehow finally tries to dodge or ignore the logical consequences of the preceding text. Gwenda Bond draws attention to the scope for self-contradiction and fracture within the text, suggesting that in such realistic stories "contrived happy endings will not do, on a human or a literary level."[27] Winfred Kaminski[28] and Paul Brians complain that resolutions to teenage dystopian novels often appear naïve, sentimental, trivial, facile, or "bogus."[29] John Stephens finds much post–nuclear holocaust literature for children "simplistic and false . . . because it takes the form of an heroic narrative moving toward an optimistic outcome."[30]

It may be, however, that in many cases this is a more complex phenomenon than a straightforward attempt to help young readers to converge on a stated ideological preference by means of the so-called happy ending. Instead, I think it may fruitfully be seen as a struggle to achieve a new, more fluid style of didacticism in dystopian writing for children. As they try to adapt the form, children's writers often appear to explore ways of increasing the scope for the reader's interaction within the fictional worlds being offered, rather than simply arguing like their predecessors for moral responsibility to be exercised *outside* the novel. The text itself becomes a space that sometimes tries to create conditions for young readers to rehearse, actively, almost playfully, a way of reflective thinking that focuses on asking questions, discovering analyses, and hypothetically testing out solutions at their own pace in an imaginative environment that is affirming and supportive, but which also articulates dark truths. The reader is invited to exercise a degree of choice in the narrative, thus affecting what it will become.

This tactic means, however, that authors must find ways of progressively resisting the pessimistic thesis of the dystopian scenarios they have invoked. The task of moving from an admonitory, authorially controlled style of didacticism toward one underpinned by a spirit of learner activity and inquiry is so demanding that it is not likely to be achieved lightly, nor very often. It is not impossible, and a few novels are elaborately structured[31] to allow for multiple interpretations throughout the whole text, achieving the profound levels of imaginative and ideological coherence that overcomes the artistic dilemmas of the form. Yet, given the deep sensitivity to audience required of the children's novelist, perhaps the predominantly admonitory content and form of the dystopian novel is not as conducive to the aims of children's writers as so many authors appear to believe.

Notes

1. Eric S. Rabkin, "Atavism and Utopia," in *No Place Else*: *Explorations in Utopian and Dystopian Fictions*, ed. Eric S. Rabkin, Martin H. Greenburg, Joseph D. Olander (Carbondale and Edwardville, Ill.: Southern Illinois University Press, 1983), 1.

2. Barbara Harrison, "Howl Like the Wolves," *Children's Literature* 15 (1987): 86; hereafter cited in text.

3. Robert Scholes, *Structural Fabulation*: *An Essay on Fiction of the Future* (Notre Dame and London: University of Notre Dame Press, 1975), 79; hereafter cited in text.

4. Jonathon Porritt, Foreword, in *A Green Manifesto*: *policies for a green future*, ed. Sandy Irvine and Alec Ponton (London: Optima, 1988), ix.

5. Jenni Calder, *Huxley and Orwell*: Brave New World *and* Nineteen Eighty-Four, Studies in English Literature, no. 63 (London: Edward Arnold, 1976), 40.

6. Natalie Babbit, "Happy Endings? Of Course, and Also Joy," *Children's Literature*: *Views and Reviews*, ed. Virginia Haviland (London: Bodley Head, 1973), 158; hereafter cited in text.

7. Perry Nodelman, "Doing Violence to Conventions: The Work of Ilse-Margret Vogel," *Children's Literature* 15 (1987): 19.

8. Margaret R. Higonnet, "Narrative Fractures and Fragments," *Children's Literature* 15 (1987): 49.

9. George Orwell, *Nineteen Eighty-Four* (1949) (Harmondsworth, England: 1984); hereafter cited in text as *Nineteen*.

10. Aldous Huxley, *Brave New World* (London: Chatto and Windus, 1932).

11. William Golding, *Lord of the Flies* (London: Faber and Faber, 1954). In "Utopias and Antiutopias," Golding outlined his own view of the terms. Utopias represent human aspirations and propose ideal paradigms for working toward a "perfected society" or "happier order of things" which "glitters . . . against a background of social darkness" ("Utopias and Antiutopias," in *A Moving Target* [London: Faber and Faber, 1982], 174). An anti-utopia, on the other hand, paints "a more terrible picture of what man might become" in order to "forc[e] an unhappy truth upon readers" (180). It acts as a "cry for help and a cry of despair" (180). *Lord of the Flies*, he claims, is anti-utopian in tone, stemming from the awful knowledge about humankind's capacity for hate, selfishness, and lack of cooperation that emerged for him during and after the Second World War.

12. Kathleen Woodward, "On Aggression: William Golding's *Lord of the Flies*," in *No Place Else: Explorations in Utopian and Dystopian Fiction*, ed. Eric

S. Rabkin, Martin H. Greenburg, Joseph D. Olander (Carbondale and Edwardsville, Ill.: Southern Illinois University Press, 1983), 204.

13. Howard S. Babb, *The Novels of William Golding* (Columbus, Ohio: Ohio State University Press, 1970), 15; hereafter cited in text.

14. William Golding, "Fable," in *The Cool Web: The Pattern of Children's Reading*, ed. Margaret Meek, Aidan Warlow, and Griselda Barton (London: The Bodley Head, 1977), 227.

15. William Golding, "Utopias and Antiutopias," in *A Moving Target* (London: Faber and Faber, 1982), 182–84.

16. Robert Swindells, *Brother in the Land* (1984), with author's afterword (Harmondsworth, England: Puffin Books, 1986); hereafter cited in text as *Brother*, 1986.

17. Robert Swindells, *Brother in the Land* (Oxford: Oxford University Press, 1984); hereafter cited in text as *Brother*, 1984.

18. Robert Swindells, *Brother in the Land* (1984) (Harmondsworth, England: Puffin Books, 2000), 150; hereafter cited in text as *Brother*, 2000.

19. For other postnuclear holocaust children's texts see, for example: Gudrun Pausewang's *The Last Children* (1988); Victor Kelleher's *Taronga* (1986); Hugh Scott's *Why Weeps the Brogan?* (1989); Whitley Streiber's *Wolf of Shadows* (1986). These works all depict the likely realistic outcomes of a nuclear strike and are narrated from the perspective of the young people (or, in Streiber's case, a wolf pack) who, as victims, suffer the dreadful consequences of this misuse of technology and science, but who are left at the novel's end looking forward hopefully to a new beginning.

20. Examples of conditioned, highly controlled worlds that have developed along the lines of Huxley or Orwell's scenarios include G. R. Kesteven's *The Awakening Water* (1977); John Christopher's *The Guardians* (1970); John Tully's *Natfact 7* (1984); Ann Schlee's *The Vandal* (1979); Alison Prince's *The Others* (1986); Enid Richemont's *The Game* (1990); Monica Hughes's *Devil On My Back* (1984); Tom Browne's *Red Zone* (1980) and William Sleator's *House of Stairs* (1974). In these books children are physically drugged, brainwashed, tortured, or brutalized in such a systematic manner by the Party or the State that they seem powerless to resist.

21. For example, in Tom Browne's *Red Zone*, Slagerman, the hero's brutal assailant, is implausibly run over by a truck just as he is about to slaughter Clem. In Robert Swindells's *Daz for Zoe*, the hero has an incredibly lucky escape from a band of murderous vandals. The frequency with which some very accomplished writers resort to this strategy illustrates a key departure from the classic dystopian novel. Perhaps this serves to supply a hopeful view within the text itself, rather than trusting the reader to supply it.

22. William Sleator, *House of Stairs* (1974) (New York: Puffin Books, 1991).

23. G. R. Kestevan, *The Awakening Water* (London: Chatto, 1977).

24. Alison Prince, *The Others* (London: Methuen, 1986).

25. Enid Richemont, *The Game* (London: Walker Books, 1990).

26. The only exceptions I have traced are Jan Mark's *The Ennead* (1978); Elisabeth Mace's *The Travelling Man* (1976); and Louise Lawrence's *Andra* (1971). In these texts the possibility of a happy resolution is utterly denied.

The consequences of the scenario are played out relentlessly, and in each the protagonist ultimately dies. Andra's death holds the possibility of representing a heroically defiant gesture in the face of defeat, but Will in *The Travelling Man* and Isaac in *The Ennead* are, as products of the system in which they live, ruthless and morally bankrupt characters. As such they are unusual in children's fiction, as is the authorial commitment to unequivocally portray an unhappy resolution.

27.   Gwena Bond, "Honesty and Hope: Presenting Human Rights Issues to Teenagers Through Fiction," *Children's Literature in Education* 25 (1994): 52.

28.   Winfred Kaminski, "War and Peace in Recent German Children's Literature," trans. J. D. Stahl, *Children's Literature* 15 (1987): 55–66.

29.   Paul Brians, "Nuclear War Fiction for Young Readers: A Commentary and Annotated Bibliography," in *Science Fiction, Social Conflict and War*, ed. Philip Davies (Manchester: Manchester University Press, 1990), 137.

30.   John Stephens, "Post Disaster Fiction: The Problematics of a Genre," *Papers* 3 (1992): 43.

31.   I believe Robert C. O'Brien's *Z for Zachariah* (1975) is structured in such a way. The whole text is arranged to offer a spectrum of possible readings. On one level, like *Lord of the Flies*, the novel can be read as a fable predicting human decline and extinction unless a radical change in human nature occurs. Loomis invades and corrupts Ann's utopian valley, predictably driving her out in his selfish urge to possess, kill, rule, and compete. Interpreted thus, survival is not possible and the text's open ending, in which Ann leaves the valley in search of another place to live, is viewed pessimistically. The text also supports a reading, however, that views both characters sympathetically. Loomis, for instance, can be viewed as using science to foster and preserve life, rather than destroy it. The unwritten possibilities of Ann's eventual realization of her utopian dreams are rooted in many signs within the preceding text. For instance, Loomis successfully survived *his* journey in the wilderness and found the valley. A mature Ann may change and return to successfully negotiate a sustainable relationship with him. By providing considerable scope throughout the text for readers to make their own interpretive choices, O'Brien skillfully adapts the dystopian form for a child readership.

Works Cited

Babb, Howard S. *The Novels of William Golding*. Columbus, Ohio: Ohio State University Press, 1970.

Babbit, Natalie. "Happy Endings? Of Course, and Also Joy." In *Children's Literature: Views and Reviews*, ed. Virginia Haviland, 155–59. London: Bodley Head, 1973.

Bond, Gwenda. "Honesty and Hope: Presenting Human Rights Issues to Teenagers Through Fiction." *Children's Literature in Education* 25 (1994): 41–53.

Brians, Paul. "Nuclear War Fiction for Young Readers: a Commentary and Annotated Bibliography." In *Science Fiction, Social Conflict and War*, ed. Philip Davies, 132–50. Manchester: Manchester University Press, 1990.

Browne, Tom. *Red Zone*. London: MacMillan Topliner Tridents, 1980.

Calder, Jenni. *Huxley and Orwell*: Brave New World *and* Nineteen Eighty-Four. Studies in English Literature, no. 63. London: Edward Arnold, 1976.

Christopher, John. *The Guardians*. Harmondsworth, England: Puffin Books, 1970.

Golding, William. *Lord of the Flies*. London: Faber and Faber, 1954.

———. "Fable." In *The Cool Web*: *The Pattern of Children's Reading*, ed. Margaret Meek, Aidan Warlow, and Griselda Barton, 226–40. London: Bodley Head, 1977.

———. "Utopias and Antiutopias." In *A Moving Target*, 171–84. London: Faber and Faber, 1982.

Harrison, Barbara. "Howl Like the Wolves." *Children's Literature* 15 (1987): 67–90.

Higonnet, Margaret R. "Narrative Fractures and Fragments." *Children's Literature* 15 (1987): 37–54.

Hughes, Monica. *Devil on My Back*. London: MacRae, 1984.

Huxley, Aldous. *Brave New World*. London: Chatto and Windus, 1932.

Kaminski, Winfred. "War and Peace in Recent German Children's Literature." Translated by J. D. Stahl. *Children's Literature* 15 (1987): 55–66.

Kelleher, Victor. *Taronga*. Ringwood, Vic.: Puffin Books, 1986.

Kesteven, G. R. *The Awakening Water*. London: Chatto, 1977.

Lawrence, Louise. *Andra*. 1971. Harlow: Longman, 1986.

Mace, Elisabeth. *The Travelling Man*. London: Andre Deutsch, 1976.

Mark, Jan. *The Ennead*. Harmondsworth, England: Kestrel Books, 1978.

O'Brien, Robert C. *Z for Zachariah*. London: Victor Gollancz, 1975.

Orwell, George. *Nineteen Eighty-Four*. 1949. Harmondsworth, England: Penguin Books, 1984.

Nodelman, Perry. "Doing Violence to Conventions: The Work of Ilse-Margret Vogel." *Children's Literature* 15 (1987): 19–36.

Pausewang, Gudrun. *The Last Children* [Die Letzen Kinder von Schewenborn]. Translated by Norman Watt. 1988. London: Walker, 1990.

Porritt, Jonathon. Foreword. In *A Green Manifesto*: *Policies for a Green Future*, eds. Sandy Irvine and Alec Ponton, ix-xi. London: Optima, 1988.

Prince, Alison. *The Others*. London: Methuen Children's, 1986.

Rabkin, Eric S. "Atavism and Utopia." In *No Place Else*: *Explorations in Utopian and Dystopian Fiction*, ed. Eric S. Rabkin, Martin H. Greenburg, and Joseph D. Olander, 1–10. Carbondale and Edwardsville, Ill.: Southern Illinois University Press, 1983.

Richemont, Enid. *The Game*. London: Walker Books, 1990.

Schlee, Ann. *The Vandal*. London: Macmillan, 1979.

Scholes, Robert. *Structural Fabulation*: *An Essay on Fiction of the Future*. London and Notre Dame: University of Notre Dame Press, 1975.

Scott, Hugh. *Why Weeps the Brogan?* London: Walker, 1989.

Sleator, William. *House of Stairs*. (1979). New York: Puffin Books, 1991.

Stephens, John. "Post Disaster Fiction: the Problematics of a Genre." *Papers* 3 (1992): 126–130.

Streiber, Whitley. *Wolf of Shadows*. London: Hodder & Stoughton, 1986.

Swindells, Robert. *Brother in the Land*. Oxford: Oxford University Press, 1984.

———. *Brother in the Land*. 1984. With author's afterword. Harmondsworth, England: Puffin Books, 1986.

————. *Brother in the Land*. 1984. Harmondsworth, England: Puffin Books, 2000.
Swindells, Robert. *Daz 4 Zoe*. London: Hamish Hamilton, 1990.
Tully, John. *Natfact 7*. London: Methuen, 1984.
Woodward, Kathleen. "On Aggression: William Golding's Lord of the Flies." In *No Place Else*: *Explorations in Utopian and Dystopian Fiction*, ed. Eric S. Rabkin, Martin H. Greenburg, and Joseph D. Olander, 199–224. Carbondale and Edwardsville, Ill.: Southern Illinois University Press, 1983.

14

The Quest for the Perfect Planet: The British Secondary World as Utopia and Dystopia, 1945–1999

KAREN SANDS-O'CONNOR

"We are living in an age of migration, change, and uncertainty. Our unease about the places and spaces we inhabit has been reinforced by the contemporary shifting of racial, class and sexual boundaries."
—JONATHAN RUTHERFORD, *Forever England*[1]

National image is determined by a variety of factors, one of which is its literature. Children's literature, in particular, has an effect on national image because it is often a young person's first understanding of a place and its people. The stereotypes of groups, classes, and races encountered in children's literature may stay with a child reader for life, whether consciously or not, and therefore this literature becomes of great importance. This essay seeks to examine how national image is portrayed in one particular type of children's literature, the secondary world novel in Britain after 1945. It is instructive to examine the fantastic fiction of a time period when Britain was redefining itself, in order to see what kind of national images the literature was producing. Does British fantastic fiction face the future, or does it return to its paradigms of Empire, and what does the answer to this question mean for child readers and the notion of childhood, both in Britain and throughout the world? The idea of a "perfect" or utopian England/Britain is used by several important authors of the time. It is an almost exclusively male, white, and regressive version of perfection, and it often requires the destruction of the child in order to maintain itself. This "national utopia" contrasts starkly with the possible worlds that British authors provide for their child characters.

British secondary worlds after 1945 seem to be on a hunt for utopia. The successful secondary worlds, whether in fantasy or science fiction, of the last fifty years, have nonetheless entertained a bleak and pessimistic outlook, not just on the primary world, but on the secondary world as well. Whereas the secondary world formerly had been a place of respite, if not from serious problems then at least from the boredom of existence in the primary world, secondary world fantasy and science fiction after 1945 posit no such escape. The primary world, because of its impersonal and power-hungry structures and leaders, harms the child characters and is generally beyond redemption. Escape to a secondary world does not suffice after 1945, as no world is safe, and despite temporarily saving this new world from evil, in the end the child character has no choice but to leave the secondary world behind and either return to the doomed primary world, or move beyond it to a transcendent but indescribable (because impossible) tertiary world. W. R. Irwin notes this trend in utopian fiction when he writes, "[o]ver the past forty years, . . . such constructs of the impossible have often represented societies that would be intolerable. More and more, utopia seems desirable only when dreamed of from far off; too near, it becomes ominous."[2] Children do not have to carry the blame for the condition of any of the worlds, but they often have the charge of rescuing the secondary world, even though in the end their efforts yield little fruit, as all worlds face destruction anyway. While authors of other types of fantasy seem to hold out hope for this world—even if the responsibility for rescuing it weighs heavily on the shoulders of children—authors of British post-1945 secondary world fantasy and science fiction suggest that any attempts to salvage this world will fail, and other worlds cannot offer any better opportunities, except in death.

The idea of utopia is frequently related to the field of science fiction, and it is therefore unsurprising that some of the early novels for children to examine this topic during this period fall under that category. W. E. Johns, who had made his name starting in the 1920s by writing stories of Biggles, the flying ace who always conquered the enemy for Britain,[3] after the war added science fiction to his repertoire. In part, this was a reaction to the Cold War fervor for all things connected with outer space, at a time when many Western nations (including Britain) felt they had a chance of achieving space travel equal to that of the United States and the newly formed Soviet Union. Johns's series, which he produced at a rate of one book per year between 1954 and 1962, begins on an optimistic note. Professor Lucius Brane, living in a castle in the Scottish highlands, has built a spaceship that he hopes to use to find a "perfect planet" for Britain to colonize. Group Captain "Tiger" Clinton of the Royal Air Force and his son Rex, out deer-hunting, meet the professor and agree to help him with his plan. It soon becomes clear, however, that the mission is more urgent than earlier British attempts at colonization, due to one factor. As Professor Brane puts it in *Return to Mars* (1955), "[t]he world is sick with fear. It lost its peace of mind when it became possible for one man to destroy it by pressing a button."[4] Krishan Kumar writes that "[f]ears about nuclear war were the persistent anti-utopian undercurrent to the industrial utopia of the 1950s."[5] However, the scientist, whom Kumar calls a "kind of culture-hero" (Kumar, 389), can think of solutions to possible world destruction. Colonization, then, is a means of re-creating a paradise lost through the threat of nuclear annihilation.

Throughout the series, Brane and the Clintons examine several planets, particularly focusing on the peaceful society they discover living on Mars. However, their quest to re-create a livable world is ultimately unsuccessful. Tiger Clinton complains, at the end of *The Quest for the Perfect Planet* (1961), "[t]alk about finding the perfect planet! Each one we try seems to be worse than the last. I'm beginning to agree with Vargo. There's no such thing as a perfect planet."[6] Utopia is indeed no place, according to Johns.

Curiously, however, near-utopia is not good enough either. Although they admire the Martian society, the earth adventurers reject the idea of becoming a part of it. Even though young Rex Clinton has fallen in love with a Martian woman, and even though the Martians themselves are willing to share their planet with any Earth emigrants, the final pages of the last book in the series, *Worlds of Wonder* (1962), has the travelers returning to Earth. Brane's earlier pronouncements of doom have become the mildly pessimistic, "[a]h well, life on Earth could be worse."[7] Rex responds to this by saying, "[a]t least we know where we are" (*Worlds*, 160). At the end of the day, familiar life in dystopian Britain is better than taking a risk on an unknown utopia.

This notion of a rejected utopia is common in other science fiction of the period, particularly where the utopia is shared with creatures from other planets. M. Keith Booker suggests that "dystopian warnings of the dangers of 'bad' utopias still allow for the possibility of 'good' utopias,"[8] and it seems that in children's fiction, any utopia not created by humans is probably bad for them. Even though the Tripods, invading conquerors from another planet in John Christopher's The Tripods trilogy (*The White Mountains, The City of Gold and Lead, The Pool of Fire*),[9] create a world where all human needs are met, the humans choose to rebel in the cause of individual freedom of will. Although they succeed in defeating the Tripods, Christopher does not give readers hope that the world will be particularly better. Instead, he echoes both Professor Brane by saying that the new world would have "no great triumphs at in the end,"[10] and Rex Clinton when he writes " '[w]e have heard petty bickering, abuse of a great man. The history books told us that this was what Europeans were like, that they could never change, but we did not believe them. Well, we believe them now' " (*Pool*, 216). The search for utopia, according to science fiction writers in Britain, leads to two places: disillusionment and home. All utopias are dystopian under the surface, but the troubles of British society after 1945 are at least out in the open, and can be therefore better dealt with.

This notion that "home may not be sweet, but at least it is home" provides both a starting point for and a sharp contrast to the fantastic fiction of the period. Certainly, the Britain these books represent is far from utopia.

However, British fantastic fiction in general does not argue that the only option is to make do with society as is. Instead, the authors of the period from 1945–1999 offer child characters a variety of solutions, ranging from overthrowing the current order to escaping to other worlds. Nonetheless, this does not make fantastic fiction more optimistic than its science fiction counterpart. In fact, the new solutions posited by these books require a heavy price for the children who want to live in new worlds: sacrifice of family, an abandonment of knowledge and learning, and even self-annihilation.

An excellent example of all three of these can be found in one of the most enduring fantastic series of the period, C. S. Lewis's Chronicles of Narnia. Lewis begins the first of this series, *The Lion, the Witch and the Wardrobe* (1950),[11] with a picture of Britain at its darkest. Lucy, Edmund, Susan, and Peter Pevensie are leaving war-torn London for a pastoral setting.[12] The countryside is frequently used as a safe haven in children's fiction. Kenneth Grahame's *The Wind in the Willows* (1908)[13] provides a good model; Peter Hunt argues that writers such as Grahame "looked out to the countryside, to an arcadian past."[14] Even John Christopher's The Tripods trilogy recognizes this; humans in the Tripod utopia live a sort of pseudo-medieval existence in small villages rather than great cities. Lewis would reemphasize the theme of London as the dystopian urban setting by removing other children and even adults from it as well. Jill Pole and Eustace Scrubb are the victims of relentless bullying at their London school in *The Silver Chair* (1953).[15] Victorian Britain was not much better, according to Lewis; although the sweets were cheaper, "schools were usually nastier than now."[16] London, for Lewis, is a place of violence at all levels of society, and escape is necessary.

The Pevensie children, however, do not remain in the countryside. At the end of the day, Lewis did not see just London as unsafe. The learned behavior of violence, greed, and jealousy pervade the country house as well; Edmund bullies his little sister Lucy until she desires a further level of escape. She finds another world, Narnia, and quickly prefers it to her own. Narnia, as Lewis creates it, is a further regressive step: more rural (the Pevensies do not encounter towns on their journey, although later in the series there are separate "kingdoms" that are more urban), more pastoral (helpful animals such as the Beavers indicate an even more complete return to nature), and governed by a medieval order.

The Lion, the Witch and the Wardrobe provides a complete journey from dystopia to utopia. First, the Pevensie children leave London for the countryside, the nearest thing to utopia in our world; then they travel through Narnia, a land that is prevented from being a utopia only by the grip of the power-hungry White Witch. Once they conquer her, the Pevensie children become rulers over a land so perfect that the only occupation for King Peter, Queen Susan, King Edmund, and Queen Lucy is hunting the occasional deer. Having thus achieved utopia, Lewis must end his story. He makes room for sequels to the novel by sending the Pevensie children home to face an England that remains unchanged; the contrast is so great that the children eventually reject their own native land. Jill Pole, who together with the Pevensies sees the end of Narnia, comments, "I'd rather be killed fighting for Narnia than grow old and stupid at home."[17]

But the children do not settle permanently in Narnia either, because Narnia does not remain a utopia—or, perhaps, like the Tripod world, Narnia only begins to reveal the dystopian qualities that upheld the utopian Narnia. A comparison between Narnia during the Pevensie children's rule and the Narnia that Aslan, the godlike figure who maintains the secondary world, seeks to destroy in the final book of the series, *The Last Battle*, is instructive. Lewis created a seemingly perfect world under the colonizing reign of four white English children. The Pevensies bring no advantages from their world to Narnia: science and technology are seemingly forgotten. A male-dominated religion has been restored through faith in Aslan, the divine figure of the book, and the appearance of Father Christmas. The power of women—both in the "bad" form of the White Witch as well as the "good" form of Lucy Pevensie, the prophet of the book—has been quashed by Aslan granting Peter the title of High King;[18] there is no High Queen. No native Narnian objects to being ruled by outsiders, and all accept the feudal system under which at least some must be servants to others. This may be utopia for some, but only for the very few and privileged.

The utopia starts to fall apart in the following book, *Prince Caspian*, when native-born Narnians have been overtaken by the Telmarines. Prince Caspian, who at long last is restored to the throne, learns that he is neither a proper Telmarine nor a Narnian: " 'You, Sir Caspian,' said Aslan, 'might have known that you could be no true King of Narnia unless, like the Kings of old, you were a son of Adam and came from the world of Adam's sons' " (*Prince*, 210). Narnians can only live in peace when ruled by outsiders.

It is rare, however, that Narnia can live in peace at all. In *The Silver Chair* Narnia is once again threatened, and as in *The Lion, the Witch and the Wardrobe*, it is female power that initially causes the trouble. Unlike in *The Lion, the Witch and the Wardrobe*, however, English children can no longer restore Narnia to its peaceful state. Other factors have broken down the utopia that ultimately cause Aslan to destroy his creation. Towns and cities have sprung up. Groups begin to challenge the feudal system. One group in particular is the Calormenes, a dark-skinned people who, along with the disfigured dwarfs, represent the ultimate evil for the last three books of the series. Lewis's fear of the dark-skinned invader, portrayed in Narnia, only mirrors the society of the time.[19] Folarin Shyllon notes that "[t]he Second World War had supposedly been fought in order to defeat Hitler's racism, but post-1945 Britain was disfigured by the naked and undisguised racism of the

British authorities and British people towards the Black community."[20] In setting the Chronicles of Narnia against the backdrop of a Britain that, as the decade of the 1950s went on, was becoming increasingly urbanized, saw more women in the workplace, and saw a marked increase in the number of former colonists emigrating to Britain from places like the West Indies and India, Lewis reveals a distinct unease with his own situation.

All of these problems come to a head in *The Last Battle*. Lewis shows his complete disillusionment with modern-day Britain when he brings Jill Pole, Eustace Scrubb, and Lucy, Edmund, and Peter Pevensie to Narnia by killing them in a train wreck. Susan, left behind, is not considered the lucky one—she survives in Britain because she has turned away from the ideals of Narnia by wearing makeup, a symbol of her increasing power as a woman (a dangerous thing in Lewis's world). Rather, the other three prefer self-annihilation, sacrifice of family (the Pevensie parents join the children at the end of the novel, but not until after they have accepted the exchange of their parents for a place in New Narnia by entering the golden gates) and a regression to a prescientific world to life in Britain. But even bringing the three children to Narnia is not enough, as the secondary world has been corrupted by the very same influences that damaged Britain: urbanization and the increased power of women and minority groups. Aslan, creator of Narnia, becomes destroyer as well, in order to take the chosen few to a tertiary world, a new utopia. This new utopia is "the England within England, the real England just as this is the real Narnia. And in that inner England no good thing is destroyed" (*Last*, 172). For Lewis, escape backward is the only answer.

Lewis does not make the same mistake with the New Narnia/England as he did when he made Peter, Susan, Edmund, and Lucy the kings and queens of utopia. *The Last Battle* is truly the last book in the series; Lewis claims to be unable to write more because "the things that began to happen after that were so great and so beautiful that I cannot write them. And for us this is the end of all the stories" (*Last*, 173). Utopia is only possible when indescribable, but certain aspects, such as who is in charge and who is salvageable, are clear.

In fact, most of the post-1945 secondary worlds repeat the themes found in Chronicles of Narnia to varying degrees. In the 1960s, Roald Dahl created a secondary world that was, like Lewis's world, a utopia that depended on everyone agreeing to white, male rule. *Charlie and the Chocolate Factory* (1964)[21] is less class-bound than the Chronicles of Narnia—the deserving child, Charlie Bucket, is from a working-class family as compared with the middle-class Pevensies—but otherwise, the book focuses on many of the same problems and provides many of the same solutions. Charlie Bucket must be rescued from the city in which he lives because it has become an urbanized slum. The only work his father can get is screwing caps on tubes of toothpaste—a recession ends even that. The family has nothing to fall back on: the government and the community offer no support, and Charlie's other relatives (two sets of grandparents) are all too feeble to be of help. Charlie and his family begin to starve to death.

The utopia that Dahl offers for Charlie Bucket is more radical and geared much more toward children than Lewis's Narnia (or New Narnia, for that matter), the stuff of dreams: a chocolate factory. Dahl's choice had obvious appeal, but also had obvious precedent in his own life. The Cadbury chocolate factory, where Dahl had once worked, was built in the town of Bournville, four miles west of Birmingham, as a factory in a garden, a company town where the workers lived in beautiful surroundings and had every need provided for, including the same daily smell that Charlie Bucket loved: the odor of rich, melted chocolate. Cadbury's worker facilities were designed in direct opposition to the slums of Birmingham where most of the workers had lived prior to the creation of the Cadbury village. One worker, Bertha Fackrell, "stressed that 'it was always the ardent desire of the heads of the Firm to take the workpeople out of the town, and to build "a factory in a garden" with plenty of ground for outdoor recreation.' The new estate would allow this aim to be fulfilled. Away from the industrial pollution of Birmingham it was a healthy spot surrounded by five farms."[22] The Firm's altruistic, even utopian, vision was realized in 1879, when the Bournville plant opened and the little homes surrounding the factory were first offered to workers.

Dahl's version of the chocolate factory utopia has one difference—it is self-enclosed. Obviously, the Cadbury workers could come and go from the village as they pleased on their free time; but Willy Wonka's factory is different. As Grandpa Joe points out to Charlie, "All factories have workers streaming in and out of the gates in the mornings and evenings—except Wonka's! Have *you* ever seen a single person going into that place—or coming out?" (*Charlie*, 17). The postal system is the only link between the two worlds for years. In this way, Wonka can prevent the problems inherent at the real Cadbury plant—workers who left to get married, labor disputes, globalization, and spying. Dahl realized that no secondary world could be perfect when outsiders could come and go as they pleased. When Willy Wonka finally does let the public in, it is only a select few, those lucky enough or greedy enough or rich enough to find chocolate bars containing golden tickets.

Of the five children who enter the factory, only Charlie recognizes that the true meaning behind the factory is in appreciating its beauty and not in consumption. Wonka takes pains to show that his is no ordinary factory, but a veritable garden. Certainly there are machines, but they are an integral and almost hidden part of a paradise created out of edible materials. As Wonka himself says, "I *insist* upon my rooms being beautiful! I can't *abide* ugliness in factories!" (*Charlie*, 68). The pastoral setting of the chocolate waterfall room is a vision of what one man can achieve. While the other children see only the chocolate and eat their way to an early exit, Charlie sees the world

Wonka has created and admires it. When Wonka asks Charlie what he thinks of the factory, Charlie says he loves it, and that "it's the most wonderful place in the whole world!" (156). He does not see it as a place filled with delicious creations, but a wonderful place in itself. Charlie sees Wonka's vision without trying to consume it, and thus he ends by "gaining the kingdom": Wonka gives his factory to Charlie. Wonka indicates his approval of Charlie by saying, "[m]ind you, there are thousands of clever men who would give anything for the chance to come in and take over from me, but I don't *want* that sort of person. I don't want a grown-up person at all. A grownup won't listen to me; he won't learn. He will try to do things his own way and not mine" (157). Wonka wants someone who will keep the factory just as it is, and sustain the utopia he has created separate from the outside world.

Wonka's factory may be a utopia for Wonka himself and for Charlie, but the fairy-tale image of the ending, with formerly poor Charlie turned ruler of the most wonderful place in the world, belies this utopia's dystopian underpinnings. Wonka's self-enclosed system depends on the compliance and complacency of its workers. Wonka's factory, like the real Cadbury's, requires workers, not just machines. Cadbury picked his from the urban poor of Birmingham. Wonka captured his from a country called Loompaland, and has kept them in happy enslavement. It is well known that the original Oompa-Loompas were portrayed as members of an African tribe,[23] but Dahl's revision of the workers as of uncertain racial origin does not excuse his depiction of colonialism. Wonka does not pay his workers in currency, only in cacao beans, so they cannot venture outside the factory and mix in the ordinary world with any success. The Oompa-Loompas who work without complaint for Wonka do not receive the chance to run the factory—despite their loyalty as workers, Wonka gives this to an outsider, Charlie Bucket, who like him is a native of the country.[24] Again, this vision of utopia is complicated by the real England of 1964, a world where Birmingham was rapidly becoming a much more diverse city, primarily because of an influx of a new minority population—particularly from Jamaica and the other former British colonies in the West Indies.[25] In this context, the implication that the Oompa-Loompas would happily cede power to a white person uneducated in the way to run a factory is distinctly troubling. Once again, utopia is a place that only exists for the chosen few, and those few are predominantly white, male, and in positions of power.

Very few authors after Dahl attempted to depict true utopias for their child protagonists, and if they did, these utopias were temporary resting places only rather than permanent solutions. Alan Garner's *Elidor* (1965)[26] suggests, rather than actually portrays, a utopia. The four children in the book have recently moved to an outer suburb of Manchester. Their mother feels that the move, even though to a smaller home, "was worth the sacrifice for the children to be able to grow up in the country" (53). Growing up in the country, a return to the pastoral, is not just a longing for "fields half a mile away" (53), as Garner initially presents it. The countryside is presented in contrast with the picture we have been given of the city of Manchester, where "[i]t was not one or two houses that were empty, but row after row and street after street. Grass grew in the cobbles everywhere, and in the cracks of the pavement. Doors hung awry. Nearly all the windows were boarded up, or jagged with glass. Only at a few were there any curtains, and these twitched as the children approached. But they saw nobody" (4). White flight can there-fore, in Garner's *Elidor*, be seen as merely an innocuous escape from a decaying city. They are not leaving any particular group of people behind, just an empty setting.

This notion that the middle class leaves the city to find pastoral utopia and not to escape the poor or minority groups who have moved in is chal-lenged by a later scene in the book. When the family is troubled by the char-acters who try to enter from the secondary world of Elidor, the parents blame the mysterious night noises on transplanted city dwellers—and not those like themselves. " 'That's what you must expect when you have overspill in a decent area,' said Mrs. Watson. "They shouldn't be allowed to build out in the country. People aren't going to change when they move from the city. And goodness knows what it will do to property values' " (*Elidor*, 97). Garner does not state who "they" are directly, but three paragraphs later, the reader learns that some council houses (the British equivalent of American low-income housing projects) have recently been built nearby. It was certainly a common misconception that people, particularly nonwhite people, who lived in council houses were responsible for more of the crime, although studies often proved the opposite.[27] Garner reinforces this message by showing a city that has been destroyed, and a countryside that is no longer a utopia for the white middle class either.

The child characters in *Elidor* live seemingly unaware of and uninter-ested in the slums that surround them, except as these slums can provide a playground for their games. The children themselves are not of this urban decay. Nor are they of the moral decay that Garner seems to suggest goes with these urban ruins. In fact, they seem transplanted from many of the ear-lier "four children and an adventure" stories, such as those by E. Nesbit, Enid Blyton, or Hilda Lewis: white, middle class, and untroubled. In many ways, by creating this type of character, Garner seems to be encouraging the white middle-class English child to ignore or accept racism and urban decline in his or her own world.

And yet, these children are again the ones called upon to save the sec-ondary world. Elidor is the only true utopia in the book, but it is in need of rescue. Significantly, the children reach this secondary world through an abandoned and crumbling church. The decline in religious values in Eng-land began in the 1950s; Judith Ryder and Harold Silver note that "[t]he established aristocracy maintained its former positions of authority even into the twentieth century. But new power groups emerged—those of the large corporation, of organized labour and of mass communications for example. The influence of . . . the established Church was considerably eroded."[28] Garner takes note of this fact but, unlike C. S. Lewis, he does not turn the children back to the Christian religion, but toward a reverence for mythological and ancient religions, where unicorns roamed in a pastoral land. Lewis's children learn about God through mythical creatures such as fauns, but the children in Elidor learn to revere the unicorn itself. They are entranced by Elidor, and work to save it. Saving it, by bringing dangerous magical objects to their own world, threatens their own existence, however, and they must then save the modern-day world as well. Once they do, Elidor is closed to them forever, a reversal of the situation that Lewis's children encounter in the Chronicles of Narnia. Garner's children only ever get glimpses of Elidor, and never see it fully restored. Perhaps Garner, like Lewis, realized that the only possible utopia is the one not visible.

The child characters in Lewis's, Dahl's, and Garner's novels are all reasonably uncritical of their society, accepting the primary world as normal, if not ideal. It is left to the narrators to delineate and comment on problems in the primary world and the need for an alternative. Later British authors, however, made their child characters both more critical of the primary world and more involved in its replacement. Both Louise Lawrence, in her Llandor books (*Journey Through Llandor*, 1995; *The Road to Irryan*, 1996; *The Shadow of Mordican*, 1996),[29] and Diana Wynne Jones, in two of her Chrestomanci novels (*Charmed Life*, 1977; *The Lives of Christopher Chant*, 1988),[30] depict their secondary worlds as dangerous choices, but nonetheless ultimately better choices for children than the modern-day world. Both authors complain about urbanization and about the adults' lack of interest in children in our world. In Jones's *Charmed Life*,[31] children cannot simply disappear from one world; instead, since there are many worlds, an "even" exchange is made so that children who move to another world are merely changing places with another child. This erases the time difference between worlds found in some earlier novels (such as the Chronicles of Narnia) but also allows Jones to make a point about her view of our world. Even though Janet Chant, in *Charmed Life*, faces grave danger if she remains in a magical secondary world when she is completely void of magical powers, she chooses it because her parents do not notice the difference between her and a substitute girl (*Charmed*, 198). The world she travels to is no utopia, but it is better than the dystopian vision of a world where parents cannot distinguish their own children from strangers.

Similarly, in Louise Lawrence's Llandor Trilogy, the children do not have a choice about entering the secondary world of Llandor, but in the end they choose to stay there, even though it means they must subject themselves first to mortal danger, then to a deathlike sleep, and finally to even more mortal danger. Roderick rejects his home in the primary world because he personally felt unhappy there, describing it as "the world of a fat boy [himself] who had nothing going for him and nothing to hope for, to which he never wanted to return."[32] Carrie, however, had been a success in the primary world, one of the prefects who—like Jill and Eustace's torturers in *The Silver Chair*—bullied those younger and weaker than her at school. She does not have Roderick's personal reasons for wanting to remain in the secondary world, and must be brought to the realization that her own world was "a world where no one, apart from the famous, seemed to matter—where millions died each day in wars and droughts and famines" (*Journey*, 267), whereas Llandor was made up of a caring society, "living souls in a living land" (267). Her own world, a world of death, she rejects, and then thinks no more of those she left behind. She concludes, "[i]t was as if she had been born in the wrong place, in the wrong world, and now, finally, she had come home" (267). All children, Lawrence suggests, suffer in the primary world— our world—whether or not they face physical threat, because simply living in the primary world makes them complicit in a world of death and hate. The only unfortunate part of their transfer to the secondary world is that they bring some of that hate of the primary world into Llandor with them, and spoil the utopia. The children spend the next two books trying to rectify this mistake, but find it hard to get out of the habit of hating that they learned in their own corrupt and uncaring world.

Neither author stops there, either. Both Jones and Lawrence complain in their novels of the physical ugliness of our world, brought about by technology. Jones has one of her magical-world natives visit our world, but he quickly leaves because it was "the worst Anywhere he had ever been in."[33] Lawrence calls our world "a world of wars and abattoirs, winners and losers and unfair competition . . ." (*Journey*, 253). Whereas children in fantastic novels before 1945 had merely tried to escape a boring world—Alice escaping from her sister down the rabbit hole, the Darling children leaving a near-idyllic London home for increased excitement in Neverland—children in novels after the war leave a dangerous one—ugly, ruined, corrupt, and dystopian. And again unlike their earlier counterparts, they rarely find perfection without accepting death in their own native land.

Philip Pullman's powerful His Dark Materials Trilogy (*The Golden Compass*, 1996; *The Subtle Knife*, 1997; *The Amber Spyglass*, 2000)[34] is the most recent to disparage the modern world as a place where children are doomed, religion is dead, technology is out of control, and women and minorities have no place in society except as outcasts. Like Diana Wynne Jones, Pullman depicts our world as one of multiple worlds, but Pullman's worlds are more closely connected than those in Jones's books: all of them are dying because a strange material, called dust or dark matter, is escaping into oblivion. Dust only seems to escape from postpuberty humans, making children the focus of Pullman's works. The Church in *The Golden Compass* tries to restore the world, but it does so by severing children from their daemons, which are animal-like representations of their souls. Children without souls cannot do wrong, and the "dust" that would escape from them once they become adults will no longer disappear.

Minorities in these books are represented (unlike in many other fantasies) but they are only ever useful, not central to the action. The gyptians (gypsies) and witches aid the two main characters, both of whom are white Oxford natives. However, by the end of the novels, these minority characters have receded into the background; ultimately, they are powerless to change or improve their world. Similarly, gender is a factor in the novels that determines ultimate power. Typical of many fantastic novels, Lyra, the main girl character, becomes the subordinate character in the second novel when she meets Will, the main boy character two years her senior. Lyra has the power of knowledge, represented by the alethiometer, but Will has the power of force, represented by the subtle knife. Although Will survives for a while without Lyra, she never is able to continue without him; she even ends up in a Sleeping Beauty–like coma during part of *The Amber Spyglass*. Pat Pinsent's comment that, "[i]n view of the power of fantasy for transcending boundaries and helping readers to experience situations which are otherwise totally unfamiliar, it is surprising how relatively little use is made of it as a means to showing the triviality of some of the apparent differences between people"[35] applies to Pullman's novels. Although they challenge many assumptions by initially foregrounding minorities and females, ultimately power remains with the white males.

It might seem that Pullman's His Dark Materials Trilogy is more friendly than most fantastic novels of this time period are to technology. After all, Will and Lyra are guided in their quest by a scientific instrument (the alethiometer) and a finely crafted tool (the subtle knife). But the end of the trilogy belies this, because this knowledge and technology must be destroyed if peace is to return to the world. Lyra's understanding of the alethiometer disappears, and the only way for her to retrieve it is through years of hard study. Will is required simply to destroy the knife. In addition, all traffic between the worlds—which increased knowledge and understanding between the different places—has to be halted, and people of each world are left to survive on their own. In all cases, the individual populations will have to rebuild a world that has destroyed its environment (Lyra's world, for example, has been heavily damaged by the war fought by her father), lost its religious institutions, and threatened its children.

Typically, for a British trilogy, these worlds are made safe for re-creation by the English. However, also typically, it is not the English adults who save the world, but the children. And like other children in fantastic novels after

1945, Will and Lyra pay a heavy price for their worlds: they must save the universe by never seeing each other again. These two young people, who have just reached puberty at the end of the trilogy and discovered their love for each other, are forced to sacrifice the one thing in their lives that has meaning for them: each other. Eric S. Rabkin makes a link between the end of utopian ideals and the end of childhood when he writes, "[t]he writers of utopian literature . . . know they must deal with the power of sex and they often remind us of the paradise that sex once cost us."[36] Pullman makes Will and Lyra sacrificial lambs to societies that not only care nothing for them, but in fact had up to this time actively worked to destroy them. Utopia can never happen for them because, as Pullman sees it, utopia is selfish as it can only exist for the few.

The idea of utopia in British fantastic fiction after 1945 remains fairly constant throughout the works of several authors. Typically, they represent a conservative vision of British society that, as Amy Elizabeth Ansell describes it, is "identified with a particular (that is, white) ethnic group. Moreover, its culture embodies Victorian values such as work, respectability, the need for social discipline, and respect for the law."[37] Utopian societies are for the chosen few, and generally these few are those who obey the laws of an older, pastoral Britain where the population was more patriarchal and monochromatic. The modern world is always depicted as generally dystopian, but never redeemable; the secondary world, which is flawed but not doomed, again represents an older form of Britain. Children are the only possible saviors of these secondary worlds, and usually they must not only save the secondary world, but sacrifice themselves in the process. The authors presented here do not offer a rosy picture of life in the modern world, but neither do they present child readers with much in the way of workable alternatives. The new worlds they create require the annihilation of childhood in order to come closer to utopia. Perhaps the quest for the perfect planet is, as W. E. Johns suggests, a dangerous one, and we are better off with the dystopia we know. Or perhaps, as many of the other authors suggest, we are doomed to receive only glimpses of heaven.

Notes

1. Jonathan Rutherford, *Forever England: Reflections on Race, Masculinity and Empire* (London: Lawrence & Wishart, 1997), 5.
2. W. R. Irwin, *The Game of the Impossible: A Rhetoric of Fantasy* (Urbana, Ill.: University of Illinois Press, 1976), 110. See also Robert C. Elliott's chapter "Fear of Utopia" in *The Shape of Utopia: Studies in a Literary Genre* (Chicago: University of Chicago Press, 1970), 84–101.
3. Peter Hollindale and Zena Sutherland call the Biggles books "a testament to the durability of imperial attitudes and values, if only as nostalgic chauvinistic myth, in the changed world of contemporary Britain" ("Internationalism,

Fantasy, Realism (1945–1970)," in *Children's Literature: An Illustrated History*, ed. Peter Hunt (Oxford: Oxford University Press, 1995), 262; the science fiction that Johns writes seems to be more wistful than nostalgic.

4. W. E. Johns, *Return to Mars* (1995) (London: May Fair, 1970), 155.

5. Krishan Kumar, *Utopia and Anti-Utopia in Modern Times* (Oxford: Basil Blackwell, 1987), 389; hereafter cited in text.

6. W. E. Johns, *The Quest for the Perfect Planet* (London: Hodder and Stoughton, 1961), 154.

7. W. E. Johns, *Worlds of Wonder* (London: Hodder and Stoughton, 1962), 159; hereafter cited in text as *Worlds*.

8. M. Keith Booker, *The Dystopian Impulse in Modern Literature: Fiction as Social Criticism* (Westport, Conn.: Greenwood, 1994), 15.

9. John Christopher's The Tripods trilogy consists of *The White Mountains* (London: Hamish Hamilton, 1967), *The City of Gold and Lead* (London: Hamish Hamilton, 1967), and *The Pool of Fire* (London: Hamish Hamilton, 1968).

10. John Christopher, *The Pool of Fire* (1968) (New York: Collier Books, 1968), 218; hereafter cited in text as *Pool*.

11. C. S. Lewis, *The Lion, the Witch and the Wardrobe* (1950) (New York: Macmillan, 1970); hereafter cited in text as *Lion*.

12. Kathryn Hume, in *Fantasy and Mimesis: Responses to Reality in Western Fiction* (New York: Methuen, 1984), points out the link between the pastoral and utopia in her section "The pastoral: retreat from society" (60–64).

13. Kenneth Grahame, *The Wind in the Willows* (1908) (Oxford: Oxford University Press, 1983).

14. Peter Hunt, *The Wind in the Willows: A Fragmented Arcadia* (New York: Twayne, 1994), 6.

15. C. S. Lewis, *The Silver Chair* (1953) (New York: Macmillan, 1970).

16. C. S. Lewis, *The Magician's Nephew* (1955) (New York: Scholastic, 1988), 1.

17. C. S. Lewis, *The Last Battle* (1956) (New York: Macmillan, 1970), 90; hereafter cited in text as *Last*.

18. C. S. Lewis, *Prince Caspian* (1951) (New York: Macmillan, 1970), 25; hereafter cited in text as *Prince*.

19. Both Joe R. Christopher, in *C. S. Lewis*, and Peter Schakel, in *Reading With the Heart: A Way into Narnia* (Grand Rapids, Mich.: William B. Eerdmans, 1979), comment on the Calormenes and compare them to medieval Moors. Schakel suggests that Lewis is not being racist, but only employing "the traditional enemy in medieval romances" (13–14). However, this explanation does not seem to take into account that Lewis was, as A. N. Wilson writes, "the despondent conservative man living in the post-war Britain" (*C. S. Lewis: A Biography*, London: HarperCollins, 1991), 227, and Narnia is his way of commenting on those times.

20. Folarin Shyllon, "The Black Presence and Experience in Britain: An Analytical Overview," in *Essays on the History of the Blacks in Britain: From Roman Times to the Mid-Twentieth Century*, ed. Jagdish S. Gundara and Ian Duffield (Aldershot, England: Avebury, 1992), 214–15.

21. Roald Dahl, *Charlie and the Chocolate Factory* (New York: Knopf, 1964); hereafter cited in text as *Charlie*.

22. Quoted in Carl Chinn, *The Cadbury Story: A Short History* (Studley, England: Brewin Books, 1998), 19.

23. See Jane Yolen's "Turtles All the Way Down," in *Only Connect: Readings on Children's Literature*, 3rd ed., ed. Sheila Egoff, Gordon Stubbs, Ralph Ashley and Wendy Sutton (Toronto: Oxford University Press, 1996), 164–74.

24. The question of the setting of *Charlie and the Chocolate Factory* is at times confused by the fact that U.S. editions of the book were "translated" to include American money and other familiar terminology. However, British editions of the book confirm a British setting, as Charlie finds "*a fifty-pence piece!*" (59) near the "kerb" (59) (London: Penguin, 2001).

25. For patterns of immigrant settlement in Britain, see Sheila Patterson's *Immigration and Race Relations in Britain 1960–1967* (Oxford: Oxford University Press, 1969), especially 194–205, or Sheila Allen's *New Minorities, Old Conflicts: Asian and West Indian Migrants in Britain* (New York: Random House, 1971). In Allen's study, she notes that between 1951 and 1961, the increase in the percentage of the population born in the "coloured Commonwealth" increased 162 percent, whereas the percentage of the population born in Great Britain increased only 4 percent (Allen, 47).

26. Alan Garner, *Elidor* (New York: Ballantine, 1965); hereafter cited in text as *Elidor*.

27. See John R. Lambert's 1970 study, *Crime, Police, and Race Relations: A Study in Birmingham* (Oxford: Oxford University Press, 1970), especially 122–30. In it, he writes that "[i]t is very apparent that the housing market operates in such a way that immigrants, and particularly coloured immigrants, live in certain typical conditions and areas, one of whose features is high rates of crime" (Lambert, 122); in spite of this, "coloured immigrants are very much less involved in the crime and disorder that surround them in the areas where they live than their white neighbours" (124).

28. Judith Ryder and Harold Silver, *Modern English Society: history and structure, 1850–1970* (London: Methuen, 1977), 272.

29. Louise Lawrence's Llandor trilogy consists of *Journey Through Llandor* (London: HarperCollins, 1995); *The Road to Irryan* (London: Collins, 1996); and *The Shadow of Mordican* (London: Collins, 1996).

30. Diana Wynne Jones, *Charmed Life* (1977) (Harmondsworth, England: Puffin Books, 1979) and *The Lives of Christopher Chant* (1988) (London: Methuen, 1988).

31. Diana Wynne Jones, *Charmed Life* (1977) (Harmondsworth, England: Puffin Books, 1979); hereafter cited in text as *Charmed*.

32. Louise Lawrence, *Journey Through Llandor* (London: HarperCollins, 1995), 253; hereafter cited in text as *Journey*.

33. Diana Wynne Jones, *The Lives of Christopher Chant* (London: Methuen, 1988), 131.

34. Philip Pullman's His Dark Materials trilogy consists of *The Golden Compass* (New York: Alfred A. Knopf, 1996; original publication as *Northern Lights*, London: Scholastic, 1995), *The Subtle Knife* (New York: Alfred A. Knopf, 1997), and *The Amber Spyglass* (New York: Alfred A, Knopf, 2000).

35. Pat Pinsent, *Children's Literature and the Politics of Equality* (London: David Fulton, 1997), 103.
36. Eric S. Rabkin, "Atavism and Utopia," in *No Place Else: Explorations in Utopian and Dystopian Fiction*, ed. Eric S. Rabkin, Martin H. Greenberg and Joseph D. Olander (Carbondale, Ill.: Southern Illinois University Press, 1983), 3.
37. Amy Elizabeth Ansell, *New Right, New Racism: Race and Reaction in the United States and Britain* (New York: New York University Press, 1997), 168.

Works Cited

Allen, Sheila. *New Minorities, Old Conflicts: Asian and West Indian Migrants in Britain*. New York: Random House, 1971.

Ansell, Amy Elizabeth. *New Right, New Racism: Race and Reaction in the United States and Britain*. New York: New York University Press, 1997.

Booker, M. Keith. *The Dystopian Impulse in Modern Literature: Fiction as Social Criticism*. Westport, Conn.: Greenwood Press, 1994.

Chinn, Carl. *The Cadbury Story: A Short History*. Studley, England: Brewin Books, 1998.

Christopher, Joe R. *C. S. Lewis*. Boston: Twayne, 1987.

Christopher, John. *The Pool of Fire*. 1968. New York: Collier Books, 1988.

Dahl, Roald. *Charlie and the Chocolate Factory*. New York: Knopf, 1964.

———. *Charlie and the Chocolate Factory*. London: Penguin Books, 2001.

Elliott, Robert C. *The Shape of Utopia: Studies in a Literary Genre*. Chicago: University of Chicago Press, 1970.

Garner, Alan. *Elidor*. New York: Ballantine, 1965.

Hollindale, Peter and Zena Sutherland. "Internationalism, Fantasy, Realism (1945–1970)." In *Children's Literature: An Illustrated History*, ed. Peter Hunt, 252–88. Oxford: Oxford University Press, 1995.

Hume, Kathryn. *Fantasy and Mimesis: Responses to Reality in Western Literature*. New York: Methuen, 1984.

Hunt, Peter. *The Wind in the Willows: A Fragmented Arcadia*. New York: Twayne, 1994.

Irwin, W. R. *The Game of the Impossible: A Rhetoric of Fantasy*. Urbana, Ill.: University of Illinois Press, 1976.

Johns, W. E. *The Quest for the Perfect Planet*. London: Hodder and Stoughton, 1961.

———. *Worlds of Wonder*. London: Hodder and Stoughton, 1962.

———. *Return to Mars*. 1955. London: May Fair, 1970.

Jones, Diana Wynne. *Charmed Life*. 1977. Harmondsworth, England: Puffin Books, 1979.

———. *The Lives of Christopher Chant*. London: Methuen Children's, 1988.

Kumar, Krishan. *Utopia and Anti-Utopia in Modern Times*. Oxford: Basil Blackwell, 1987.

Lambert, John R. *Crime, Police, and Race Relations: A Study in Birmingham*. Oxford: Oxford University Press, 1970.

Lawrence, Louise. *Journey Through Llandor*. London: Collins, 1995.

Lewis, C. S. *The Lion, the Witch and the Wardrobe*. 1950. New York: Macmillan, 1970.

————. *Prince Caspian*. 1951. New York: Macmillan, 1970.

————. *The Silver Chair*. 1953. New York: Macmillan, 1970.

————. *The Magician's Nephew*. 1955. New York: Scholastic, 1988.

————. *The Last Battle*. New York: Macmillan, 1956.

Patterson, Sheila. *Immigration and Race Relations in Britain 1960–1967*. Oxford: Oxford University Press, 1969.

Pinsent, Pat. *Children's Literature and the Politics of Equality*. London: David Fulton, 1997.

Pullman, Philip. *The Golden Compass*. New York: Alfred A. Knopf, 1995.

————. *The Subtle Knife*. New York: Alfred A. Knopf, 1997.

————. *The Amber Spyglass*. New York: Alfred A. Knopf, 2000.

Rabkin, Eric S. "Atavism and Utopia." In *No Place Else: Explorations in Utopian and Dystopian Fiction*, ed. Eric S. Rabkin, Martin H. Greenberg and Joseph D. Olander, 1–10. Carbondale, Ill.: Southern Illinois University Press, 1983.

Rutherford, Jonathan. *Forever England: Reflections on Masculinity and Empire*. London: Lawrence & Wishart, 1997.

Ryder, Judith and Harold Silver. *Modern English Society: history and structure, 1850–1970*. London: Methuen, 1977.

Schakel, Peter J. *Reading with the Heart: The Way into Narnia*. Grand Rapids, Mich.: William B. Eerdmans, 1979.

Shyllon, Folarin. "The Black Presence and Experience in Britain: An Analytical Overview." In *Essays on the History of Blacks in Britain: From Roman Times to the Mid-Twentieth Century*, ed. Jagdish S. Gundara and Ian Duffield, 202–24. Aldershot, England: Avebury, 1992.

Wilson, A. N. *C. S. Lewis: A Biography*. London: Collins, 1991.

Yolen, Jane. "Turtles All the Way Down." In *Only Connect: Readings on Children's Literature*. 3rd ed. Ed. Sheila Egoff, Gordon Stubbs, Ralph Ashley, and Wendy Sutton, 164–74. Toronto: Oxford University Press, 1996.

Interview with Lois Lowry, Author of *The Giver*

CARRIE HINTZ AND ELAINE OSTRY

The following is an interview with Lois Lowry, conducted by e-mail on March 9, 2001. Lois Lowry has written scores of books for children and young adults. Of greatest interest to the utopian field are *The Giver* (1993) and *Gathering Blue* (2000). *The Giver* in particular has achieved iconic status in a short time, and is widely taught in the classroom.

Q: *Most of your writing in the utopian mode is actually dystopian. Are you more drawn to the nightmarish scenario of the dystopia, or could you imagine writing a pure utopia? If so, what would it consist of?*

A: This choice is pure pragmatism. The writer looks for the plot with elements of conflict and ambiguity. A pure utopian setting would make for dull fare, I'm afraid.

Q: *In* The Giver, Gathering Blue, *and* Number the Stars, *you emphasize the lies adults, even teachers, tell children. Why do you stress the lie? Do you think that* The Giver *and* Gathering Blue *pit adolescents against adults, especially since the adults control knowledge?*

A: I think these books pit the young protagonists against society and the form it has taken. A society is, of course, controlled by adults . . . and so the logical outcome pits children against adults.

Q: *How do you envision the link between personal deception and the wider political deceptions of the state in* Gathering Blue *and* The Giver?

A: It's a trickle-down situation, as we've seen in real life. The political deception in Hitler's Germany, for example, so pervaded the German culture of that time that it led to massive personal deception, even self-deception. Totalitarianism always has that very insidious element.

Q: *Many of your adolescent characters are able to act heroically in a way that their adult counterparts cannot. Is the emphasis on the adolescent or child hero a political statement about the relative power of young people to criticize their society? Are children more likely to be agents of utopia, or at least more capable of combating dystopia?*

A: In my opinion it is the task of a writer for young people to present, as a fictional protagonist, a young person who makes moral choices. I don't make political statements . . . although sometimes my books are seen in that light; probably political statements emerge intrinsically from the material. I'm not aware of putting them there.

Having said that, I will add that I do think young people have a very strong moral sense before they enter the adult world with its unfortunate compromises and trade-offs. I think as readers they relate to a protagonist faced with moral dilemmas and acting heroically. And who knows . . . if perhaps as young people, they identify with such heroes, even fictional ones . . . they will be more inclined to back off from moral compromise in the adult world they'll eventually enter.

Q: *As you were writing* The Giver, *were you conscious of a parallel between a dystopian society and the trauma of adolescence itself, such as the exposure of adult hypocrisy, dissociation from family, and testing of values?*

A: As a writer I am only aware of STORY as I write. What leads to this . . . what depends upon that . . . and making it all flow together in a logical and absorbing narrative way.

Then, after it is written, I can look back at it and see what is there on other levels. These things, these parallels—and also the religious parallels that many people have pointed out and found meaningful—are there, no question. But they were intrinsic to the story and I did not put them there consciously.

Q: *Have you been influenced by other writers who produce utopian/dystopian writing for children and young adults?*

A: No. I don't read children's literature, and so I am not familiar with any utopian/dystopian writing for that audience.

Q: *Was* Brave New World *an influence (conscious or unconscious) when writing* The Giver? *What about Orwell's use of language in* Nineteen Eighty-Four? *Was this a conscious influence on your own Newspeak or euphemisms in* The Giver?

A: I read both *Brave New World* and *Nineteen Eighty-Four* in college, in the 1950s. And—though you didn't mention it—*The Handmaid's Tale* much later. So they are there, in my consciousness, although I haven't reread them so wouldn't be able to describe details. (Interestingly, though, the names in *The Handmaid's Tale* stayed with me: Offred, for example, making the female a subsidiary to the male: Of Fred.) I think there are certain elements that one's imagination might postulate into a future society. The concept of NAMING may be one; and I have used that concept in *Gathering Blue.*

Language, of course, is the governing criterion in any society. So the attention paid to language and its usage in all of these books is no whim or accident.

Q: *Did real-life utopian experiments and communities influence you while you were writing* The Giver? *For example, the absence of the nuclear family might recall the kibbutzim of Israel, and the emphasis on celibacy could be reminiscent of the Shakers. Did you self-consciously echo any "real life" experiments in social organization?*

A: Certainly my awareness of various social experiments has informed my work. Probably the one with which I am most closely attuned is the Shakers, since I own a home in New Hampshire very near a Shaker village. Not only the celibacy practiced in that community—but the "sameness,"—and the element of socialism in everyday life—are reflected in the world of *The Giver.* (Coincidentally, the Shakers—at least in the Canterbury community near my house—were also great gardeners and growers of herbs; and that art found its way into my book *Gathering Blue.*)

The Shakers, though, had music. The loss of music, art, and literature was the truly dystopian element in *The Giver* for me.

Q: Gathering Blue *is a commentary on creativity and coercion. What is the role of the artist in an ideal society? How can adults develop the creativity of children without destroying it?*

A: Every repressive society has restrained artistic expression. (As I write this we are aware of the destruction taking place in Afghanistan of Buddhist art.) Books were burned in Nazi Germany. "Modern art" was outlawed under Stalin, and poets and writers were banished to Siberia.

I think it is something we must be vigilant about. In this country we've seen—we see today—attempts made to restrict artistic expression. It's not a question of whether we, as a people, like or loathe certain types of art (in its broadest sense, including literature and music) . . . but it is essential that all artistic exploration be unreined.

On a very simplistic level, I presented, in *Gathering Blue*, three artists who were being not only coerced, but seduced. How quickly the little singer, Jo, went from mourning the loss of her own unfettered song to loving the attention she would gain by the rote performance of the memorized anthem.

In our own culture the coercion is as often financial as political, though the two are closely allied. We've seen many writers and performers sell out. In my imagined truly utopian world, the artist would be honored and valued and rewarded but left completely exempt from commercial incentives.

How can adults develop or foster creativity in children? I wish they would disconnect the commercial implications. I am saddened when, so often in schools, I hear children ask questions about publishing, agents, royalties. . . . If only those who guide them could focus on the joy of language, of creating, of the magic that happens when sentences sing and connect and tell a story. Every time I see that a child has put a small copyright symbol on a piece of his own work, I know that a bit of creativity has been lost.

Q: *Why do you often choose fantasy as a genre? What can it do that a more realistic mode cannot?*

A: Actually, I don't often choose fantasy. Out of twenty-seven books only two have fallen into that category. But the world of fantasy does offer a writer an amazing avenue of creative expression. To recapitulate an existing world in an intriguing way is the usual task of a writer; but to create and explore a nonexistent world—and to make it seem REAL—is a wonderful and exciting challenge to the writer's imagination.

Q: *One of the most startling things about the community in* The Giver *is the absence of color, and Jonas's awakening to color is one of the most power- ful moments in the book. You continue to use color symbolically in* Gathering Blue. *How does the use of color relate to the formation of a utopia/dystopia?*

A: I don't think it does. I happen to be a very visual person, a very visual writer (I was once a professional photographer). Because color is important to me—I wanted to explore how a world would be diminished without it. I used it as metaphor, really. It was a literary gimmick, as it were, having noth- ing to do with the question of utopia/dystopia.

Q: *You refer to previous times in the history of Kira's community as alternating between periods of holocaust and utopia, of ruin and rebirth. Why do you emphasize this kind of alternation? Can utopia be sustained?*

A: History, of course, is a series of cycles. There was a long period of peace and prosperity during the Roman Empire that makes our own brief flir- tations with stability seem like one-night-stands. In depicting the history of Kira's world I simply tried to re-create the ongoing history of our own.

Q: *What do you hope children will learn about utopian and political organization from your books? From reader responses, have they learned what you hoped they would?*

A: At the conclusion of *Number the Stars*, in the afterword, I said that I hoped the story of Denmark and its people would remind us that a world of human decency is possible. My hope is that young people reading *The Giver* and *Gathering Blue* will perceive something about the importance of choices that humans make as they fashion their societies.

From the response of readers, I know that both books have caused young people—often guided by gifted teachers—to think, argue, debate, explore, and no longer to take certain things for granted.

I don't hope for young people to "learn" from my books. I hope only that they learn to question.

Q: *One of our contributors, Monica Hughes, stresses that when writing for children, the dystopia must show light at the end of the tunnel, or hope. Do you agree? Can children/young adults handle pure dystopia?*

A: "Handle?" Young people handle dystopia every day: in their lives, their dysfunctional families, their violence-ridden schools. They watch dystopian television and movies about the real world where firearms bring about explosive conclusions to conflict.

Yes, I think they need to see some hope for such a world. I can't imagine writing a book that doesn't have a hopeful ending.

Annotated Bibliography of Utopian and Dystopian Writing for Children and Young Adults

CARRIE HINTZ, ELAINE OSTRY, KAY SAMBELL, AND
REBECCA CAROL NOËL TOTARO

This is the first annotated bibliography of utopian and dystopian fiction for children and young adults. Utopia and dystopia are slippery categories. For this bibliography, we have limited the categories to books that present nonexistent communities with an elaborated social system that is posited as significantly better than that of the reader; in dystopias, the society is significantly worse, often to a nightmarish degree. We have looked for books that elaborate on the social formation of a utopian/dystopian community, and which propose to teach young readers about governance. In most cases, children and young adults are the protagonists.

With an eye to space and feasibility, we have decided to focus on books that give an abstract formulation of utopia or dystopia. As a result, most of the books listed here are fantasy or science fiction. We do not claim to be all-inclusive. For the most part, we have omitted the following categories from our bibliography: historical fiction (including historical fantasy), traditional folk and fairy tales, classical utopias abridged for children, Arthurian fantasies, school stories, picture books, poetry, drama, domestic stories, Robinsonnades, pastoral fantasies, short stories, and books written originally for an adult audience but that have been often taught to, or appropriated by, children and young adults (such as *Fahrenheit 451*). We have also eliminated books that contain elements of utopianism but that do not delineate the social structure of the utopia or dystopia in detail.

We hope that this annotated bibliography will help scholars and other interested readers locate books for children and young adults that present a utopia or dystopia. We foresee increased interest in the field, and this bibliography can act as a springboard for such research.

Adams, Richard. *Watership Down*. London: Rex Collings, 1972. This novel portrays both utopian and dystopian communities from the point of view of a band of rabbits who leave the endangered warren of Sandleford, including Hazel, Fiver, and Bigwig. A great deal is revealed about rabbit political and social organization, including the powerful military officers or Owsla. As the rabbits journey to a safer world, they encounter "Efrafa," a totalitarian warren controlled by the powerful General Woundwort, who imposes his strict rule on everyone. After escaping with several does, the rabbits find the "promised land" of Watership Down, a well-situated, prosperous warren where they can live peacefully.

Anderson, Margaret Jean.
  In the Keep of Time. New York: Knopf, 1977.
  In the Circle of Time. New York: Knopf, 1979.
  The Mists of Time. New York: Knopf, 1984.
In *In the Keep of Time*, the four Elliot children discover a time portal in an ancient tower. Through it, they experience fifteenth-century Scotland in a seeming Dark Age of war and hunger. The children accidentally step into the future where worldwide floods have returned civilization as they know it to nature. Tribes of peoples remain to hunt and gather. The children discover that these tribes believe that they are in an age of progress compared to the prior "Technological Civilization" that brought about environmental disaster through greedy over-mechanization. In *In the Circle of Time*, two teens, Robert and Jennifer, find a time portal among the Scottish Stones of Arden. In a future Scotland, they befriend Kartan, a young man whose pastoral, peace-loving society struggles to survive attacks from the technological, dystopian society ("the Barbaric Ones") that has emerged in the postflood years of the twenty-second century. Kartan's community includes sharing children, meals, and all property. The teenagers experience a successful, entirely positive utopia challenged by its opposite, and they see clearly what they have in their own time—and most important, in their own homes—in comparison. A description of this society continues in *The Mists of Time*.

Applegate, K. A. Animorphs [series]. The first of the series is *Animorphs: The Invasion* (New York: Scholastic, 1996). The world is invaded by Yeerks, who take over human bodies, as they have taken over many planets' inhabitants. Five children meet a dying Andalite who warns them of the coming peril and gives them the ability to morph into animals. They form a resistance group against the increasingly Yeerk-dominated society, which plans not only to dominate politically, but also to destroy the environment. The Yeerks "are a plague that spreads from world to world, leaving nothing but desolation and slavery and misery in their wake" (*Animorphs: The Message*, 18–19).

―――――. Remnants [series]. The first of the series is *The Mayflower Project* (New York: Scholastic, 2001). Earth is destroyed by an asteroid; eighty people are "saved" by being put into hibernation and sent out into space. When they awake five hundred years later, most of them are dead. The survivors (mostly teenagers) find themselves on what seems to be a planet, but is really a huge, sophisticated spaceship called Mother. Mother creates an environment that she thinks will make them feel at home, by downloading art from one of the CD-ROMS on board. However, moving through Hieronymus Bosch's hell is hardly comfortable, especially when pursued by alien Riders and Blue Meanies. Worse, the group is divided by various power struggles and factions. Some want power at all costs; others use business models and democratic ideals for their social structures. The burden of being the remnants of the human race, obliged to be humane no matter what the circumstances, weighs heavily on some characters. Mother can create a fake Earth, but at the price, it suggests by the latest part of the series, of their humanity.

Baird, Thomas. *Smart Rats*. New York: Harper and Row, 1990. In the twenty-first century, the Earth's resources dwindle and a worldwide governing force takes over all rations. The leaders abuse their power; they create slogans like "an unrationed life isn't worth living"; they institute measures including the "Progeny Reduction and Relocation Program" that, they claim, will help with distribution of dwindling supplies. The removed children discover instead a "Progeny Reduction Center" in a region of the earth that houses all unwanted humans, from the mentally ill to the aged. Laddie Grayson, the teenage protagonist, faces removal. Through several stunning choices, Laddie turns the table on the leaders, deciding that in order to beat them, he must first join them.

Barrie, J. M. *Peter and Wendy* [*Peter Pan*]. London: Hodder and Stoughton, 1911. Peter Pan leads Wendy and her brothers to Neverland, an island that resembles the children's own fantasies. Neverland is a place of adventure (the very danger of it lends it utopian appeal) where the children rule and conquer. It is associated with childhood itself, corresponding to a Romantic, utopian notion of childhood.

Bartholomew, Barbara. The Time Keeper Trilogy.
  The Time Keeper. Signet Vista: New American Library, 1985.
  Child of Tomorrow. Signet Vista: New American Library, 1985.
  When Dreamers Cease to Dream. Signet Vista: New American Library, 1985.
Throughout the trilogy a group of children can travel forward in time, experiencing an apparently perfect society that is formed to ensure the "best good"

for its people. The utopia, however, is really an elaborate robot-run prison in which the human race has rendered itself obsolete in the cause of happiness and stability. The children reassert the right to choose to be unhappy in the brave new world of the future.

Baum, L. Frank. *The Wonderful Wizard of Oz*. Illustrated by W. W. Denslow. Chicago: Geo. M. Hill Co., 1900. Oz is a utopian land of beauty and wonder, especially when contrasted with ugly, poor Kansas. However, it also contains danger in the form of wicked witches and wild beasts. Dorothy and her friends the Tin Woodman, the Scarecrow, and the Cowardly Lion rid the land of the wicked witches and, with the exception of Dorothy, establish themselves as rulers of different countries of Oz.

—————. *The Emerald City of Oz*. Illustrated by John R. Neill. Chicago: Reilly & Britton, 1910. This is the most utopian of the Oz books, and it emphasizes the socialist economic organization of Oz. Instead of being a reassuring home, Kansas is seen as a brutal world, and hence Dorothy arranges to bring Aunt Em and Uncle Henry to Oz for good.

Bawden, Nina. *Off the Road*. New York: Clarion Books, 1998. Tom follows his grandfather outside their walled community where only one child per family is allowed, and the old are euthanized. However, he finds the outside world to be a hierarchical system that is similarly exclusive, and so he returns to his walled community to try to reach a balance between the two worlds.

Bova, Ben. *City of Darkness*. New York: Scribner, 1976. Ron Morgan becomes inextricably mixed up in the racial conflict and savage warfare of a domed New York City, the only place fit for human habitation in a future United States. Learning that this violent environment has been brought about by bitter racial conflict, he vows to bring about change.

Bowkett, Stephen. *Ice* [The Wintering]. London: Dolphin, 2001. Kell lives in the Enclave, an enclosed community governed by the All Mother. The inhabitants believe that she protects them from wild beasts and ice outside. In the name of harmony, the weather is controlled; children do not grow up knowing their birth parents, and individual choice does not exist. The All Mother gives Kell nightmares to check his questioning. Kell joins a band of rebels, and finds out that the All Mother spies constantly on her people; she has also inserted a membrane into everyone's eyes so that they see exactly what she wants them to see. His membrane ripped from his eyes, he leaves the Enclave with his new comrades.

Browne, Frances. *Granny's Wonderful Chair*. Illustrated by Kenneth Meadows. London: Griffith & Farrar, 1857. Prince Wisewit's time was one of good government, with no lawsuits, crime, or illness. When his brother, King Winwealth, marries greedy Queen Wantall, the kingdom grows unhappy as the people are robbed and disenfranchised. Snowflower, with the antimaterialistic stories in her magical chair (which happens to contain Prince Wisewit under a spell), restores the court to its better self. Prince Wisewit returns, and brings harmony with him.

Browne, Tom. *Red Zone*. London: Macmillan Topliner Tridents, 1980. Britain in the twenty-second century is strictly zoned according to class. Kara is from the privileged, computerized Inner Zone. Clem lives in the brutalized Red Zone, in which warring Vandos' fights to the death are viewed as entertainment by city-dwellers. Both teenagers ultimately escape to the Green Zone to begin a new life together.

Brunhoff, Jean de. *Babar the King*. 1933. Translated by Merle S. Haas. New York: Random House, 1935. Celesteville is the utopian capital of the country ruled by King Babar. All inhabitants are happy and productive. When various mishaps plague the city, it is saved by "graceful winged elephants who chase Misfortune away from Celesteville and bring back Happiness" (44–45).

Burgess, Melvin. *Bloodtide*. London: Anderson Press, 1999. A ruined London of the future dominated by warring ganglords provides the imaginative backdrop to this dystopian vision. The novel combines its brutalized futuristic science fiction setting with a reworking of the myth of the Icelandic Volsunga saga. This is a cautionary tale of betrayal, hatred, and the corrosive nature of power.

Burnett, Frances Hodgson. *The Secret Garden*. Philadelphia: Lippincott, 1911. Mary discovers and cultivates a garden that has been locked up for ten years. She creates a utopian space where the healing powers of nature—or "the magic," as the children call it—transform her and her sickly cousin Colin. The influence of the garden extends beyond the circle of children to the adult world.

Christopher, John [Christopher Samuel Youd]. The Tripods Trilogy.
    The White Mountains. London: Hamish Hamilton, 1967.
    The City of Gold and Lead. London: Hamish Hamilton, 1967.
    The Pool of Fire. London: Hamish Hamilton, 1968.
In a neoprimitive dystopian society, humans are ruled by the Masters. They travel in Tripods, huge machines into which young men are taken and made to wear a Cap that controls their minds and ensures blind obedience to the

Masters. Some teenagers escape such slavery, and attempt to overcome the Masters, who are ultimately revealed as aliens who plan to emerge from their domed cities once they have adjusted the earth's atmosphere to suit their needs; this is fatal to their human "pets." The books concentrate on the difficult moral questions posed by fighting for freedom, and finally settle on the difficulty of humans establishing world unity in the face of national rivalries once the aliens have been overcome.

———— [Christopher Samuel Youd]. *The Guardians*. London: Hamish Hamilton, 1970. Set in an Orwellian twenty-first-century England, *The Guardians* projects a society characterized by strict class divisions between the masses in the Conurbs and the gentry in the County. When Rob Randall learns that this society is maintained by a few "guardians," who are prepared to murder and operate on the brains of dissidents to achieve the "perfection" of such a stable state, he pledges to overthrow the system.

———— [Christopher Samuel Youd]. The Winchester Trilogy.
The Prince in Waiting. London: Hamish Hamilton, 1970.
Beyond the Burning Lands. London: Hamish Hamilton, 1971.
The Sword of the Spirits. London: Hamish Hamilton, 1972.
In a postdisaster, neoprimitive Britain, a simpler way of life has emerged as people have turned against science and technology, but this is no pastoral utopia. Society has developed along feudal lines, with warring factions relying on deception and violence in a constant struggle for power. A secret elite of religious Seers has kept scientific knowledge alive, and chooses the ambitious Luke as a figurehead who can be exploited to unite the country and reinstate machine culture. Each volume explores the means by which society is governed and the tensions that emerge in the quest for social stability and the greater good. In the final book Luke's motivation, and hence the concept of heroic leadership, is questioned, as revenge and jealousy rather than honor fuel his desire to rule. Although he finally balks in the face of passive resistance from some citizens, the trilogy ends with Luke's unhappy reflections on his personal and public past, in which he has lost his family and has been instrumental in the Seers' domination of society.

———— [Christopher Samuel Youd]. *Wild Jack*. London: Hamish Hamilton, 1974. In the near future, humanity has plundered Earth's natural resources to the point of breakdown, and a small elite band of scientists protect themselves in walled cities. The comfort and control of an ordered city life is contrasted with the risk and freedom of a savage life lived in the Outlands. Three children have to consider the advantages and disadvantages of each society and decide where they prefer to live.

———— [Christopher Samuel Youd]. *Empty World*. Harmondsworth, England: Puffin, 1977. A deadly plague, which rapidly ages and kills its victims, is ravaging an England of the future. Neil struggles to survive, but these adverse future circumstances bring out the worst in human nature and he can depend on no one. Ultimately he joins forces with two girls, but jealousy and resentment soon tear their utopian enclave apart. The novel questions people's capacity for peaceful cooperation when altruism may cost one's life.

Ciencin, Scott. *Windchaser* [Dinotopia]. New York: Random House, 1995. The book is set in Dinotopia, and explores the education of two boys, Raymond and Hugh, in the ways of this ideal world where dinosaurs and humans interact in peace and prosperity. Raymond and Hugh are "dolphinbacks," accidentally carried into Dinotopia after a mutiny has grounded a prison ship headed for Australia. Hugh, a London pickpocket, has particular difficulty adjusting to life in Dinotopia; his suspicious hostility and sinister plans underscore the contrast between the utopian Dinotopia and the rest of the world. Eventually Hugh finds a place in Dinotopia as an apprentice to the saurian philosopher-diplomat Laegreffon.

————. *Lost City* [Dinotopia]. New York: Random House, 1996. Adolescents Andrew, Liam, and Ned discover an isolated culture living within the idyllic world of Dinotopia. This culture offers a strong contrast to the non-martial culture of Dinotopia. The tribe that lives in the city, the Troodons or "Unrivalled," is essentially a warrior culture. Like Dinotopia, however, the Lost City is posited as an ideal world based on respect and without violence, although competition not cooperation is the ethos of the community.

————. *Thunder Falls* [Dinotopia]. New York: Random House, 1996. Joseph, a human, and Fleetfeet, his saurian companion, must work together to survive a task set by their mentor, Steelgaze. The book underlines the fundamental importance of human-animal cooperation in Dinotopian society.

Cooper, Claire. *Earthchange*. Minneapolis: Lerner Publications Company, 1985. After a global catastrophe plunges the world into a dystopia ruled by poverty, superstition, and absolute rule, young Rose and her grandmother struggle for survival and try to find scientists who might offer a technological solution to their problems.

Cooper, Susan. *Green Boy*. New York: Margaret K. McElderry Books, 2002. In the Bahamas, a pair of brothers whose beloved cay is under proposed development find themselves traveling to Pangaia. In this dictatorial world, developers and scientists have ruined the environment and climate, experimented in bizarre genetic engineering, and created huge concrete cities. A resistant group has been living underground for a hundred years, engaging in the Greenwar on Gaia's behalf. The mute brother, Lou, becomes the huge Green Man who pours out greenery over the city, destroying it. The work is informed by the Gaia Hypothesis, which argues that the world is itself a living organism that should be respected.

Correy, Lee [G. Harry Stine]. *Starship through Space.* New York: Henry Holt and Company, 1954. A space team, including some young adults, discovers humans on Mars, called the Ainsath. The Ainsath have manipulated their environment by changing its biological components. This means biochemical feats such as having trees grow into houses, and developing animals for precise uses through mutations. The women, most of whom were killed or weakened by a gender-selective plague, created the laws, customs, and religion of this peaceful group.

Dahl, Roald. *Charlie and the Chocolate Factory.* Illustrated by Quentin Blake. New York: Knopf, 1964. Willy Wonka presides over the chocolate factory, which includes countless edible delights and seemingly endless inventions. The factory is mysteriously enclosed, with no one ever entering or leaving. Five children tour the factory, meeting the Oompa-Loompa workers, and learning about Wonka's singular vision. Undesirable children are weeded out, until only Charlie is left to take over the enterprise.

Danzinger, Paula. *This Place Has No Atmosphere.* New York: Dell, 1986. When fourteen-year-old Aurora Borealis Wilcox's parents inform her that they are moving the family to the moon, she is horrified. In the year 2057, the Earth is crowded. Most families live in dystopian malls over one hundred stories high. The moon will soon become a way station en route to a permanent Mars colony, but in the meantime it functions as a colony of scientists, artists, and others who intend to experiment with colonial life. After some adventures, Aurora starts to feel at home, and then she realizes that this colony is a better place, permitting improved social, physical, and familial interactions because "with a small population everyone is more important, more useful" (111).

David, Peter. *The Maze.* [Dinotopia]. New York: Random House, 1999. When a farmer is infected with a deadly disease, two adolescents and a dinosaur companion seek out an accomplished healer, Odon the Megaraptor. Odon, one of the original inhabitants of the island before the advent of humans, has retreated behind a deadly maze, due to his strong objections to the mingling of humans and dinosaurs in Dinotopian society. Jason, Gwen, and their saurian companion Booj must convince him to return to Dinotopian life, and embrace the cooperative existence of human and dinosaur: they succeed in this task, and the farmer is saved.

DeWeese, Gene. *Firestorm*. [Dinotopia]. New York: Random House, 1997. In this *Dinotopia* sequel, a powerful blight is wiping out important plants on Dinotopia, including *Arctium longevus*, the plant that ensures that Dinotopians have a long life. Olivia and Albert team up with their dinosaur partners Hightop and Thunderfoot, again underscoring the ethic of cooperation in Dinotopian society. As is typical of many books in the Dinotopia series, the adolescent protagonist learns an important lesson in life—in this case the often-impetuous Olivia learns patience and the need to work slowly and cooperatively on tasks.

Dickinson, Peter. The Changes Trilogy.
    The Weathermonger. London: Victor Gollancz, 1968.
    Heartsease. London: Victor Gollancz, 1969.
    The Devil's Children. London: Victor Gollancz, 1970.
Dickinson's books all explore the probable implications of a neoprimitive society in a future in which people have turned against machine culture. England has reverted to superstition and brutal violence. Intolerance is rife, and anyone different is stoned or cast out, even children. The books raise questions about ordinary people's capacity for dogmatism, fanaticism, and prejudice.

―――. *Eva*. London: Victor Gollancz, 1988. In an overcrowded future dominated by commercialism and technology, the human victim of a horrific car crash, Eva, is given life by having her brain implanted in the body of a chimp. Human and chimp life are experienced simultaneously through Eva's perspective. The invasive nature of human society's impact on the natural world is questioned throughout, especially as Eva and her fellow city-bred chimps are released on an island as an experiment: they escape the cameras and try out a utopian existence devoid of human interference.

Dickson, Gordon R. *Secret under Antarctica*. New York: Holt, Rinehart and Winston, 1963. Young Robby Hoenig accompanies his father on an International Department of Fisheries expedition to Antarctica and is captured by Tropicans. In their underwater station he learns that the Tropicans are members of a movement determined to enact a supposedly utopian program of returning the world to a balmier condition prior to the shifting of the continents and the forming of huge glaciers. But they plan to use bombs to shift the earth. With the help of a highly intelligent seal, Cerebus, and International Police Agent Lillibulero, Robby saves the planet from the mad plan.

Eldridge, Roger. *Shadow of the Gloom-World*. New York: Dutton, 1977. In the cavern community of shadows, Fernfeather, the young adult protagonist, begins to question his society's restrictive practices: commoners are killed once the community leaders, the "Vigilants," deem them useless; dreams and pictures are forbidden; the people have no communal or private memories of the deceased, and so there is no history. Visions of something beyond this realm of shadows give him the courage to journey outside the restrictions of the Vigilants. Once beyond the walls, he meets Harebell, another who has escaped, and with her Fernfeather finds a new people whose history and kindness show them a way to help his own society.

Elliott, Janice.
    The King Awakes. London: Walker, 1987.
    The Empty Throne. London: Walker, 1988.
Both of Elliott's books explore a dystopian neoprimitive future society that ensues after a huge disaster. Savage intolerance, superstition, and violence are commonplace and the populace is ruled by tyrants who will stop at nothing, including torture and murder, to maintain power.

Farmer, Nancy. *The Ear, the Eye and the Arm*. New York: Puffin Books, 1994. In the Zimbabwe of 2194, three children discover a country called Resthaven that was created to protect ancient African culture from European customs. It has a traditional village life (which makes it a dystopia for the women who must do the bulk of the work). Those who are weary of modern life can apply for citizenship—and, if accepted, cannot leave. The country has symbolic meaning: "[a]s long as Resthaven exists, the Heart of Africa is safe" (148).

Faville, Barry. *The Keeper*. Auckland, N.Z.: Oxford University Press, 1986. Life in this postnuclear holocaust scenario is governed by fear of outsiders and superstition. Secrecy, intolerance, and a lack of freedom fuel this society, which the young protagonist, Michael, ultimately rejects. He leaves to seek a utopian community on an island far from the village of his birth.

Fisk, Nicholas. *A Rag, a Bone and Hank of Hair*. London: Kestrel, 1980. A nuclear power leak has resulted in a severe population crisis at the end of the twenty-second century. Society is strictly controlled to preserve peace, and cloning is used to experiment with the manufacture of families who need to fit in with the submissive populace. Brin tries to produce a new kind of "reborn" in his struggle for freedom.

Fleischman, Paul. Illustrated by Kevin Hawkes. *Weslandia*. New York: Walker Books, 1999. Persecuted by his classmates, Wesley devises his own utopian world one summer, complete with staple crop, clothing, music, language, and architecture. Fascinated by Wesley's world, his classmates join him in "Weslandia."

Foster, Alan Dean. *Dinotopia Lost* [Dinotopia]. Atlanta: Turner Publishing Ltd., 1996. An adventure story set in Dinotopia, this novel follows Will Denison and his friends as they rescue dinosaurs held hostage by human pirates shipwrecked in Dinotopia. The pirates ultimately renounce crime and join Dinotopian society.

——. *The Hand of Dinotopia* [Dinotopia]. New York: HarperCollins, 1999. The adventurous Sylvia Romano and Will Denison, along with their sardonic saurian companion Chaz, go on a quest to find "the Hand of Dinotopia," a rock formation that will point the way out of Dinotopia, a realm formerly considered to be completely isolated. In the desert, they meet Khorip, an embittered dinosaur who seeks to leave Dinotopia for the "Realm Without." When he learns about war and other terrors of the outside world, he elects to stay within Dinotopia. The novel is also notable for its depiction of the pluralism of Dinotopian society. This includes a portrayal of the intentional community "Family Helth" [sic] which lives outside mainstream society pursuing a special diet and a life of meditation.

Gee, Maurice. *The World Around the Corner*. Oxford: Oxford University Press, 1980. Caroline stumbles into a world where goblinlike Grimbles terrorize innocent elves: "The Grimbles have turned their half into a desert. They have cut down all the trees, levelled the hills, damned up all the rivers. They live in great walled cities. Their world is one of smoke and poison and darkness . . . they have burrowed under the mountains into our half of the world. They want to turn that into desert too" (38).

——. *The Halfmen of O*. Auckland, N. Z.: Oxford University Press, 1982.
The Priests of Ferris. Auckland, N. Z.: Oxford University Press, 1984.
In *The Halfmen of O*, Susan and Nick find themselves in a world in which people have been divided: half of them are good, half are bad. The pair must restore balance, wresting control from the dictator Otis Claw. The City where he resides is an industrial zone full of pollution, cruel inhabitants, and suffering. Susan is fated to restore the balance of the stones called the Halves, which together look like the yin/yang symbol. To do so, she must elicit the help of the creatures of the woods, sea, air, and stone. In *The Priests of Ferris*, the harmony Susan had restored has been lost again, through the dictatorial, murderous priests who claim that they are acting in her name. Religion is a cloak for political power in this ordered, cruel state. An alliance between the different species of the world, in which equality is stressed, allows a revolution to succeed.

Glut, Donald F. *Chomper* [Dinotopia]. New York: Random House, 2000. Adolescent Perry adopts a baby Gigantosaurus, only to be forced to send it back to its original town when it becomes clear that it does not fit into a calm, suburban setting. The book probes the idea of the need for appropriate dwellings for all members of the dinosaur-human utopian community, as well as the cooperation between Perry and his Gigantosaurus that wins him admission into the Gigantosaurus community.

Gurney, James. *Dinotopia: A Land Apart from Time*. Illustrated by James Gurney. Atlanta: Turner Publishing, 1992. Arthur Denison and his young son, Will, are shipwrecked on the isolated and advanced society of Dinotopia. The book presents Arthur's journal, an explorer's record that is somewhat reminiscent of that of Robinson Crusoe's writing. Some of Will's written responses to this new land are presented as well. The book is illustrated with detailed, colorful views of everyday life in Dinotopia. The timeless quality of Dinotopia is underscored, as well as the emphasis on dinosaur-human cooperation typical of all books set in Dinotopia.

———. *The World Beneath*. Atlanta: Turner Publishing, 1995. In this sequel to *Dinotopia*, Victorian explorer Arthur Denison decides to seek out machines and a special energy-producing stone to advance Dinotopia's technology. Oriana, his female companion and eventual partner, convinces him that this is not necessary: "the golden age is here right now" (126). We learn in this book that Egypt and Atlantis were influenced by Dinotopia as well.

Haddix, Margaret Peterson. *Running Out of Time*. New York: Simon & Schuster, 1995. Jessie finds out that she is living in a "living history" village in 1996, watched by tourists through hidden cameras, and run by scientists experimenting on them with diphtheria strains to develop a stronger gene pool.

———. *Among the Hidden*. New York: Simon & Schuster, 1998.
Among the Impostors. New York: Simon & Schuster, 2001.
Among the Betrayed. New York: Simon & Schuster, 2002.
Famine leads to a totalitarian society where it is forbidden to have more than two children. In *Among the Hidden*, Luke, a third child, lives like a fugitive in his own home. His new neighbor Jen Talbot is also a third child, who has formed an Internet community of shadow children and plots a protest march that results in slaughter. In *Among the Impostors*, Mr. Talbot arranges for Luke to attend a windowless school that acts as a hiding place for many third children, who are betrayed by a boy pretending to be one of them. In *Among the Betrayed*, third-child Nina is urged by the Population Police to betray some other third children; instead, she saves them from the

prison. As it turns out, it was an elaborate test of her reliability, and she and Luke join forces.

————. *Turnabout*. New York: Simon & Schuster, 2000. Two women are part of an anti-aging experiment gone wrong. They cannot, as promised, halt their age when they want to, but continue to grow "down." At age fifteen, they decide to break the rules and find their descendants, who may take care of them as they continue to become more vulnerable and helpless. The modern society is one of total surveillance through computers, debit cards, and satellites.

Halam, Ann. The Transformations Trilogy.
  The Daymaker. London: Orchard, 1987.
  Transformations. London: Orchard, 1988.
  The Skybreaker. London: Orchard, 1990.
In the far future a "new web of reality" has emerged in which magic is the new power, and human society has turned its back on its former lack of care for the natural environment. Zanne, a Covenor, has been brought up to use her magical powers to give a "good death" to technology, which has been outlawed by superstitious communities, in an attempt to control and deny the past. The "new web" is, however, far from utopian in its repressive, intolerant ways. Zanne must learn to understand and transform, rather than kill, the past to achieve a truly utopian existence.

Hamilton, Virginia. The Justice Cycle.
  Justice and Her Brothers. New York: Greenwillow, 1978.
  Dustland. New York, Greenwillow: 1980.
  The Gathering. New York: Greenwillow, 1981.
A group of children psychically connect to form the First Unit and travel into the future, which is an apparently barren wasteland of dust. Despite the inhospitable landscape, however, mutant human life forms thrive and new beginnings are legion, based on choice, variety, tolerance of difference, and openness to change. Via the biological metaphor of evolutionary theory, Hamilton explores the themes of power, interpretation, uncertainty, and the uncalculated imperfection that underlies possible future change in the ceaseless human quest for utopia.

Handler, Daniel [Lemony Snicket]. *The Vile Village*. Illustrated by Brett Helquist. New York: HarperCollins Publishers, 2001. The Baudelaire orphans are exiled to the V.F.D. (Village of Fowl Devotees), which has been designed on the principle "it takes a village to raise a child." This is no benign community, however: the three youngsters are forced to do all of the work of the town, which is creepily covered with crows. It features a highly regimented structure and thousands of rules which beset the children: "The council of Elders has so many rules that you can scarcely do anything without breaking one of them" (56).

Harris, Rosemary.
>*A Quest for Orion.* London: Faber, 1978.
>*Tower of the Stars.* London: Faber, 1980.

Neo-Stalinist "Freaks" have enslaved Western Europe by using germ warfare. A group of children form a resistance movement at first to evade, but ultimately to challenge and overthrow the regime that rules the populace by fear and violence.

Hesse, Karen. *The Music of Dolphins.* New York: Scholastic, 1996. Mila is a feral child, raised by dolphins after a plane crash. As a teenager, she is discovered and studied, and taught human ways. Human society, to her, is cold, controlling, aggressive, and full of rules and governmental regulations. She is not free. Contrasted to human society is the society of dolphins, which is marked by music, instinctive cooperation, communication, and nurturing. She forces the scientists to return her to the sea.

Holloway, Emory. *Janice in Tomorrow-Land.* New York: American Book Company, 1936. The vivacious yet discontented Janice imaginatively visits a world in the future that offers material, educational, entertainment, culinary, and social opportunities far beyond those she experiences in her own world.

Hoover, H. M. *Children of Morrow.* New York: Four Winds Press, 1973. The consequences of environmental destruction are traced and counted in this novel set in the 2300s. Neither of the surviving colonies—the primitive Base society ruled by religious and martial laws, or the elite bunker society of Morrow—is attractive. The novel explores the notions of ownership, intolerance, selfishness, and exploitation that have led humans to destroy the natural environment and inherit such a dystopian future.

———. *The Delikon.* New York: Viking Press, 1977. A highly evolved alien species fails in its efforts to help humankind mature into complex social beings. Serious questions are raised about people's capacity to imagine utopia when human nature is governed by short-term self-interest. The book invites the reader to weigh individuality against a merged social consciousness.

———. *This Time of Darkness.* New York: Viking Press, 1980. Amy and Axel inhabit a squalid underground city. Escaping to a higher level they discover a domed city of privilege, where people live in fear of riots from the people beneath them. Cast out by the authorities into the wilderness beyond the city, the children finally join a community based on kindness, not fear. Although the villagers cannot challenge and change the corruption of the city, they form a utopian enclave in which the children can find security and happiness.

Hopf, Alice Lightner. *The Galactic Troubadours*. New York: Norton, 1965. Nicholas and his young musician friends live on Hercules V, an entirely automated planet where there is no room for the impractical—no room for troubadours or gourmets, as all inhabitants work in the essentials of running a new world. But soon Nicholas and his friends get the opportunity to explore other planets. They take their musical abilities with them and play for the inhabitants of other worlds. On their tour, they encounter other societies and learn to appreciate their own. They return to Hercules V with joy and find awaiting them a community that has heard of their travels and now welcomes their talents.

———. *Day of the Drones*. New York: Norton, 1969. Fifteen-year-old Amhara is a dark-skinned native of Afria and a prominent member of her community, selected to become a high-level Medic. Her dark skin helps her to succeed, because five hundred years after a global disaster, her people have determined that light-skinned people were the evil ones who destroyed the planet. Amhara's people in turn destroy all children whose skin is too light. Amhara and her cousin N'Gobi go on an expedition: they travel the globe, discover a rich culture from which to learn, and return hopeful that they can transform their world into one that embraces diversity.

Hughes, Monica. *The Tomorrow City*. Toronto: HarperCollins, 1978. A computer is programmed to administer a perfect city, with the needs of the city's children foremost. When the computer destroys the elderly and homeless and brainwashes all residents, creating a dystopian "city of tomorrow," the adolescent protagonists Caro and David disable the computer and bring an end to its rule.

———. *The Guardian of Isis*. London: Hamish Hamilton, 1981. [Isis Trilogy.] In 2136 the planet Isis has deteriorated under the tyranny of one ruler, who has imposed rituals, taboos, and strict laws. Jody is unable to conform to the repressive regulations of this dystopian community and is banished from the settlement.

———. *Devil on My Back*. New York: Atheneum, 1984.
    The Dream Catcher. London: Julia MacRae, 1986.
In *Devil on My Back*, in the underground postdisaster colony of ArcOne (originally "Ark One"), Tomi is a privileged overlord in a rigidly stratified society where the elite use their knowledge to control the "slaves" and

"workers" beneath them. After a revolt by the slaves, Tomi accidently leaves his contained society, where he meets a group of freed slaves who convince him of the injustice of ArcOne. *The Dream Catcher* explores a postdisaster community based on the psychic linking of minds and equality. Ruth, however, is a misfit who questions the lack of risk, uncertainty, and independence Ark 3's society represents. She challenges its claustrophobic comfort and, like Tomi, dreams of freedom Outside.

―――. *The Other Place*. Toronto: HarperCollins, 1999. In an overcrowded earth of the future, the "Botany Bay" project sends a colony of children to an uninhabited planet to found an ideal society. The innocence and resourcefulness of the children helps them succeed where adults have failed.

Hughes, Ted. *The Iron Giant: A Story in Five Nights*. Illustrated by George Adamson. London: Faber, 1968. A British boy nullifies the threat of the Iron Giant, and engages him in the fight against the space-bat-angel-dragon that has just sat on Australia and threatened to eat every living thing on Earth. The creature ends up inside the moon singing Earth to universal harmony.

Ibbotson, Eva. *The Secret of Platform 13*. London: Pan Macmillan, 1994. The floating island, accessible to London only once every nine years, is also called Avalon and St. Martin's Land. Its people live peacefully with animals and all kinds of bizarre creatures like ogres. They are hidden from the modern world by mistmakers. Their rulers see themselves as subservient to the people. The prince, however, has been kidnapped from the island and a rescue team must find him.

―――. *Monster Mission*. Illustrated by Teresa Sdralevich. London: Macmillan Children's Books, 1999. [U.S. title *The Island of the Aunts*. New York: Dutton Children's Books, 2000.] Three children, unhappy with their lives in England, are kidnapped by a mysterious group of aunts who tend to outlandish creatures on a remote island. This is a utopia in which hard work, cooperation, and environmental protection are valued. Every creature is equal, no matter how small or ugly. The utopia is blessed by the kraken, who travel the seas, protecting them and spreading good karma; it is also threatened by one child's father, who wants to capture the creatures and make money off them.

James, Lawrence.
   The Revengers. London: Bantam, 1992.
   Beyond the Grave. London: Bantam, 1992.
Although life is simpler in these postdisaster novels of the future, it is far from idealized. Instead, intolerance and aggression characterize the social

groups that have emerged. Daunting questions are raised about the fundamental fabric of human society.

Juster, Norton. *The Phantom Tollbooth*. Illustrated by Jules Feiffer. London: Epstein & Carroll, 1961. Milo journeys to the Kingdom of Wisdom. It is ruled by Azaz, king of words, and the Mathemagician, ruler of numbers, who are rivals. The kingdom is in disarray because the princesses Rhyme and Reason have been banished. Milo retrieves them in an attempt to restore harmony.

Karl, Jean E. *But We Are Not of Earth*. New York: Dutton, 1981. Romula Linders lives on Meniscus F in a seemingly utopian "School/Home" for children orphaned and exiled from Earth. She and three friends, known as the "Terrible Four," are trained for practical, efficient jobs, until one day when they are selected for a mission to a new planet, Ariel. They find a more utopian world of beauty than they had thought imaginable; they feel that they have found home, until mysterious creatures attack. They learn of their teacher's plot to remain on the planet forever, and they must decide where they belong.

Kelleher, Victor. *Taronga*. Ringwood, Vic.: Viking Kestrel, 1986. In the near future humanity is perilously close to bringing about its own extinction as, due to war and ongoing threats of global nuclear hostility, civilization is breaking down irreparably. In Sydney marauding gangs fight savagely for possession of Taronga Zoo's resources, exemplifying the selfish greed and sadistic pleasure that has resulted in this scenario of violence and brutality. The teenager Ben learns to turn his back on humanity's "Last Days" and frees the animals, setting out into the bush to create a utopian alternative based on cooperation between species.

———. *The Makers*. Ringwood, Vic.: Puffin, 1987. The future is a wasteland due to humanity's incapacity to control its violent, aggressive nature. Two evolutionary lines have evolved. One line, "The Makers," is peaceful and meek. They are cast as parents who hope to use education and technology to oversee and contain the aggressive nature of the other line, the primitive "Children of Violence." The Makers must learn that, to avoid becoming despots and creating a dystopia, they have to allow their children the freedom to make their own choices.

———. *Parkland*. Ringwood, Vic.: Viking Children's Books, 1995. Parkland is a zoo, in which biologically manipulated hybrid human-animals are imprisoned. The unjust values of a society that is prepared to mistreat other species in such a way are laid bare in this violent vision of a credible dystopian future.

Kesteven, G. R. *The Awakening Water*. London: Chatto, 1977. In this futuristic dystopia the Party drugs, imprisons, and subdues the populace to prevent fighting and destruction. Watford Nine John escapes to recreate a utopian community of young people by democratic, honest means. The novel explores the tension between freedom and government.

Kress, Nancy. *David Brin's Out of Time: Yanked!* New York: Avon Books, 1999. This novel is set in a utopian 2339, where there is no crime, pollution, or disease. However, to face a threat from an alien race, this utopian society needs heroes with "grit," which it takes from past societies ranging from tenth-century Iceland to twentieth-century America.

Lally, Soinbhe. *A Hive for the Honeybee*. New York: Scholastic, 1996. Mo is a young drone who constantly questions the political and social structure of his hive. He argues for change: for a better life for the workers, and expanded opportunities for females. Why should the drones simply laze about and be fed and cleaned by the workers? "Somebody had to debunk all the silly accepted ideas that could accumulate in an old hive" (45). However, the forces of instinct in this traditional and quasi-religious society are too strong to suffer change.

Larrabeiti, Michael. *The Borribles*. New York: Macmillan, 1976. In the alleys of London, the Borribles live and play and try to elude the police who see them as hoodlums. They are children who drop out of society—those who stop going to school, those who had a "bad start." The sign of their membership in their group is that they grow pointy ears, stop aging, and join with their peers to survive in a world set against them. Their primary goal is to survive in the alleys, so they spend most of their time looking for food and shelter and defending themselves against their enemies, the Rumbles, who are giant rodents. In their adventures, they earn their new Borrible names and prove themselves among their peers, with whom they maintain a child's version of a city where no adults can structure their lives.

Lawrence, Louise. *Andra*. London: Collins, 1971. Two thousand years in the future, life in Sub-City One is artificially controlled and dreary in its perfection and conformity. Andra alone recognizes the dystopian nature of this existence, realizing what has been lost when humans were forced to live underground because she has received a small graft from a surface-dweller's brain. When she dies at the end of the novel, the possibility of an alternative way of life to the stultifying torpor of such an ordered existence dies too.

———. *Children of the Dust*. London: Bodley Head, 1985. In the aftermath of a full-scale nuclear war, life has become a competition for scant resources between those who live in nuclear bunkers and those who struggle with the effects of fallout in the devastated natural world. Homo Sapiens is, however, ultimately replaced by "Homo Superior," a mutant strain with psychic abilities allowing the species to cooperate and rise above the socially aggressive ways of its destructive predecessors.

L'Engle, Madeleine.
>	*A Wrinkle in Time.* New York: Farrar, Straus & Giroux, 1962.
>	*A Wind in the Door.* New York: Farrar, Straus & Giroux, 1973.
>	*A Swiftly Tilting Planet.* New York: Farrar, Straus & Giroux, 1978.

A group of children travel in time to understand and counter the forces of evil in the past and future that threaten their world. They encounter and revoke various forms of repressive social structures. The books explore freedom and individualism as principles that underpin a just society. In *A Wrinkle in Time*, evil is defined as the extermination of individuality on a planet ruled by IT, a huge brain that controls the lives of the conformist, unthinking populace.

Levitin, Sonia. *The Cure.* San Diego: Harcourt Brace, 1999. In the year 2407, the United Social Alliance of Earth under the rule of Elders assures peace through conformity. Those citizens who do not conform willingly choose to be "recycled," but when Gemm 16884 is caught celebrating his passions with song, he opts for "The Cure" instead. Using virtual reality as a tool, the Elders allow Gemm to experience life as a sixteen-year-old Jew in 1348 who, along with his entire community, is accused of causing the plague and is burned to death. Upon awakening, Gemm understands the danger of diversity. Gemm is cured and promoted to the role of Elder, but soon he plans to change his world from the inside out by honoring love and difference.

Lowry, Lois. *The Giver.* Boston: Houghton Mifflin, 1993. When he is chosen to be the receiver of historical memory, Jonas comes to realize that his perfect society, in which there is no pain and much cooperation, is really a dystopia, as those who do not fit the community's standard of perfection are "released," or put to death. He leaves, forcing the community to face complexity.

———. *Gathering Blue.* New York: Houghton Mifflin, 2000. Kira's society isolates the artists and directs their gifts to its own uses. Those who are deemed burdens to the community are killed or left to die in the Fields. However, they are often rescued by another community made up of the rejects, where harmony thrives. Kira learns of this society and pledges to bridge the gaps between the communities.

Macdonald, Caroline. *The Lake at the End of the World.* Ringwood, Vic.: Viking Kestrel, 1988. The world has almost been destroyed by pollution.

Hector leaves the confines of his underground colony to make contact with a family that still struggles to live outside freely. The novel explores the choice between living in a safe, but restrictive, society as opposed to experiencing danger and freedom.

————. *The Eyewitness*. Sydney, Aus.: Hodder & Stoughton, 1991. *The Eyewitness* is set in a future world where citizens are divided into those with IN numbers and those "feral" individuals who stand outside the rigid order of the "Whole World Government." There is omnipresent surveillance, punishment for any individuals who consort with the "ferals," and a particularly strong taboo against suicide. The protagonist Leo and the time-traveling Jack fight against this repressive government.

MacDonald, George. *The Princess and Curdie*. London: Chatto & Windus, 1877. Reflecting the Fisher King tale, Curdie restores the ill king to power, and punishes the evil court. He and Princess Irene rule over a contented and good people. However, when they die, a king is elected who, in his quest for gold, literally undermines and destroys the capital city.

Mace, Elisabeth.
> *Ransome Revisited*. London: Andre Deutsch, 1975.
> *The Travelling Man*. London: Andre Deutsch, 1976.

The Travelling Man traces the journey of Will, a ruthless schemer, in his determined quest to find the "Clever Men," whom he believes are able to rise above his world's regressive superstition and rituals. The novel ends, though, with his disillusionment and death, as Will's dreams of attaining utopia are systematically extinguished. He learns that there can be no clever men due to fundamental flaws in human nature. Prequel to *Ransome Revisited*. In the postdisaster Britain of *Ransome Revisited*, life is almost intolerable, as children are denied names, brutally treated in school and made to toil purposelessly in slate mines. The story follows some children who leave to seek a better place. Although some are killed on the way, two find the Colony, which offers the (illusory?) promise of a pastoral utopia.

Mark, Jan. *The Ennead*. Harmondsworth, England: Kestrel Books, 1978. This novel is underpinned by a sense of nihilism and failure. In the far future people live on barren planets, which act as metaphors for their barren relationships. It follows the fortunes of the unlikable, broken antihero, Isaac, who finally makes a conscious choice that under such circumstances life is not worth living.

Matas, Carol and Perry Nodelman. *More Minds*. New York: Simon & Schuster Books for Young Readers, 1996. Sequel to *Of Two Minds*. In Gepeth, there are no uncertainties due to the Balance. Even the rain is parceled out, every Sunday from two to six. However, Princess Lenora realizes that she is not alone in her dissatisfaction with this predictable way of life. The Balance is under threat. Traveling through time, Lenora discovers that she herself brought the Balance into being, in response to a world—enchanting yet ultimately chaotic—in which people could automatically alter their reality to match every whim. She determines to find some middle way between ultimate freedom and the total control of the Balance.

McNaughton, Janet. *The Secret Under My Skin*. Toronto: HarperCollins, 2000. Blay Raytee is a street kid, a ward of the government (the Commission) that succeeded the Technocaust that poisoned the environment. The Commission, distrustful of technology and wishing to retain control, hides the fact that the environment is improving. The Weavers' Guilds lead the resistance, wishing to found a democracy.

Moulton, Deborah. *Children of Time*. New York: Dial Books, 1989. David lives in a totalitarian state run by computers, or the Guardian system, which is on the brink of nuclear war. He is whisked away to a strange castle filled with children, run by the maniacal "Mommy," who plans to have him rule the world after nuclear destruction. David's father forms a democratic underground community, or "Demosee," to outlast the nuclear storm. Upon waking up after his long sleep in a hybernation chamber, David conquers the evil Sarke who leads the children, and gives the care of the brainwashed children to the "Demosee" tribe. It is hinted that with the help of Irene, who possesses seeds that can withstand radioactivity, David will usher in a better future.

———. *First Battle of Morn*. New York: Dial Books, 1988. When fourteen-year-old Torin comes of age and gains his medallion of authority from the Teachers, he believes he is on the path to success on his planet of Morn; vivid visions torment him, however, and soon the Teachers call him to join them in their city. On his journey, Torin meets a group of rebels and learns that those he saw as his leaders are tyrants; these leaders have turned the commoners of Morn into their slaves by monitoring them through the medallions and selectively breeding them for submission. At the same time, the Teachers have enhanced their own communication and procreation capabilities, so that soon no trace of their earthly or human origin will exist and the entire planet will be in their control. With the rebels, Torin disables the Teacher's main computer and saves the planet.

Naylor, Phyllis Reynolds. *Sang Spell*. New York: Atheneum Books for Young Readers, 1998. Josh discovers a community in the Appalachians made up of Melungeons, people of mixed blood who settled in the backwoods in the sixteenth century, fleeing persecution. "We are Christian, Jew, and Muslim, thousands of miles from our home. We are Portuguese, Spanish, Berber, Arab, Jew, and black, yet we all live together peaceably. Well, most of us . . ." (121). The village is hidden from society, and one cannot escape from it since it has its own physical laws. Some inhabitants have the ability to live forever.

Nelson, O. T. *The Girl Who Owned a City*. Minneapolis: Lerner Publications Co., 1975. This novel is set in a dystopian world where gangs and fierce armies are at war after a virus sweeping the earth has killed everyone over twelve years of age.

Neufeld, John. *Sleep Two, Three, Four! A Political Thriller*. New York: Harper & Row, 1971. An heir to Nixon and Spiro Agnew, President Wagenson has made the United States a totalitarian state, where people live in "homogenous communities" based on race, and are terrorized by government gangs. The teen heroes join the Underground to resist the society.

Nix, Garth. *Shade's Children*. New York: HarperCollins, 1997. In the future, Overlords raise children in Dormitories only to slaughter them for parts by the age of fourteen. Those who escape face monstrous hunting bio-machines aimed at killing them. The fortunate ones become Shade's Children, a band of young adults led by a disembodied mind that existed as a man before the Overlords took over the world. Shade's goal is to return the world to its earlier condition, but his willingness to risk the lives of his most faithful followers—Ella, Drum, Gold Eye, and Ninde—suggests Shade threatens as much as he protects the young adults. In the end, the heroes can rely only on each other as they attempt to end alien rule on Earth.

O'Brien, Robert C. *Mrs. Frisby and the Rats of NIMH*. New York: Atheneum, 1971. The rats have escaped from a lab to set up their ideal community, based on their new technological abilities. Feeling that they have become too materialistic, they decide to form a second community in Thorn Valley, based on independence and hard work.

———. *Z for Zachariah*. London: Gollancz, 1975. Ann Burden appears to be the sole survivor of a nuclear war, until a scientist, Loomis, finds her Edenic valley. The novel follows their attempts to live together. Will they create a new pastoral utopia or re-create the follies of their predecessors to ruin the environment yet again? By the end the signs are not promising, although the possibility of reconciliation is not ruled out. The values and attitudes underpinning social possibilities are explored throughout.

Oppel, Kenneth. *Sunwing*. Toronto: HarperCollins, 1999. A colony of bats is lured to a Human Building featuring an indoor forest where winter never comes, insects are plentiful, and no predators exist. Shade, however, discovers that the Humans are experimenting on his fellow bats and using them to carry explosives to a faraway war. He escapes only to encounter monster cannibal bats who plan to extinguish the sun. He uses his special sound powers to stop this Armageddon. In the process, he helps to arrange an alliance with old enemies, the owls and rats, thus establishing utopia in the forest, one in which bats can move freely in the sun again.

Parenteau, Shirley. *The Talking Coffins of Cryo-City*. New York: Elsevier/ Nelson Books, 1979. This futuristic world is explicity described as a "utopia" (10), and its motto is "PERFECT WEATHER FOR A PERFECT WORLD" (13). In this world, a computer programs the weather, dictated by the weather planners, and there is no hunger and scarcity. Criminals are sent to the cryogenic coffins of Cryo-City where they will be thawed out at a time when their criminal tendencies can be physically cured.

Park, Ruth. *My Sister, Sif*. Ringwood, Vic. and Harmondsworth, England: Viking Kestrel, 1986. Human society's exploitative relationship with nature is subjected to radical questioning by Riko, the central character of Park's novel. Riko is half-human, half mer-creature. She and her sister, Sif, experience the utopian existence of an alternative society living in harmony with whales and dolphins beneath the ocean. Human intolerance of other species and lack of care for the environment, however, fatally threaten their way of life.

Pausewang, Gudrun. *The Last Children of Schevenborn* [*Die Letzen Kinder von Schewenborn*]. Translated by Norman Watt. Toronto: Douglas & MacIntyre Ltd., 1988. Roland's carefree summer holidays are abruptly interrupted by nuclear war, and he is suddenly forced to struggle for survival in the polluted environmental and social wreckage. The gradual decline of social mores into a nightmare characterized by mistrust, deception, stealing, and killing is witnessed through the child's horrified eyes. The book underlines the fundamental importance of respect, mutual responsibility, and love in human society by depicting its absence in an uncompromisingly "hard" world.

Philbrick, Rodman. *The Last Book in the Universe*. New York: Scholastic, 2000. Spaz lives in a world of concrete, pollution, and extreme poverty after the Big Shake, or massive earthquake. The world is divided between the Urb, where the normals like Spaz live, and Eden, where the proovs, or genetically improved humans, live. The Urb is an urban chaos run by warlords and threatened by mind-degenerating drugs; Eden is orderly and still has blue sky. Spaz enters Eden in an attempt to save his little sister, and makes some of the proovs question the current system.

Prince, Alison. *The Others*. London: Methuen Children's, 1986. Life in Ergo Norm's rigidly hierarchical world is closely monitored and subject to strict rules. After a nuclear disaster, biological life, including human life, is artificially controlled and manipulated to comply with the political system. The mutant Ergo strives to overthrow this oppressive regime.

Pullman, Philip. His Dark Materials Trilogy.
 Northern Lights. London: Scholastic, 1995. [U.S. title *The Golden Compass*. New York: Alfred A. Knopf, 1996.]
 The Subtle Knife. London: Scholastic, 1997.
 The Amber Spyglass. London: Scholastic, 2000.
His Dark Materials features Lyra and, in the sequel to *Northern Lights*, Will, and their exploration of different worlds. Their mission is restore harmony, and save the souls of children, by stopping the Dust from escaping. The trilogy meditates on power, especially that of the Church and the Kingdom of Heaven. The chief dystopian world is Cittàgazze, where specters suck out adults' souls; an example of a threatened utopian world is that of the *mulefa*, in which all relationships are symbiotic and nothing is destroyed. The children end up succeeding in their mission, although to do so they must say good-bye forever. They resolve to devote the rest of their lives to improving their worlds, thus building the "Republic of Heaven."

Richemont, Enid. *The Game*. London: Walker Books, 1990. The Furies decide to give humans all the things they crave: power, greed, violence. The result is a shocking future in which the populace is brainwashed to become intolerant of individual difference, "imperfections" are wiped out, and strict racial and class segregation is the norm. The government has outlawed family life, sex, and love. A small group of children overthrow this brutal tyranny, although disquieting questions about social intolerance remain.

Robinson, Veronica. *Delos*. London: Andre Deutsch, 1980. After years living in the spaceship Delos following a catastrophe on earth, humans find a planet on which they can live in freedom and peace. Although they have difficulty adjusting to this liberating environment, they forge a utopian, peaceful society with no knowledge of destructive technology.

Rowling, J. K.
 Harry Potter and the Philosopher's Stone. London: Bloomsbury, 1997.
 Harry Potter and the Chamber of Secrets. London: Bloomsbury, 1998.

Harry Potter and the Prisoner of Azkaban. London: Bloomsbury, 1999.
Harry Potter and the Goblet of Fire. London: Bloomsbury, 2000.
In this extended battle between good and evil, Hogwarts School of Wizardry and Witchcraft is a utopian space of good government (of Professor Dumbledore), plentiful food, and chocolate as medicine. However, it is threatened by Voldemort's constant invasions in different forms. Additionally, as Hermione discovers to her horror in *The Goblet of Fire*, the school relies on an underclass of house elves.

Sachar, Louis. *Holes*. New York: Farrar, Straus & Giroux, 1998. Stanley is sent to a detention center in the heart of the desert, run by the malevolent Warden who sets the boys to digging holes all day. He escapes and finds the elusive oasis, God's Thumb.

Sargent, Pamela.
     Watchstar. New York: Pocket Books, 1980.
     Eye of the Comet. New York: Harper & Row, 1984.
     Homesmind. New York: Harper & Row, 1984.
This trilogy follows three generations of characters interested in founding harmony between inhabitants of Earth and cometdwellers. In *Watchstar*, Daiya lives in a village in which all members communicate through telepathy, forming the Net. They live in harmony; however, the children who do not have these mental powers are killed, as are those who cannot endure the Ordeal. Keeping oneself separate from others is punishable by death. She meets Reiho, a traveler from a comet, whose community is harmonious, beautiful, and nonconfrontational, bonded by Homesmind, the communal mind of the comet that aids them. In *Eye of the Comet*, Lydee has grown up in the comet world and returns to her original home, Earth. Many misunderstandings ensue between the two worlds, but the book ends with a utopian vision of harmony. In *Homesmind*, the difficulties of setting up this utopia are elaborated. Earth is threatened by an evil comet, and also by the weakening of the power of the ancient Minds, which Earth's inhabitants tap into for their telepathic powers. Disasters occur, as Homesmind and the Minds are destroyed, but the trilogy ends in hope, with the discovery of the Child of Homesmind and the Minds, who promises to unite the two peoples.

Schlee, Ann. *The Vandal*. London: Macmillan Children's, 1979. Paul lives in the ordered urban world of the Enlightenment. Citizens are quiet, law-abiding, and civilized. Paul, however, does not fit in and gradually learns that this society has been brought about by scientists who drug the masses and eradicate memories of the past in order to control human aggression. Paul, caught undertaking acts of vandalism in an instinctive rebellion against such control, is removed and made to harvest crops under large domes with other workers who maintain the city-dwellers' lifestyle. Eventually he escapes in an attempt to join other like-minded people who try to destroy the corrupt system by burning the domes.

Scott, Hugh. *Why Weeps the Brogan?* London: Walker, 1989. This book offers a commentary on the future that adults are leaving for their children to inherit. The story is based on two children who have ironically been betrayed by their mother's instructions to stay inside a museum during a nuclear attack. In this world of dust and decay, the frightful creature that they fear but serve is ultimately revealed as their mother, hideously maimed by the blast.

Shusterman, Neal. *Downsiders*. New York: Simon & Schuster Books for Young Readers, 1999. The downsiders live in a "hidden utopia" under New York City created by disenfranchised workers of the first subway. They continue to rescue those who literally fall through the cracks of Topside society. Eminently resourceful, they create everything from the garbage of Topside. Their ultimate leader—and one who "appears" rather than is elected—is always a child or teenager, as only someone young can be "the Most-Beloved." The society is threatened by the unwitting invasion of Topsiders.

Sleator, William. *House of Stairs*. New York: E. P. Dutton, 1974. A group of teenage orphans are taken by scientists and placed in a house of stairs where, in order to get food from a mysterious machine, they become conditioned to fight among each other. Two members of the group starve rather than join in, and are sent to an island for misfits. The scientists inform them at the end that they were part of a presidential experiment to create a completely obedient team of youths to serve him.

Snyder, Midori. *Hatchling* [Dinotopia]. New York: Random House, 1995. This book is set in Dinotopia, where teenager Janet Morgan is appointed as an apprentice to the Hatchery. After she falls asleep during her watch, she runs away in disgrace, only to encounter a wounded dinosaur named Kranog, who is about to lay an egg. Since Kranog is the last of her race, it is crucial that the egg survive. In keeping with the Dinotopian ethic of human-animal harmony, Kranog literally includes Janet in her account of her family lineage. Janet and her "nestfriend" Zephyr (a dinosaur) mature in this book, and understand the importance of their work at the Hatchery and beyond.

Snyder, Zilpha Keatley. The Green-sky Trilogy.
    Below the Root. Illustrated by Alton Raible. New York: Atheneum, 1975.
    And All Between. Illustrated by Alton Raible. New York: Atheneum, 1976.

Until the Celebration. Illustrated by Alton Raible. New York: Atheneum, 1977.
The Kindar live in an apparently idyllic world in the trees, where there is no violence or scarcity. When the teenage protagonist Raamo is chosen to become a member of the elite Ol-zhaan group, he and two of his friends discover that dissenters in their society have been exiled against their will to a world below the root of the tree. Although the Kindar are told that these underground people are predatory monsters (called the "Pash-shan"), they actually form a community called the Erdlings. The final two books of the series concentrate on the Erdlings and the often-difficult reunion of Kindar and Erdling societies.

Spyri, Johanna. *Heidi's Lehr-und Wanderjahre* [*Heidi*]. Gotha: Perthes, 1880. The Swiss Alps provide a natural utopia, where beauty and goodness reign. Everyone who comes in contact with the Alps is healed in some way: spiritually, emotionally, and physically. Heidi is like a Romantic embodiment of the mountains themselves.

Staig, Laurence. *The Glimpses*. London: Macmillan Children's, 1989. The Helix Party tries to use subliminal messages to brainwash the population into accepting a fascist regime. Worse still, biogenetic engineering is being developed to produce a superior race of leaders. A group of children who can "glimpse" into the structure of cells to see the horrifying truth that people are being "farmed" to fulfill social roles ultimately combine forces to prevent this nightmare.

———. *The Network*. London: Collins, 1989. In the near future three social outcasts must struggle to fathom the source of a network of evil that has consumed the sophisticated technology of the London Underground. Their quest ultimately reveals a deadly nuclear arsenal that is unleashed to annihilate its human creators. The novel questions people's naïve dependence on deceptively benign leadership.

Stone, Josephine Rector. *Green Is for Galanx*. New York: Atheneum, 1980. The artificial space community "Wally's World" controls all members of its society, taking the special gifts of unusual children and placing them in androids. Illona is a teacher of these children who seeks protect them; the large, green creature called the Galanx helps them to escape.

———. *Praise All the Moons of Morning*. New York: Atheneum, 1979. On the planet of Ix-thian, ordinary citizens are kept in thrall by the narcotic fungus "loofah," and the iron rule of the Goldmen. Cass Williams, an Earth teenager, travels in time to help the character Desta and her friends escape.

Stoutenburg, Adrien. *Out There*. New York: Viking Press, 1971. A band of unwanted children, led by Aunt Zeb, undertakes a trip outside their dystopian domed city to experience the delights and fears of risk in the pockets of natural wilderness that they hope may still exist despite the polluted environment of the twenty-first century. Although they find wildlife, they also find that it is still threatened by entrepreneurs who wish to exploit it as a new leisure industry.

Streiber, Whitley. *Wolf of Shadows*. New York: Knopf, 1985. The willful destruction not only of human society but also of the natural environment is explored in this apocalyptic story, which shows the end of the world through a wolf's eyes. Streiber provokes the reader to question the values and attitudes that could lead to such a dystopian future world.

Sutton, Jean and Jeff. *The Beyond*. New York: G. P. Putnam's Sons, 1967. The book is set on the planet Ergo in Galactic Year 3155, a place where the Federation's telepaths, mutants, and other paranormal people are sent. The Federation, despite its regressive policies, can be described as utopian: "the third millennium of the Federation was an age of play, pleasure, sensual abandon—absolute freedom from war, strife, poverty" (14).

Swindells, Robert. *Brother in the Land*. Oxford: Oxford University Press, 1984. Swindells's cautionary story of the horror, brutal rivalry, and breakdown of human relationships in the aftermath of nuclear war raises questions about human nature and humans' capacity to live cooperatively and peaceably. The outcome is a hell of humanity's own making, experienced by Danny, a teenage survivor.

————. *Daz 4 Zoe*. London: Hamish Hamilton, 1990. In the near future British society is rigidly divided into Two Nations. A privileged elite inhabits affluent suburbs; the uneducated, disadvantaged underclass is forced to live in inner-city slums, brutally controlled by the police. Two teenagers from different backgrounds seek to span the social divisions of their birth, ultimately turning their backs on the injustices of their society to start afresh elsewhere.

Thomas, Frances. *Cityscape*. London: Heinemann, 1988. An unhappy, alienated teenager, Debra, escapes contemporary London to travel into another city through a door in time. The future city has outlawed reading and is governed by military rule. Here Debra's ability to read is valued by people trying to overthrow the repressive regime, but she discovers she is only treasured as an agent of political change rather than as a person. She chooses to return to her own time with renewed insight into her own worth and identity.

Tolan, Stephanie S. *Welcome to the Ark*. New York: Morrow Junior Books, 1996. Four youngsters in an experimental mental-health group home in the Adirondacks discover special powers of ESP. They use these gifts (and the Internet) to create a global network of similarly talented children, and apply their powers to combating the terrorist violence that has engulfed the world. World peace begins in Lake Placid.

Townsend, John Rowe. *The Islanders*. Oxford: Oxford University Press, 1981. Molly lives on an isolated island inhabited by a small, Puritanical community governed by the Teaching. The Teaching is from a book, but no one can read anymore. The Teaching promotes social harmony and mutual aid, especially as resources are limited. Strangers arriving in the community, like the group of people escaping a volcano, are sent to a barren island to die. Molly and others question the Teaching, and learn that the community was founded on murder rather than righteousness. The book ends on a note of change and harmony between the inhabitants and the strangers who managed to survive exile.

————. *King Creature Come*. Oxford: Oxford University Press, 1980. A future Earth has been ravaged by major wars. Society is starkly divided between Persons, who live a languid, enervated existence of luxury, and Creatures, who live in poverty and squalor in a decaying city. The Guards who protect the Persons from the Creatures revolt, only to be overthrown themselves by the Creatures. Harmony and Vector, two misfit Persons, try to forge uneasy alliances with Guards and Creatures to make a decent society in an exploration of freedom, justice, and control.

————. *Noah's Castle*. London: Oxford University Press, 1975. Two or three years in the future, U.K. society is breaking down into disorder and violence. Food is scarce and people are starving. The fabric of society tears apart, and the novel explores various possible responses to this nightmare, from the creation of "Share Alike," a group fighting for equal distribution of resources, to the siege mentality of families who will stop at nothing to keep what they have.

Tully, John. *Natfact 7*. London: Methuen, 1984. In a socially stratified Britain of the future, political injustice is rife and punishment for lawbreaking harsh. Skip joins a revolutionary group, All Citizens Equal (ACE), which fights to bring about an alternative ideal society built on love, not greed. Disillusioned by the ensuing bloodshed, Skip wonders if the end justifies the means in the attempt to form a utopian society, as power won by violent means needs to be maintained by violence.

Turner, Gerry. *Stranger from the Depths*. Garden City, N.Y.: Doubleday and Company, 1967. A group of young adults discover Saa, the last surviving inhabitant of the underwater city of Haad. Haad was a peaceful city, replete with technological wonders, featuring sexual equality and a lack of disease (until a plague came that killed all but Saa). Saa discovers that there are signs of life deep within the earth and, with his new friends, finds the city of Gaan, a community of violence, oppression of females, and empty religious rituals. Saa takes some of the rebels back to Haad, intending to revive the city. The teens' memories are erased before their return, to protect Haad from humans.

Ure, Jean.
> *Plague 99*. London: Methuen Teen Collection, 1989. [U.S. title is *Plague*. San Diego: Harcourt Brace Jovanovich, 1991].
> *Come Lucky April*. London: Methuen, 1992. [Reprint of *After the Plague*. London: Mammoth, 1995.]

In *Plague 99*, a devastating plague all but wipes out humanity. Survivors of the disaster struggle to survive, allowing the author to explore profound social issues and raise questions about human nature and the possibility of social cooperation in a time of extreme scarcity. *Come Lucky April* takes place one hundred years after the plague. A community of women has developed, which has eliminated male aggression by sending boys away for five years to be trained and castrated. A girl from the community, Come Lucky April, meets an outsider, Daniel, who disrupts the society of women. The novel questions which community is most desirable.

Vale, Brenda. *Albion*. Barnstaple: Spindlewood, 1982. *Albion* is a utopian vision of a human future when people have opted for a simpler way of life in which society is more in tune with nature. The novel explores the hardships, but primarily the benefits, of an ecologically sensitive approach to life.

Vornholt, John. *River Quest* [Dinotopia]. New York: Random House, 1995. This book extends the lesson of cooperation in Dinotopia to the freshwater environment and the salvation of the Polongo River, which has mysteriously dried up. Thirteen-year-old Marigold and her saurian partner Paddlefoot must learn to cooperate with the prickly teenager Birch and his Triceratops friend Rogo; they form a partnership that saves a Dinotopian art treasure and helps revitalize the river. They all learn more about their vocation and life's work in Dinotopia. Aaron, a recent arrival to Dinotopia, testifies to the superiority of Dinotopian society by contrasting it to regular Earth society.

———. *Sabertooth Mountain* [Dinotopia]. New York: Random House, 1996. This adventure story set in Dinotopia focuses on the sabertooth tigers that live in the Forbidden Mountains apart from other denizens. An avalanche blocks their access to their food source; they must decide whether to follow the Dinotopian motto of "breathe deep, seek peace" or to violently hunt for food. Thirteen-year-old Cai helps them find a peaceful solution, befriending a sabertooth named Redstripe in the process. Cai both attains the personal understanding that is the hallmark of Dinotopian life and helps to integrate the sabertooths into the wider culture.

Wallis, Redmond. *The Mills of Space*. Cape Town: Purnell, 1989. Set in outer space, this is a story of a group of dissidents fighting against the evils of mind control. Their native Motherlode is being used as an experiment in which people are manipulated into hating machines and are therefore easily ruled.

Walsh, Jill Paton. *Torch*. New York: Farrar, Straus & Giroux, 1987. Set in a neoprimitive future Greece, in which scientific knowledge and memory of the past have been lost, a group of children are given responsibility for a mysterious torch. They carry it on a quest to find a place where the torch thrives, visiting many corrupt games that various dystopian societies use for selfish and cruel ends. They learn that the torch burns brightest when it finds a race that is run for its own sake, which only happens within the children's fragile utopian community.

Warburton, Nick. *Rat Squad*. Oxford: Oxford University Press, 2000. In Grace City everyone appears to be happy, safe, and free, but rats are allowed to kill people as a matter of policy and as a means of population control.

Watson, Simon. *No Man's Land*. London: Gollancz, 1975. Watson envisages a depersonalized, regimented future in which an excess of rationality has resulted in a concrete jungle controlled by a machine: "Giant." Although children overthrow the machine, the novel is unresolved on the issue of life in a gilded utopian cage.

West, Carl and Katherine MacLean. *Dark Wing*. New York: Atheneum, 1979. In Travis's United States, juveniles have full rights, and the highly organized society expands into space. Discovering by chance a paramedic's computer, Travis learns about medicine, which is illegal. The sick are blamed not only for their illnesses but also for tainting the perfect world. They are put to death. Travis works as an outlaw doctor and also learns about the negative side of his society by being a police cadet.

Westall, Robert. *Futuretrack 5*. Harmondsworth, England: Kestrel, 1983. A terrifying computer logic, devoid of human feeling, underpins the rigid hierarchy of classes in this uncompromising dystopia. Absolute social stability has been bought at a terrible cost: the young are educated to accept their social lot; the law is brutally enforced by "Paramils" who use "psychopters" to invade people's minds; nonconformists are lobotomized and the unemployed "Unnems" are controlled by their lusts in a culture of suicidal but addictive game-playing. The teenager Kitson tries to rebel, only to find there is no other way, and he is forced to assert a new form of tyranny.

Wilder, Cherry.
> *The Luck of Brin's Five.* New York: Atheneum, 1977.
> *The Nearest Fire.* New York: Atheneum, 1980.

These two books are set on the planet Torin, a world inhabited by the Moruia (the weavers) and the Tsamuia (the fire people). The books are centered on Earth explorers and their contact with these new cultures. Utopian content is apparent in the description of the city of Rintoul, and "the habit of perfection and grace [which] inspires those who build there, those who live in the city, so that it regenerates and grows more beautiful from age to age" (*Luck*, 117).

Wyndham, John [John Beynon Harris]. *The Chrysalids.* London: Michael Joseph, 1955. In a postcatastrophe Labrador, thousands of years in the future, mutants abound. However, physical deviants are destroyed in search of purity and perfection. A small group of telepathic young people make contact with a society in New Zealand that rescues them from their fundamentalist dystopia.

Afterword

LYMAN TOWER SARGENT

In the mid-1970s while I was compiling my initial bibliography of utopian literature,[1] I spent part of three days in the PZ7 (juvenile literature) stacks at the Library of Congress (you could still get a stack pass then). I was looking at as many of the PZ7s as I could find that someone, sometime, somewhere had called science fiction. As a direct result of this experience, I decided to exclude juvenile literature (which I defined as anything in the PZ7s) from the bibliography. I took this step partially from the need to avoid feeling any more overwhelmed than I already did by my project. I excluded film, but not published film scripts, for the same reason.[2] But the other reason I excluded the PZ7s is relevant to this collection: very few of the hundreds of books I looked at in those three days had any social or political content and those that did were so vague as to be virtually impossible to characterize.

Clearly there are utopian works in juvenile literature. Celesteville in the Babar stories is utopian and collectively the books might pass my vagueness test, but no single text does. The first work that forced me to abandon my blanket exclusion is one of the oldest, Edith Nesbit's "The Sorry-Present and the Expelled Little Boy" in her *The Story of the Amulet* (1906). Nesbit knew H. G. Wells very well, so it is hardly surprising that she wrote a story satirizing the Wellsian future.

But letting Nesbit in did not force me to open the door to other PZ7s. A friend of Wells was one thing; the other PZ7s were a whole other issue. And, in fact, since I was forced to open that door and go back to reconsider some of my earlier exclusions, I have had to include very few of the works I had excluded under the blanket rule. (Since stack passes are no longer available, I have not looked at all the works I excluded.)

I was forced to reconsider by Jack Lasenby's *The Conjuror* (1992) and Lois Lowry's *The Giver* (1993). A friend recommended Lasenby to me, and I included the book in my bibliography of New Zealand utopian literature[3] without thinking that I was opening a door. I first read a review of *The Giver* and then the book, and this is when I realized that something had happened that meant I had to change.

At any given age, children appeared to be older; and authors and publishers responded with books for these older children. Part was marketing, particularly the creation of the YA niche in which both the Y and the A had to be addressed. Initially these works addressed issues that young adults were facing daily, like sex, drugs, and death, but then people like Lasenby and Lowry took a further step and wrote works for this audience that included serious presentations of social and political themes, a few of which can reasonably be called utopias.

This first collection of essays on utopias written for children and young adults raises as many questions as it answers, which is good. While it is usually easy to tell when a book is aimed at the children's market, it is harder to be certain about the young adult market. The works considered here or listed in the Annotated Bibliography include some that I have always considered as aimed at an adult market. As a result, I wonder whether "young adult" is primarily a marketing category rather than one where there are clear distinctions between it and books written with an adult audience in mind.

There are similar issues regarding the way the word "utopia" is used. The authors and editors use it in quite a few different ways, some mutually exclusive, and there are texts included that do not fit any definition of utopia that I know. But that very problem raises what, to me, is the most important question brought out by considering these essays and the books they discuss: What constitutes a utopian space for a child or young adult?

I am not going to try a comprehensive analysis within the brief space of this afterword, but there do seem, at first glance, to be some commonalities. Children's and young adult positive utopias are similar in at least one area. Both provide a safe space. The child's space is primarily a play space where incidents occur that directly teach moral lessons.

While young adult dystopias are remarkably similar to those written for adults, some young adult positive utopias differ from both those written for children and those written for adults. Here the safe space is sometimes quite literally a safe place, a retreat from the problems and dangers of the world outside. But most often the safe place is also a space for testing and experimentation, a place in which to learn and grow, to become aware of who you are. And the safe place is not usually completely safe; there are dangers outside, and often inside as well, dangers to be met and overcome if the safe place is to be protected. And, of course, such testing helps the young adults define themselves vis à vis each other and the adult world.

I hope that this initial foray into an untouched field will inspire others to look more carefully at these utopias and ask basic questions such as, what are the differences between children's and young adult utopias? What are the gender, national, and racial differences (all begun here) in the literatures? I call utopianism "social dreaming," and it is particularly important that we understand the dreams and nightmares that are directed at children and young adults.

Notes

1. Lyman Tower Sargent, *British and American Utopian Literature 1516–1975*: *An Annotated Bibliography*. (Boston: G. K. Hall, 1979).
2. On utopian film, see the list in "Utopia/Dystopia and Cinema," in *Utopia*: *The Search for the Ideal Society in the Western World*, ed. Roland Schaer, Gregory Claeys, and Lyman Tower Sargent (New York and Oxford: The New York Public Library/Oxford University Press, 2000), 381–82; and the four essays on utopian film in *Utopian Studies* 4.2 (1993).
3. Lyman Tower Sargent, *New Zealand Utopian Literature*: *An Annotated Bibliography*. Occasional Paper 97/1. (Wellington, New Zealand: Stout Research Centre for the Study of New Zealand Society History & Culture, Victoria University of Wellington, 1997).

Contributors

Holly V. Blackford is Assistant Professor of English and Director of Writing at Rutgers University, where she also teaches American and Children's Literature and conducts research through the Center for Children and Childhood Studies. She recently completed her dissertation at the University of California, Berkeley. In it, she argues that young female readers identify not with characters but with literary form, a finding based on interviews with girls aged 8–16 about their reading practices. She has published articles on *Little Women*, *Incidents in the Life of a Slave Girl*, and contemporary women's fiction, film, and culture.

Fred Erisman is Professor Emeritus at Texas Christian University. He has written six books, including *Reading A. B. Guthrie's* The Big Sky (2000) and *Fifty Western Writers* (1982). He has published numerous articles in such journals as *Children's Literature*, *Journal of American Culture*, and *Extrapolation*, and held the 2002–2003 Charles A. Lindbergh Chair in Aerospace History at the National Air & Space Museum.

Cathrine Frank completed her doctorate at The George Washington University, writing a dissertation titled *Novel Bequests: Law, Literature, and the Transmission of Culture, 1837–1925*. She has presented papers on Scott, Conrad, Galsworthy, and Forster. Her article on Frances Burney and Walter Scott appeared in the Fall 2001 issue of *European Romantic Review*.

Sara Gadeken is Assistant Professor of English at Texas Tech University. She has published articles in *Studies in English Literature 1500–1900*, *Utah Foreign Language Review*, *Eighteenth-Century Novel*, and *Eighteenth-Century Fiction*. She is currently working on a book titled *Sarah Fielding and the Salic Law of Wit*.

James Gurney is the author and illustrator of the Dinotopia books, including *Dinotopia: A Land Apart from Time* (1992); *Dinotopia: The World Beneath*

(1995); and *Dinotopia: First Flight* (1999). He has completed artwork for *National Geographic* and mounted several art exhibits, including a 1993–1997 series of exhibits devoted to Dinotopia. His awards include the Hugo Award, the Chesley Award, the World Fantasy Award, and the Silver Medal of the Society of Illustrators (New York).

Carrie Hintz is Assistant Professor of English at Queens College/CUNY. She is currently completing a book titled *An Audience of One: The Letters of Dorothy Osborne to Sir William Temple*, and has published on early modern women writers (including Margaret Cavendish), utopian fiction, and pedagogy. Her article on Monica Hughes and Lois Lowry appeared in the April 2002 issue of *The Lion and the Unicorn*.

Monica Hughes is a prominent writer of young adult novels, especially speculative fiction. She has written over twenty-five books, including *The Keeper of the Isis Light* (1980), *The Dream Catcher* (1982), and *Ring-Rise, Ring-Set* (1982). *The Keeper of the Isis Light* won the 2000 Phoenix Award. She has also won the Vicky Metcalf Award (1981) and the Silver Feather Award. In 1981 and 1982 she received the Canada Council Prize for Children's Literature.

Alice Jenkins is Lecturer in the Department of English at the University of Glasgow. She is the coeditor, with Juliet John, of *Rethinking Victorian Culture* (2000) and *Rereading Victorian Fiction* (2000). She has also published on the relation between literature and the history of science, and is currently working on a study of the spatial imagination in contemporary fantasy.

Lois Lowry has written more than twenty-seven books for children and young adults, with *Gathering Blue* appearing in 2000. She received the 1994 Newbery Medal for *The Giver* and the 1990 Newbery Medal for *Number the Stars*. In addition to the Newbery, she has received the Boston Globe/Horn Book Award, the Children's Literature Award, and the National Jewish Libraries Award.

Alberto Manguel is an editor, translator, novelist, and essayist. He is the coeditor, with Gianni Guadalupi, of *The Dictionary of Imaginary Places* (2000), now in its second edition. He has edited numerous anthologies, including *Black Water: The Book of Fantastic Literature* (1984), *Black Water 2: More Tales of the Fantastic* (1990), and *Evening Games: Tales of Parents and Children* (1986). He is the author of *A History of Reading* (1996), *In the Looking-Glass Wood: Essays on Books, Reading, and the World* (1998), and *News from a Foreign Country Came* (1991).

Maureen F. Moran is Professor of English Literature at Brunel University, London, where she teaches nineteenth-century literature and culture. She has published on Walter Scott, Gerard Manley Hopkins, Walter Pater, Victorian women writers, and popular fantasy writers such as Tanith Lee. She was awarded the Russel B. Nye award in 2000 by the Association of Popular Culture for her article on attitudes toward witchcraft in Victorian writing. Her two current research interests focus on Gerard Manley Hopkins's engagement with particular religious debates of the nineteenth century, and "religious sensationalism" in Victorian writing.

Elaine Ostry is Assistant Professor of English at SUNY-Plattsburgh, where she teaches Children's and Young Adult Literature. She has published *Social Dreaming: Dickens and the Fairy Tale* (Routledge, 2002). She has also published in *The Lion and the Unicorn* and *Victorian Periodicals Review*. She is currently working on a book about metamorphosis in children's and young adult fantasy.

Katherine Paterson is the author of over twenty-nine books for children and young adults, including the 1978 Newbery Award–winner *Bridge to Terabithia* and the 1981 Newbery Award–winner *Jacob Have I Loved* (1980).

Kay Sambell has been teaching children's literature since 1989, both at the University of York and more recently at Northumbria University, U.K., where she is course leader for the B.A. in Childhood Studies. She gained her Ph.D. in 1996 for a thesis titled *The Use of Future Fictional Time in Novels for Young Readers*. Her research interests include perspectives on childhood, forms of didacticism in children's novels, and futuristic literature for teenage readers. She is a 2002 winner of a National Teaching Fellowship.

Karen Sands-O'Connor is Assistant Professor of English at Buffalo State College, where she teaches children's literature and literary criticism. Her book, co-authored with Marietta Frank, is titled *Back in the Spaceship Again*: *Juvenile Science Fiction Series after 1945*. She also examined the concept of utopia in her doctoral work at Cardiff University, Wales, where she concentrated on post-1945 British children's fantastic fiction.

Lyman Tower Sargent is Professor of Political Science at the University of Missouri–St. Louis and the author of *British and American Utopian Literature, 1516–1985: An Annotated Chronological Bibliography* (1988). He is the editor of *Utopian Studies*. He was founder and coeditor with Gregory Claeys of the Syracuse University Press Series on Utopianism and Communitarianism. He advised the Bibliothèque Nationale de France and the New York Public Library on their joint exhibit "Utopie: La quête de la société idéale en Occident/Utopia: The Quest for the Ideal Society in the West" (Paris: April to July 2000; New York: October 2000 to January 2001) and, with Roland

Schaer and Gregory Claeys, coedited the catalogue, *Utopie: La quête de la société idéale en Occident* (2000) and *Utopia: The Quest for the Ideal Society in the Western World* (2000).

Rebecca Carol Noël Totaro is Assistant Professor of English at Florida Gulf Coast University. She serves on the steering committee for the Society for Utopian Studies and has published articles on Shakespeare, utopian literature, and bubonic plague. Her book, *Suffering in Paradise: The Bubonic Plague in English Utopian Renaissance Literature*, is currently in review.

Jack Zipes is Professor of German at the University of Minnesota, and has published widely in the fields of folklore and Children's Literature. He has written numerous books, including *Sticks and Stones* (2000), *When Dreams Come True* (1999), *Happily Ever After (1997)*, *Creative Storytelling* (1995), *The Brothers Grimm* (1988), and *Fairy Tales and the Art of Subversion* (1985). He has translated and compiled anthologies of the Brothers Grimm, French fairy tales, and the fairy tales of Hermann Hesse. He has edited collections of Red Riding Hood tales, Victorian fairy tales, and feminist fairy tales.

Author Index

Subject and Title Index

CPSIA information can be obtained at www.ICGtesting.com
Printed in the USA
LVOW060528060612

284809LV00001B/102/P